SOLUTIONS TO SELECTE
EXERCISES IN

THE
LOGIC
BOOK

Second Edition

MERRIE BERGMANN   Smith College

JAMES MOOR   Dartmouth College

JACK NELSON   Temple University

McGraw-Hill, Inc.
New York St. Louis San Francisco Auckland Bogotá
Caracas Lisbon London Madrid Mexico City Milan
Montreal New Delhi San Juan Singapore
Sydney Tokyo Toronto

Solutions to Selected Exercises in The Logic Book

90 DOC DOC 95

ISBN 0-07-004940-8

This book was set in Baskerville by Science Typographers, Inc.
The editors were Steve Pensinger and Cynthia Ward;
the production supervisor was Louise Karam.
The cover was designed by Katherine Urban.
Project supervision was done by Science Typographers, Inc.
R. R. Donnelley & Sons Company was printer and binder.

Cover Photo: Jaco BAR-Portrait of *Luca Pacioli and an Unknown Man*, Capodimonte Museum, Naples.
Photo SCALA/EPA, Inc.

CONTENTS

SOLUTIONS

CHAPTER ONE

1.1E

1. Logic can tell us that a set of beliefs is inconsistent and thus that one or more of the members of that set are false. But generally logic cannot tell us which member or members are false. The inconsistency should be resolved by abandoning or modifying those beliefs that are not strongly supported by the evidence available to us. Evidence is a product of our investigation of the way the world is.

3. The most sincerely held beliefs can be false, and false beliefs can adversely affect one's interactions with the world. For example, one can very sincerely believe that a piece of pork has been thoroughly cooked. But if the pork has not been thoroughly cooked, trichinosis is a real danger, and sincerity is no antidote.

1.3E

1. Argument

His power, we allow, is infinite.

Whatever he wills is executed.

Neither man nor any other animal is happy.

He does not will their happiness.

3. Argument

The table, which we see, seems to diminish, as we remove farther from it.

The real table, which exists independent of us, suffers no alteration.

The table which we saw was nothing but its image, which was present to the mind.

5. Argument

Things which lack intelligence, such as natural bodies, act for an end.

Whatever lacks intelligence cannot move toward an end, unless it be directed by some being endowed with knowledge and intelligence.

Some intelligence exists by whom all natural things are directed to their ends; and this being we call God.

Note: In our paraphrase of the original argument portions of some of the sentences have been deleted because they can be regarded as giving evidence for or an explanation of the *premises* of the argument.

7. Argument

If it is inferred that the brain of a woman is smaller than that of a man merely because a woman's bodily frame generally is of less dimensions than a man's, this criterion would lead to strange consequences.

A tall and large-boned man must in this showing be wonderfully superior in intelligence to a small man, and an elephant or a whale must prodigiously excel mankind.

It is by no means established that the brain of a woman is smaller than that of a man.

9. Argument

If the teacher happens to be a man of sense, it must be an unpleasant thing to him to be conscious, while he is lecturing his students, that he is either speaking or reading nonsense, or what is little better than nonsense.

It must, too, be unpleasant to him to observe that the greater part of his students desert his lectures, or perhaps attend upon them with plain enough marks of neglect, contempt, and derision.

If he is obliged to give a certain number of lectures, these motives alone, without any other interest, might dispose him to take some pains to give tolerably good ones.

11. Argument

Sexual Selection depends, not on a struggle for existence in relation to other organic beings or to external conditions, but on a struggle between the individuals of one sex, generally the males, for the possession of the other sex.

The result is not death to the unsuccessful competitor, but few or no offspring.

Sexual Selection is less rigorous than natural selection.

13. Argument

Either death is a state of nothingness and utter unconsciousness, or there is a change and migration of the soul from this world to another.

If you suppose that there is no consciousness, but a sleep like the sleep of him who is undisturbed even by dreams, death will be an unspeakable gain.

If death is a journey to another place and there all the dead abide, that will be a great good—I shall then be able to continue my search into true and false knowledge.

Death is good.

Note: The question in the original argument has been paraphrased as a declarative sentence.

15. Argument

Some whales have been captured far north in the Pacific, in whose bodies have been found the barbs of harpoons darted in the Greenland seas.

In some of these instances it has been declared that the interval of time between the two assaults could not have exceeded very many days.

It has been believed by some whalemen, that the Nor'-West Passage, so long a problem to man, was never a problem to the whale.

1.4E

1.a. False. Many valid arguments have false premises. Here is an example:

All Doberman pinschers are friendly.

All friendly creatures are dogs.

All Doberman pinschers are dogs.

c. False. A valid argument all of whose premises are true cannot have a false conclusion. But if a valid argument has at least one false premise, it may well have a false conclusion. Here is an example:

> If collies undergo photosynthesis, then collies are plants.
> Collies undergo photosynthesis.
> _____
> Collies are plants.

e. True. If one of the sentences in the set is logically false, then it is not possible for all of the sentences in the set to be true at the same time because the logically false sentence is never true.

g. False. A valid argument is sound if it has all true premises but not if it has one or more false premises. Valid arguments can have false premises. See, for example, the argument given in answer to exercise c.

i. False. A sound argument is a valid argument with true premises. Hence all sound arguments have true conclusions.

k. False. An argument may have true premises and a true conclusion and not be valid. Consider the following argument:

> Chicago is in Illinois.
> _____
> Madrid is in Spain.

m. True. An argument that has a conclusion which is logically equivalent to one of its premises is valid. For an argument to be invalid it must be possible for all of the premises to be true and the conclusion false. If the premises are all true, then the conclusion which is logically equivalent to one of the premises must also be true. The argument cannot be invalid and must, therefore, be valid.

2.a. No, the sentences that this person believes need not form an inconsistent set. Consistent sets can have false sentences as members. What is important for consistency is that the truth of one or more of the members of a set of sentences not require the falsity of some other member of the set.

c. Normally logic cannot tell us whether a sentence is true or false. For most of the sentences we normally deal with, truth is a matter of how things are with the world. And, to determine whether or not a valid argument is sound, we do need to determine whether or not the premises are true. However, in one case logic can tell us that an argument is sound: if the argument is valid and all its premises are logical truths.

e. If an argument has a logical falsehood as one of its premises, it is impossible for that premise to be true. If one premise cannot be true, then surely it cannot be that all the premises are true and the conclusion false. So the argument must be valid.

g. If an argument has a logical truth for its conclusion, it is impossible for that conclusion to be false. And if the conclusion cannot be false, then surely it cannot be that the premises are true *and* the conclusion false. Hence an argument with a logical truth for a conclusion will be valid, regardless of what its premises are. But it will be sound only if those premises are true. So some such arguments will be sound (those with true premises), and some will not (those with one or more false premises).

     i. If a set of one million sentences is consistent and a new set of sentences is constructed so that every sentence in the new set is logically equivalent to at least one of the sentences in the old set, the new set must be consistent. Because the first set is consistent, it is possible for all of the sentences in the set to be true at the same time. Because all of the sentences in the new set are logically equivalent to the sentences in the old set, it is possible for all of them to be true at the same time, namely when the sentences in the original set are all true.

CHAPTER TWO

2.1E

1.a. Both Bob jogs regularly and Carol jogs regularly.

    B & C

c. Either Bob jogs regularly or Carol jogs regularly.

    B ∨ C

e. It is not the case that either Bob jogs regularly or Carol jogs regularly.

    ~(B ∨ C)

    [or]

Both it is not the case that Bob jogs regularly and it is not the case that Carol jogs regularly.

       ~B & ~C

g. Either it is not the case that Bob jogs regularly or Carol jogs regularly.

     ~B ∨ C

    i. Both (either Bob jogs regularly or Albert jogs regularly) and it is not the case that (both Bob jogs regularly and Albert jogs regularly).

      (B ∨ A) & ~(B & A)

k. Both it is not the case that (either Carol jogs regularly or Bob jogs regularly) and it is not the case that Albert jogs regularly.

~(C ∨ B) & ~A

m. Either Albert jogs regularly or it is not the case that Albert jogs regularly.

A ∨ ~A

2.a. Albert jogs regularly and so does Bob.
c. Either Albert or Carol jogs regularly.
e. Neither Albert nor Carol jogs regularly.
g. Bob jogs regularly and so does either Albert or Carol.
i. Albert, Carol, and Bob jog regularly.
k. Either Bob or Carol jogs regularly, or neither of them jogs regularly.

3. c and k are true; and a, e, g, and i are false.

4. Paraphrases
a. It is not the case that all joggers are marathon runners.
c. It is not the case that some marathon runners are lazy.
e. It is not the case that somebody is perfect.

Symbolizations

a. Using 'A' for 'All joggers are marathon runners':

~A

c. Using 'L' for 'Some marathon runners are lazy':

~L

e. Using 'P' for 'Somebody is perfect':

~P

5.a. If Bob jogs regularly then it is not the case that Bob is lazy.

B ⊃ ~L

c. Bob jogs regularly if and only if it is not the case that Bob is lazy.

B ≡ ~L

e. Carol is a marathon runner if and only if Carol jogs regularly.

M ≡ C

g. If (both Carol jogs regularly and Bob jogs regularly) then Albert jogs regularly.

(C & B) ⊃ A

i. If (either   it is not the case that   Carol   jogs   regularly   or it is not the case that Bob jogs regularly) then it is not the case that Albert jogs regularly.

$$(\sim C \lor \sim B) \supset \sim A$$

k. If (both Albert is healthy and it is not the case that Bob is lazy) then (both Albert jogs regularly and Bob jogs regularly).

$$(H \& \sim L) \supset (A \& B)$$

m. If it is not the case that Carol is a marathon runner then [Carol jogs regularly if and only if (both Albert jogs regularly and Bob jogs regularly)].

$$\sim M \supset [C \equiv (A \& B)]$$

o. If [both (both Carol is a marathon runner and it is not the case that Bob is lazy) and Albert is healthy] then [both Albert jogs regularly and (both Bob jogs regularly and Carol jogs regularly)].

$$[(M \& \sim L) \& H] \supset [A \& (B \& C)]$$

q. If (if Carol jogs regularly then Albert jogs regularly) then (both Albert is healthy and Carol is a marathon runner).

$$(C \supset A) \supset (H \& M)$$

s. If [if (either Carol jogs regularly or Bob jogs regularly) then Albert jogs regularly)] then (both Albert is healthy and it is not the case that Bob is lazy).

$$[(C \lor B) \supset A] \supset (H \& \sim L)$$

6.a. Either Bob is lazy or he isn't.
c. Albert jogs regularly if and only if he is healthy.
e. Neither Bob nor Carol jogs regularly.
g. If either Albert or Carol does not jog regularly, then Bob does.
i. Carol jogs regularly only if Albert does but Bob doesn't.
k. Carol does and does not jog regularly.
m. If Bob is lazy, then he is; but Bob jogs regularly.
o. If Albert doesn't jog regularly, then Bob doesn't jog regularly only if Carol doesn't.
q. Albert doesn't jog regularly, and Bob jogs regularly if and only if he is not lazy.

2.2E

1.a. Either the French team will win at least one gold medal or either the German team will win at least one gold medal or the Danish team will win at least one gold medal.

$$F \lor (G \lor D)$$

c. Both (either the French team will win at least one gold medal or either the German team will win at least one gold medal or the Danish team will win at least one gold medal) and (either [it is not the case that either the French team will win at least one gold medal or the German team will win at least one gold medal] or [either (it is not the case that either the French team will win at least one gold medal or the Danish team will win at least one gold medal) or (it is not the case that either the German team will win at least one gold medal or the Danish team will win at least one gold medal)]).

$$[F \lor (G \lor D)] \mathbin{\&} (\mathord{\sim}(F \lor G) \lor [\mathord{\sim}(F \lor D) \lor \mathord{\sim}(G \lor D)])$$

e. Either both the French team will win at least one gold medal and the German team will win at least one gold medal or either both the French team will win at least one gold medal and the Danish team will win at least one gold medal or both the German team will win at least one gold medal and the Danish team will win at least one gold medal.

$$(F \mathbin{\&} G) \lor [(F \mathbin{\&} D) \lor (G \mathbin{\&} D)]$$

g. Either both both the French team will win at least one gold medal and the German team will win at least one gold medal and it is not the case that the Danish team will win at least one gold medal or either both both the French team will win at least one gold medal and the Danish team will win at least one gold medal and it is not the case that the German team will win at least one gold medal or both both the German team will win at least one gold medal and the Danish team will win at least one gold medal and it is not the case that the French team will win at least one gold medal.

$$[(F \mathbin{\&} G) \mathbin{\&} \mathord{\sim}D] \lor ([(F \mathbin{\&} D) \mathbin{\&} \mathord{\sim}G] \lor [(G \mathbin{\&} D) \mathbin{\&} \mathord{\sim}F])$$

2.a. None of them will win a gold medal.

c. None of them will win a gold medal.

e. At least two of them will win a gold medal.

g. The French team will win a gold medal and exactly one of the other two teams will win a gold medal.

3.a. If either the French team will win at least one gold medal or either the German team will win at least one gold medal or the Danish team will win at least one gold medal then both the French team will win at least one gold medal and both the German team will win at least one gold medal and the Danish team will win at least one gold medal.

$$[F \lor (G \lor D)] \supset [F \mathbin{\&} (G \mathbin{\&} D)]$$

c. If the star German runner is disqualified then if the German team will win at least one gold medal then it is not the case that either the French team will win at least one gold medal or the Danish team will win at least one gold medal.

$$S \supset [G \supset \mathord{\sim}(F \lor D)]$$

e. The Danish team will win at least one gold medal if and only if both the French team is plagued with injuries and the star German runner is disqualified.

$$D \equiv (P \& S)$$

g. If the French team is plagued with injuries then if the French team will win at least one gold medal then both it is not the case that either the Danish team will win at least one gold medal or the German team will win at least one gold medal and it rains during most of the competition.

$$P \supset (F \supset [\sim(D \vee G) \& R])$$

4.a. If the German star is disqualified then the German team will not win a gold medal, and the star is disqualified.

c. The German team won't win a gold medal if and only if the Danish as well as the French will win one.

e. If a German team win guarantees a French team win and a French team win guarantees a Danish team win then a German team win guarantees a Danish team win.

g. Either at least one of the three wins a gold medal or else the French team is plagued with injuries or the star German runner is disqualified or it rains during most of the competition.

5.a. If both the United States will negotiate seriously and Russia will negotiate seriously then the nuclear disarmament talks will succeed.

Both (if there is a strong conventional military force in Europe then the United States will negotiate seriously) and (the Russia will negotiate seriously if and only if the Kremlin has something to gain).

Both the Kremlin has something to gain and there is a strong conventional military force in Europe.

The nuclear disarmament talks will succeed.

U: The United States will negotiate seriously.
R: Russia will negotiate seriously.
S: The nuclear disarmament talks will succeed.
C: There is a strong conventional military force in Europe.
K: The Kremlin has something to gain.

$(U \& R) \supset S$

$(C \supset U) \& (R \equiv K)$

$K \& C$

S

c. Either either the maid committed the murder or the butler committed the murder or the cook committed the murder.

Both (if the cook committed the murder then a knife was the murder weapon) and (if a knife was the murder weapon then it is not the case that either the butler committed the murder or the maid committed the murder).

A knife was the murder weapon.

The cook committed the murder.

M: The maid committed the murder.
B: The butler committed the murder.
C: The cook committed the murder.
K: A knife was the murder weapon.

(M ∨ B) ∨ C

(C ⊃ K) & (K ⊃ ~(B ∨ M))

K

C

e. If the candidate is perceived as conservative then both it is not the case that the candidate will win New York and both the candidate will win California and the candidate will win Texas.

Both if the candidate has an effective advertising campaign then the candidate is perceived as conservative and the candidate has an effective advertising campaign.

Either both the candidate will win California and the candidate will win New York or either (both the candidate will win California and the candidate will win Texas) or (both the candidate will win New York and the candidate will win Texas).

P: The candidate is perceived as conservative.
N: The candidate will win New York.
C: The candidate will win California.
T: The candidate will win Texas.
E: The candidate has an effective advertising campaign.

P ⊃ [~N & (C & T)]

(E ⊃ P) & E

(C & N) ∨ [(C & T) ∨ (N & T)]

2.3E

1. Since we do not know how these sentences are being used (e.g., as premises, conclusions, or as isolated claims) it is best to symbolize those which are non-truth-functional compounds as atomic sentences of *SL*.

a. 'It is possible that' does not have a truth-functional sense. Thus the sentence should be treated as a unit and abbreviated by one letter, for example, 'E'. Here 'E' abbreviates not just 'Every family on this continent owns a television set' but the entire original sentence, 'It is possible that every family on this continent owns a television set'.

c. 'Necessarily' has scope over the entire sentence. Abbreviate the entire sentence by one letter such as 'N'.

e. This sentence can be paraphrased as a truth-functional compound:

Both <u>it is not the case that</u> Tamara will stop by <u>and</u> Tamara promised to phone early in the evening

which can be symbolized as ' ~ B & E', where 'B' abbreviates 'Tamara will stop by' and 'E' abbreviates 'Tamara promised to phone early in the evening'.

g. 'John believes that' is not a truth-functional connective. Abbreviate the sentence by one letter, for example 'J'.

i. 'Only after' has no truth-functional sense. Therefore abbreviate the entire sentence as 'D'.

2.a. The paraphrase is

<u>Either</u> the maid committed the murder <u>or</u> the maid believed her life was in danger.

If the butler committed the murder <u>then</u> (<u>both</u> the murder was done silently <u>and</u> <u>it is not the case that</u> the <u>body</u> was mutilated).

<u>Both</u> the murder was done silently <u>and</u> <u>it is not the case that</u> the maid's life was in danger.

The butler committed the murder <u>if and only if</u> <u>it is not the case that</u> the maid committed the murder.

The maid committed the murder.

Notice that 'The maid believed her life was in danger' (first premise) and 'The maid's life was in danger' (third premise) make different claims and cannot be treated as the same sentence. Further, since the subjunctive conditional in the original argument is a premise, it can be weakened and paraphrased as a truth-functional compound. Using the abbreviations

M: The maid committed the murder.
D: The maid believed that her life was in danger.
B: The butler committed the murder.
S: The murder was done silently.
W: The body was mutilated.
L: The maid's life was in danger.

the symbolized argument is

$$M \lor D$$
$$B \supset (S \;\&\; \sim W)$$
$$S \;\&\; \sim L$$
$$B \equiv \sim M$$
___
$$M$$

c. The paraphrase is

If (both Charles Babbage had the theory of the modern computer and Charles Babbage had modern electronic parts) then the modern electronic computer was developed before the beginning of the twentieth century.

Both Charles Babbage lived in the early nineteenth century and Charles Babbage had the theory of the modern computer.

Both it is not the case that Charles Babbage had modern electronic parts and Charles Babbage was forced to construct his computers out of mechanical gears and levers.

___

If Charles Babbage had had modern electronic parts available to him then the modern computer would have been developed before the beginning of the twentieth century.

In the original argument subjunctive conditionals occur in the first premise and the conclusion. Since it is correct to weaken the premises but not the conclusion, the first premise, but not the conclusion, is given a truth-functional paraphrase. The conclusion will be abbreviated as a single sentence. Using the abbreviations

T: Charles Babbage had the theory of the modern computer.
E: Charles Babbage had modern electronic parts.
C: The modern computer was developed before the beginning of the twentieth century.
L: Charles Babbage lived in the early nineteenth century.
F: Charles Babbage was forced to construct his computers out of mechanical gears and levers.
W: If Charles Babbage had had modern electronic parts available to him then the modern computer would have been developed before the beginning of the twentieth century.

the paraphrase can be symbolized as

$$(T \;\&\; E) \supset C$$
$$L \;\&\; T$$
$$\sim E \;\&\; F$$
___
$$W$$

2.4E

1.a. True

    c. False. The chemical symbol names or designates the metal copper not the word 'copper'.

    e. False. The substance copper is not its own name

    g. False. The name of copper is not a metal.

2.a. The only German word mentioned is 'Deutschland' which has eleven letters.

    c. The phrase 'the German name of Germany' here refers to the word 'Deutschland', so 'Deutschland' is mentioned here.

    e. The word 'Deutschland' occurs inside single quotation marks in exercise e, so it is there being mentioned, not used.

    3.a. A sentence of *SL*.

    c. A sentence of *SL*.

    e. A sentence of *SL*.

    g. A sentence of *SL*.

    i. A sentence of *SL*.

    4.a. The main connective is '&'. The immediate sentential components are '~A' and 'H'. '~A & H' is a component of itself. Another sentential component is 'A'. The atomic sentential components are 'A' and 'H'.

    c. The main connective is '∨'. The immediate sentential components are '~(S & G)' and 'B'. The other sentential components are '~(S & G) ∨ B' itself, '(S & G)', 'S', and 'G'. The atomic components are 'B', 'S', and 'G'.

    e. The main connective is the first occurrence of '∨'. The immediate sentential components are '(C ≡ K)' and '(~H ∨ (M & N))'. Additional sentential components are the sentence itself, '~H', '(M & N)', 'C', 'K', 'H', 'M', and 'N'. The last five sentential components listed are atomic components.

    5.a. No. The sentence is a conditional, but not a conditional whose antecedent is a negation.

    c. Yes. Here $\mathscr{P}$ is the sentence 'A' and $\mathscr{Q}$ is the sentence '~B'.

    e. No. The sentence is a negation, not a conditional.

    g. No. The sentence is a negation, not a conditional.

    i. Yes. Here $\mathscr{P}$ is 'A ∨ ~B' and $\mathscr{Q}$ is '~(C & ~D)'.

    6.a. 'H' can occur neither immediately to the left of '~' nor immediately to the right of 'A'. As a unary connective, '~' can immediately precede but not immediately follow sentences of *SL*. Both 'H' and 'A' are sentences of *SL*, and no sentence of *SL* can immediately precede another sentence of *SL*.

    c. '(' may not occur immediately to the right of 'A', as a sentence of *SL* can be followed only by a right parentheses or by a binary connective. But '(' may occur immediately to the left of '~', as in '(~A & B)'.

    e. '[' may not occur immediately to the right of 'A' but may occur immediately to the left of '~', as it functions exactly as does '('.

3.1E

1.a. $2^1 = 2$
  c. $2^2 = 4$

2.a.

E	~~(E	&	~E)
	↓		
T	F T T	F	F T
F	F T F	F	T F

c.

A	J	A	≡	[J	≡	(A	≡	J)]
			↓					
T	T	T	T	T	T	T	T	T
T	F	T	T	F	T	T	F	F
F	T	F	T	T	F	F	F	T
F	F	F	T	F	F	F	T	F

e.

A	H	J	[~A	∨	(H	⊃	J)]	⊃	(A	∨	J)
								↓			
T	T	T	F T	T	T	T	T	T	T	T	T
T	T	F	F T	F	T	F	F	T	T	T	F
T	F	T	F T	T	F	T	T	T	T	T	T
T	F	F	F T	T	F	T	F	T	T	T	F
F	T	T	T F	T	T	T	T	T	F	T	T
F	T	F	T F	T	T	F	F	F	F	F	F
F	F	T	T F	T	F	T	T	T	F	T	T
F	F	F	T F	T	F	T	F	F	F	F	F

g.

A	B	~(A	∨	B)	⊃	(~A	∨	~B)
					↓			
T	T	F T	T	T	T	F T	F	F T
T	F	F T	T	F	T	F T	T	T F
F	T	F F	T	T	T	T F	T	F T
F	F	T F	F	F	T	T F	T	T F

i.

			↓						
B	E	H	~(E	&	[H	⊃	(B	&	E)])
T	T	T	F T	T	T	T	T	T	T
T	T	F	F T	T	F	T	T	T	T
T	F	T	T F	F	T	F	T	F	F
T	F	F	T F	F	F	T	T	F	F
F	T	T	T T	F	T	F	F	F	T
F	T	F	F T	T	F	T	F	F	T
F	F	T	T F	F	T	F	F	F	F
F	F	F	T F	F	F	T	F	F	F

k.

								↓					
D	E	F	~[D	&	(E	∨	F)]	≡	[~D	&	(E	&	F)]
T	T	T	F T	T	T	T	T	T	F T	F	T	T	T
T	T	F	F T	T	T	T	F	T	F T	F	T	F	F
T	F	T	F T	T	F	T	T	T	F T	F	F	F	T
T	F	F	T T	F	F	F	F	F	F T	F	F	F	F
F	T	T	T F	F	T	T	T	T	T F	T	T	T	T
F	T	F	T F	F	T	T	F	F	T F	F	T	F	F
F	F	T	T F	F	F	T	T	F	T F	F	F	F	T
F	F	F	T F	F	F	F	F	F	T F	F	F	F	F

m.

										↓			
A	H	J	(A	∨	(~A	&	(H	⊃	J)))	⊃	(J	⊃	H)
T	T	T	T	T	F T	F	T	T	T	T	T	T	T
T	T	F	T	T	F T	F	T	F	F	T	F	T	T
T	F	T	T	T	F T	F	F	T	T	F	T	F	F
T	F	F	T	T	F T	F	F	T	F	T	F	T	F
F	T	T	F	T	T F	T	T	T	T	T	T	T	T
F	T	F	F	F	T F	F	T	F	F	T	F	T	T
F	F	T	F	T	T F	T	F	T	T	F	T	F	F
F	F	F	F	T	T F	T	F	T	F	T	F	T	F

3.a.

			↓					
A	B	C	~	[~A	∨	(~C	∨	~B)]
F	T	T	F	T F	T	F T	F	F T

c.

						↓			
A	B	C	(A	⊃	B)	∨	(B	⊃	C)
F	T	T	F	T	T	T	T	T	T

e.

```
              ↓
A  B  C | (A  ≡  B)  ∨  (B  ≡  C)
────────────────────────────────────
F  T  T |  F  F  T   T   T  T  T
```

g.

```
                              ↓
A  B  C | ~[B  ⊃  (A  ∨  C)]  &  ~~B
──────────────────────────────────────
F  T  T | FT  T   F   T  T    F  TFT
```

i.

```
                                   ↓
A  B  C | ~  [~(A  ≡  ~B)  ≡  ~A]  ≡  (B  ∨  C)
──────────────────────────────────────────────────
F  T  T | T   FF   T   FT  F  TF   T   T  T  T
```

4.a.

```
              ↓
D  F  G | F  ∨  (G  ∨  D)
──────────────────────────
T  T  T | T  T   T   T  T
T  T  F | T  T   F   T  T
T  F  T | F  T   T   T  T
T  F  F | F  T   F   T  T
F  T  T | T  T   T   T  F
F  T  F | T  T   F   F  F
F  F  T | F  T   T   T  F
F  F  F | F  F   F   F  F
```

c.

```
                            ↓
D F G |[F ∨ (G ∨ D)]  &  (~(F ∨ G) ∨ [~(F ∨ D) ∨ ~ (G ∨ D)])
──────────────────────────────────────────────────────────────
T T T | T T  T T T    F   F T T T   F   F T T T   F F T T T
T T F | T T  F T T    F   F T T F   F   F T T T   F F F T T
T F T | F T  T T T    F   F F T T   F   F F T T   F F T T T
T F F | F T  F T T    T   T F F F   T   F F T T   F F F T T
F T T | T T  T T F    F   F T T T   F   F T T F   F F T T F
F T F | T T  F F F    T   F T T F   T   F T T F   T T F F F
F F T | F T  T T F    T   F F T T   T   T F F F   T F T T F
F F F | F F  F F F    F   T F F F   T   T F F F   T T F F F
```

e.

D	F	G	(F	&	G)	↓ ∨	[(F	&	D)	∨	(G	&	D)]
T	T	T	T	T	T	T	T	T	T	T	T	T
T	T	F	T	F	F	T	T	T	T	T	F	F	T
T	F	T	F	F	T	T	F	F	T	T	T	T	T
T	F	F	F	F	F	F	F	F	T	F	F	F	T
F	T	T	T	T	T	T	T	F	F	F	T	F	F
F	T	F	T	F	F	F	T	F	F	F	F	F	F
F	F	T	F	F	T	F	F	F	F	F	T	F	F
F	F	F	F	F	F	F	F	F	F	F	F	F	F

(Main connective: the standalone ∨, marked ↓. Column values: T, T, T, F, T, F, F, F.)

g.

[(F & G) & ~D] ∨ ([(F & D) & ~G] ∨ [(G & D) & ~F])

Value columns in order: F, &, G, &, ~D, ↓∨, F, &, D, &, ~G, ∨, G, &, D, &, ~F

D F G	[(F	&	G)	&	~D]	↓ ∨	([(F	&	D)	&	~G]	∨	[(G	&	D)	&	~F])
T T T	T	T	T	F	F	F	T	T	T	F	F	F	T	T	T	F	F
T T F	T	F	F	F	F	T	T	T	T	T	T	T	F	F	T	F	F
T F T	F	F	T	F	F	T	F	F	T	F	F	T	T	T	T	T	T
T F F	F	F	F	F	F	F	F	F	T	F	T	F	F	F	T	F	T
F T T	T	T	T	T	T	T	T	F	F	F	F	F	T	F	F	F	F
F T F	T	F	F	F	T	F	T	F	F	F	T	F	F	F	F	F	F
F F T	F	F	T	F	T	F	F	F	F	F	F	F	T	F	F	F	T
F F F	F	F	F	F	T	F	F	F	F	F	T	F	F	F	F	F	T

(Main connective: the ∨ following [(F & G) & ~D], marked ↓.)

5.a.

D	F	G	[F	∨	(G	∨	D)]	↓ ⊃	[F	&	(G	&	D)]
T	T	T	T	T	T	T	T	T	T	T	T	T	T
T	T	F	T	T	F	T	T	F	T	F	F	F	T
T	F	T	F	T	T	T	T	F	F	F	T	T	T
T	F	F	F	T	F	T	T	F	F	F	F	F	T
F	T	T	T	T	T	T	F	F	T	F	T	F	F
F	T	F	T	T	F	F	F	F	T	F	F	F	F
F	F	T	F	T	T	T	F	F	F	F	T	F	F
F	F	F	F	F	F	F	F	T	F	F	F	F	F

(Main connective: ⊃, marked ↓.)

c.

D	F	G	S	S	↓ ⊃	[G	⊃	~	(F	∨	D)]
T	T	T	T	T	F	T	F	F	T	T	T
T	T	T	F	F	T	T	F	F	T	T	T
T	T	F	T	T	T	F	T	F	T	T	T
T	T	F	F	F	T	F	T	F	T	T	T
T	F	T	T	T	F	T	F	F	F	T	T
T	F	T	F	F	T	T	F	F	F	T	T
T	F	F	T	T	T	F	T	F	F	T	T
T	F	F	F	F	T	F	T	F	F	T	T
F	T	T	T	T	F	T	F	F	T	T	F
F	T	T	F	F	T	T	F	F	T	T	F
F	T	F	T	T	T	F	T	F	T	T	F
F	T	F	F	F	T	F	T	F	T	T	F
F	F	T	T	T	T	T	T	T	F	F	F
F	F	T	F	F	T	T	T	T	F	F	F
F	F	F	T	T	T	F	T	T	F	F	F
F	F	F	F	F	T	F	T	T	F	F	F

e.

D	L	S	D	↓ ≡	(L	&	S)
T	T	T	T	T	T	T	T
T	T	F	T	F	T	F	F
T	F	T	T	F	F	F	T
T	F	F	T	F	F	F	F
F	T	T	F	F	T	T	T
F	T	F	F	T	T	F	F
F	F	T	F	T	F	F	T
F	F	F	F	T	F	F	F

g.

D	F	G	L	R	L	↓ ⊃	(F	⊃	[~	(D	∨	G)	&	R])
T	T	T	T	T	T	F	T	F	F	T	T	T	F	T
T	T	T	T	F	T	F	T	F	F	T	T	T	F	F
T	T	T	F	T	F	T	T	F	F	T	T	T	F	T
T	T	T	F	F	F	T	T	F	F	T	T	T	F	F
T	T	F	T	T	T	F	T	F	F	T	T	F	F	T
T	T	F	T	F	T	F	T	F	F	T	T	F	F	F
T	T	F	F	T	F	T	T	F	F	T	T	F	F	T
T	T	F	F	F	F	T	T	F	F	T	T	F	F	F
T	F	T	T	T	T	T	F	T	F	T	T	T	F	T
T	F	T	T	F	T	T	F	T	F	T	T	T	F	F
T	F	T	F	T	F	T	F	T	F	T	T	T	F	T
T	F	T	F	F	F	T	F	T	F	T	T	T	F	F
T	F	F	T	T	T	T	F	T	F	T	T	F	F	T
T	F	F	T	F	T	T	F	T	F	T	T	F	F	F
T	F	F	F	T	F	T	F	T	F	T	T	F	F	T
T	F	F	F	F	F	T	F	T	F	T	T	F	F	F
F	T	T	T	T	T	F	T	F	F	F	T	T	F	T
F	T	T	T	F	T	F	T	F	F	F	T	T	F	F
F	T	T	F	T	F	T	T	F	F	F	T	T	F	T
F	T	T	F	F	F	T	T	F	F	F	T	T	F	F
F	T	F	T	T	T	T	T	T	T	F	F	F	T	T
F	T	F	T	F	T	F	T	F	T	F	F	F	F	F
F	T	F	F	T	F	T	T	T	T	F	F	F	T	T
F	T	F	F	F	F	T	T	F	T	F	F	F	F	F
F	F	T	T	T	T	T	F	T	F	F	T	T	F	T
F	F	T	T	F	T	T	F	T	F	F	T	T	F	F
F	F	T	F	T	F	T	F	T	F	F	T	T	F	T
F	F	T	F	F	F	T	F	T	F	F	T	T	F	F
F	F	F	T	T	T	T	F	T	T	F	F	F	T	T
F	F	F	T	F	T	T	F	T	T	F	F	F	F	F
F	F	F	F	T	F	T	F	T	T	F	F	F	T	T
F	F	F	F	F	F	T	F	T	T	F	F	F	F	F

3.2E

1.a. Truth-functionally indeterminate

A	~A	↓ ⊃	A
T	F T	T	T
F	T F	F	F

c. Truth-functionally true

A	(A	≡	~A)	⊃ ↓	~(A	≡	~A)
T	T	F	F T	T	T T	F	F T
F	F	F	T F	T	T F	F	T F

e. Truth-functionally indeterminate

B	D	(~B	&	~D)	∨ ↓	~(B	∨	D)
T	T	F T	F	F T	F	F T	T	T
T	F	F T	F	T F	F	F T	T	F
F	T	T F	F	F T	F	F F	T	T
F	F	T F	T	T F	T	T F	F	F

g. Truth-functionally indeterminate

A	B	C	[(A	∨	B)	&	(A	∨	C)]	⊃ ↓	~(B	&	C)
T	T	T	T	T	T	T	T	T	T	F	F T	T	T
T	T	F	T	T	T	T	T	T	F	T	T T	F	F
T	F	T	T	T	F	T	T	T	T	T	T F	F	T
T	F	F	T	T	F	T	T	T	F	T	T F	F	F
F	T	T	F	T	T	T	F	T	T	F	F T	T	T
F	T	F	F	T	T	F	F	F	F	T	T T	F	F
F	F	T	F	F	F	F	F	T	T	T	T F	F	T
F	F	F	F	F	F	F	F	F	F	T	T F	F	F

i. Truth-functionally true

J	K	(J	∨	~K)	≡ ↓	~~(K	⊃	J)
T	T	T	T	F T	T	T F T	T	T
T	F	T	T	T F	T	T F F	T	T
F	T	F	F	F T	T	F T T	F	F
F	F	F	T	T F	T	T F F	T	F

k. Truth-functionally true

A	D	[(A	∨	~D)	&	~(A	&	D)]	⊃ ↓	~D
T	T	T	T	F T	F	F T	T	T	T	F T
T	F	T	T	T F	T	T T	F	F	T	T F
F	T	F	F	F T	F	T F	F	T	T	F T
F	F	F	T	T F	T	T F	F	F	T	T F

2.a. Not truth-functionally true

F	H	(F	∨	H)	↓ ∨	(~F	≡	H)
F	F	F	F	F	F	T F	F	F

c. Truth-functionally true

A	B	C	~A	↓ ⊃	[(B	&	A)	⊃	C]
T	T	T	F T	T	T	T	T	T	T
T	T	F	F T	T	T	T	T	F	F
T	F	T	F T	T	F	F	T	T	T
T	F	F	F T	T	F	F	T	T	F
F	T	T	T F	T	T	F	F	T	T
F	T	F	T F	T	T	F	F	T	F
F	F	T	T F	T	F	F	F	T	T
F	F	F	T F	T	F	F	F	T	F

e. Truth-functionally true

C	[(C	∨	~C)	⊃	C]	↓ ⊃	C
T	T	T	F T	T	T	T	T
F	F	T	T F	F	F	T	F

3.a. Truth-functionally false

B	D	(B	≡	D)	↓ &	(B	≡	~D)
T	T	T	T	T	F	T	F	F T
T	F	T	F	F	F	T	T	T F
F	T	F	F	T	F	F	T	F T
F	F	F	T	F	F	F	F	T F

c. Not truth-functionally false

A	B	A	↓ ≡	(B	≡	A)
T	T	T	T	T	T	T

e. Not truth-functionally false

C	D	[(C	∨	D)	≡	C]	↓ ⊃	~C
F	T	F	T	T	F	F	T	T F

4.a. False. For example, while '(A ⊃ A)' is truth-functionally true, '(A ⊃ A) & A' is not.

c. True. There cannot be any truth-value assignment on which the antecedent is true and the consequent false, because there is no truth-value assignment on which the consequent is false.

e. False. For example, although '(A & ~A)' is truth-functionally false, 'C ∨ (A & ~A)' is not.

g. True. Since a sentence ~𝒫 is false on a truth-value assignment if and only if 𝒫 is true on the truth-value assignment, 𝒫 is truth-functionally true if and only if ~𝒫 is truth-functionally false.

i. False. For example, '(A ∨ ~A)' is truth-functionally true, but '(A ∨ ~A) ⊃ B' is truth-functionally indeterminate.

5.a. On every truth-value assignment, 𝒫 is true and 𝒬 is false. Hence 𝒫 ≡ 𝒬 is false on every truth-value assignment. Therefore 𝒫 ≡ 𝒬 is truth-functionally false.

c. No. Both 'A' and '~A' are truth-functionally indeterminate, but 'A ∨ ~A' is truth-functionally true.

3.3E

1.a. Not truth-functionally equivalent

A	B	~(A	&	B)	~(A	∨	B)
		↓			↓		
T	T	F T	T	T	F T	T	T
T	F	T T	F	F	F T	T	F
F	T	T F	F	T	F F	T	T
F	F	T F	F	F	T F	F	F

(The row T F is circled.)

c. Truth-functionally equivalent

H	K	K	≡	H	~K	≡	~H
			↓			↓	
T	T	T	T	T	F T	T	F T
T	F	F	F	T	T F	F	F T
F	T	T	F	F	F T	F	T F
F	F	F	T	F	T F	T	T F

e. Truth-functionally equivalent

F	G	(G	⊃	F)	⊃	(F	⊃	G)	(G	≡	F)	∨	(~F	∨	G)
					↓							↓			
T	T	T	T	T	T	T	T	T	T	T	T	T	F T	T	T
T	F	F	T	T	F	T	F	F	F	F	T	F	F T	F	F
F	T	T	F	F	T	F	T	T	T	F	F	T	T F	T	T
F	F	F	T	F	T	F	T	F	F	T	F	T	T F	T	F

g. Not truth-functionally equivalent

							↓								↓		
H	J	K	~	(H	&	J)	≡	(J	≡	~	K)	(H	&	J)	⊃	~	K
T	T	T	F	T	T	T	T	T	F	F	T	T	T	T	F	F	T
T	T	F	F	T	T	T	F	T	T	T	F	T	T	T	T	T	F
T	F	T	T	T	F	F	T	F	T	F	T	T	F	F	T	F	T
T	F	F	T	T	F	F	F	F	F	T	F	T	F	F	T	T	F
F	T	T	T	F	F	T	F	T	F	F	T	F	F	T	T	F	T
F	T	F	T	F	F	T	T	T	T	T	F	F	F	T	T	T	F
F	F	T	T	F	F	F	T	F	T	F	T	F	F	F	T	F	T
F	F	F	T	F	F	F	F	F	F	T	F	F	F	F	T	T	F

(Row T T T and second formula column circled)

i. Not truth-functionally equivalent

								↓									↓			
A	C	D	[A	v	~	(D	&	C)]	⊃	~	D	[D	v	~	(A	&	C)]	⊃	~	A
T	T	T	T	T	F	T	T	T	F	F	T	T	T	F	T	T	T	F	F	T
T	T	F	T	T	T	F	F	T	T	T	F	F	F	F	T	T	T	T	F	T
T	F	T	T	T	T	T	F	F	F	F	T	T	T	T	T	F	F	F	F	T
T	F	F	T	T	T	F	F	F	T	T	F	F	T	T	T	F	F	F	F	T
F	T	T	F	F	F	T	T	T	T	F	T	T	T	T	F	F	T	T	T	F
F	T	F	F	T	T	F	F	T	T	T	F	F	T	T	F	F	T	T	T	F
F	F	T	F	T	T	T	F	F	F	F	T	T	T	T	F	F	F	T	T	F
F	F	F	F	T	T	F	F	F	T	T	F	F	T	T	F	F	F	T	T	F

(Row T F F circled)

k. Not truth-functionally equivalent

				↓										↓	
F	G	H	F	v	~	(G	v	~H)	(H	≡	~F)	v	G
T	T	T	T	T	F	T	T	F T	T	F	F T	T	T
T	T	F	T	T	F	T	T	T F	F	T	F T	T	T
T	F	T	T	T	T	F	F	F T	T	F	F T	F	F
T	F	F	T	T	F	F	T	T F	F	T	F T	T	F
F	T	T	F	F	F	T	T	F T	T	T	T F	T	T
F	T	F	F	F	F	T	T	T F	F	F	T F	T	T
F	F	T	F	T	T	F	F	F T	T	T	T F	T	F
F	F	F	F	F	F	F	T	T F	F	F	T F	F	F

(Row T F T circled)

2.a. Truth-functionally equivalent

			↓			↓	
G	H	G	v	H	~G	⊃	H
T	T	T	T	T	F T	T	T
T	F	T	T	F	F T	T	F
F	T	F	T	T	T F	T	T
F	F	F	F	F	T F	F	F

c. Truth-functionally equivalent

A	D	(D	≡	A)	&	D		D	&	A
					↓			↓		
T	T	T	T	T	T	T		T	T	T
T	F	F	F	T	F	F		F	F	T
F	T	T	F	F	F	T		T	F	F
F	F	F	T	F	F	F		F	F	F

e. Not truth-functionally equivalent

A	A	≡	(~A	≡	A)		~(A	⊃	~A)		
		↓					↓				
T	T	F	F T	F	T		T T	F	F T		

3.a. Not truth-functionally equivalent.

C: The sky clouds over.
N: The night will be clear.
M: The moon will shine brightly.

C	M	N	C	∨	(N	&	M)		M	≡	(N	&	~C)
				↓						↓			
T	T	T	T	T	T	T	T		T	F	T	F	F T
T	T	F	T	T	F	F	T		T	F	F	F	F T
T	F	T	T	T	T	F	F		F	T	T	F	F T
T	F	F	T	T	F	F	F		F	T	F	F	F T
F	T	T	F	T	T	T	T		T	T	T	T	T F
F	T	F	F	F	F	F	T		T	F	F	F	T F
F	F	T	F	F	T	F	F		F	F	T	T	T F
F	F	F	F	F	F	F	F		F	T	F	F	T F

c. Truth-functionally equivalent

D: The *Daily Herald* reports on our antics.
A: Our antics are effective.

A	D	D	⊃	A		~A	⊃	~D	
			↓				↓		
T	T	T	T	T		F T	T	F T	
T	F	F	T	T		F T	T	T F	
F	T	T	F	F		T F	F	F T	
F	F	F	T	F		T F	T	T F	

e. Not truth-functionally equivalent

M: Mary met Tom.
L: Mary liked Tom.
G: Mary asked George to the movies.

G	L	M	(M	&	L)	↓⊃	~G	(M	&	~L)	↓⊃	G
T	T	T	T	T	T	F	F T	T	F	F T	T	T
T	T	F	F	F	T	T	F T	F	F	F T	T	T
T	F	T	T	F	F	T	F T	T	T	T F	T	T
T	F	F	F	F	F	T	F T	F	F	T F	T	T
F	T	T	T	T	T	T	T F	T	F	F T	T	F
F	T	F	F	F	T	T	T F	F	F	F T	T	F
F	F	T	T	F	F	T	T F	T	T	T F	F	F
F	F	F	F	F	F	T	T F	F	F	T F	T	F

4.a. Yes. 𝒫 and 𝒬 have the same truth-value on every truth-value assignment. On every truth-value assignment on which they are both true, ~𝒫 and ~𝒬 are both false, and on every truth-value assignment on which they are both false, ~𝒫 and ~𝒬 are both true. It follows that ~𝒫 and ~𝒬 are truth-functionally equivalent.

c. If 𝒫 and 𝒬 are truth-functionally equivalent then they have the same truth-value on every truth-value assignment. On those assignments on which they are both true, the second disjunct of ~𝒫 ∨ 𝒬 is true and so is the disjunction. On those assignments on which they are both false, the first disjunct of ~𝒫 ∨ 𝒬 is true and so is the disjunction. So ~𝒫 ∨ 𝒬 is true on every truth-value assignment.

3.4E

1.a. Truth-functionally consistent

A	B	C	A	↓⊃	B	B	↓⊃	C	A	↓⊃	C
T	T	T	T	T	T	T	T	T	T	T	T
T	T	F	T	T	T	T	F	F	T	F	F
T	F	T	T	F	F	F	T	T	T	T	T
T	F	F	T	F	F	F	T	F	T	F	F
F	T	T	F	T	T	T	T	T	F	T	T
F	T	F	F	T	T	T	F	F	F	T	F
F	F	T	F	T	F	F	T	T	F	T	T
F	F	F	F	T	F	F	T	F	F	T	F

c. Truth-functionally inconsistent

			$\overset{\downarrow}{\sim}$ [J	∨	(H	⊃	L)]	L	$\overset{\downarrow}{\equiv}$	(~J	∨	~H)	H	$\overset{\downarrow}{\equiv}$	(J	∨	L)
T	T	T	F	T	T	T	T	T	F	F	T	F	F	T	T	T	T	T
T	T	F	F	T	T	T	F	F	F	T	F	T	F	F	T	T	T	T	T	F
T	F	T	F	F	T	T	T	T	T	T	T	F	T	F	T	T	T	F	T	T
T	F	F	T	F	F	T	F	F	F	F	T	F	T	F	T	T	F	F	F	F
F	T	T	F	T	T	F	T	T	T	T	F	T	T	T	F	F	F	T	T	T
F	T	F	F	T	T	F	T	F	F	F	F	T	T	T	F	F	F	T	T	F
F	F	T	F	F	T	F	T	T	T	T	T	F	T	T	F	F	F	F	T	T
F	F	F	F	F	T	F	T	F	F	F	T	F	T	T	F	F	T	F	F	F

e. Truth-functionally inconsistent

H	J	(J	⊃	J)	$\overset{\downarrow}{\supset}$	H	$\overset{\downarrow}{\sim}$ J	$\overset{\downarrow}{\sim}$ H
T	T	T	T	T	T	T	F T	F T
T	F	F	T	F	T	T	T F	F T
F	T	T	T	T	F	F	F T	T F
F	F	F	T	F	F	F	T F	T F

g. Truth-functionally consistent

A	B	C	$\overset{\downarrow}{A}$	$\overset{\downarrow}{B}$	$\overset{\downarrow}{C}$
(T	T	T	T	T	T)
T	T	F	T	T	F
T	F	T	T	F	T
T	F	F	T	F	F
F	T	T	F	T	T
F	T	F	F	T	F
F	F	T	F	F	T
F	F	F	F	F	F

i. Truth-functionally consistent

A	B	C	(A	&	B)	$\overset{\downarrow}{\vee}$	(C	⊃	B)	$\overset{\downarrow}{\sim}$ A	$\overset{\downarrow}{\sim}$ B
T	T	T	T	T	T	T	T	T	T	F T	F T
T	T	F	T	T	T	T	F	T	T	F T	F T
T	F	T	T	F	F	F	T	F	F	F T	T F
T	F	F	T	F	F	T	F	T	F	F T	T F
F	T	T	F	F	T	T	T	T	T	T F	F T
F	T	F	F	F	T	T	F	T	T	T F	F T
F	F	T	F	F	F	F	T	F	F	T F	T F
(F	F	F	F	F	F	T	F	T	F	T F	T F)

2.a. Truth-functionally consistent

B	D	E		B	⊃↓	(D	⊃	E)		~D	&↓	B
T	F	T		T	T	F	T	T		T F	T	T

c. Truth-functionally consistent

F	J	K		F	⊃↓	(J	∨	K)		F	≡↓	~J
T	F	T		T	T	F	T	T		T	T	T F

e. Truth-functionally consistent

A	B		(A	⊃	B)	≡↓	(~B	∨	B)		A↓
T	T		T	T	T	T	F T	T	T		T

3.a. Truth-functionally inconsistent

S: Space is infinitely divisible.
Z: Zeno's paradoxes are compelling.
C: Zeno's paradoxes are convincing.

C	S	Z		S	⊃↓	Z		~↓(C	∨	Z)		S↓
T	T	T		T	T	T		F T	T	T		T
T	T	F		T	F	F		F T	T	F		T
T	F	T		F	T	T		F T	T	T		F
T	F	F		F	T	F		F T	T	F		F
F	T	T		T	T	T		F F	T	T		T
F	T	F		T	F	F		T F	F	F		T
F	F	T		F	T	T		F F	T	T		F
F	F	F		F	T	F		T F	F	F		F

E: Eugene O'Neill was an alcoholic.
P: Eugene O'Neill's plays show that he was an alcoholic.
I: *The Iceman Cometh* must have been written by a teetotaler.
F: Eugene O'Neill was a fake.

E	F	I	P	E	P↓	I↓	E	V↓	F
T	T	T	T	**T**	T	T	T	T	**T**
T	T	T	F	T	F	T	T	T	T
T	T	F	T	T	T	F	T	T	T
T	T	F	F	T	F	F	T	T	T
T	F	T	T	T	T	T	T	T	F
T	F	T	F	T	F	T	T	T	F
T	F	F	T	T	T	F	T	T	F
T	F	F	F	T	F	F	T	T	F
F	T	T	T	F	T	T	F	T	T
F	T	T	F	F	F	T	F	T	T
F	T	F	T	F	T	F	F	T	T
F	T	F	F	F	F	F	F	T	T
F	F	T	T	F	T	T	F	F	F
F	F	T	F	F	F	T	F	F	F
F	F	F	T	F	T	F	F	F	F
F	F	F	F	F	F	F	F	F	F

e. Truth-functionally consistent

R: The Red Sox will win next Sunday.
J: Joan bet $5.00.
E: Joan will buy Ed a hamburger.

E	J	R	R	⊃↓	(J	⊃	E)	~R	&↓	~E
T	T	T	T	T	T	T	T	F T	F	F T
T	T	F	F	T	T	T	T	T F	F	F T
T	F	T	T	T	F	T	T	F T	F	F T
T	F	F	F	T	F	T	T	T F	F	F T
F	T	T	T	F	T	F	F	F T	F	T F
F	**T**	**F**	**F**	**T**	**T**	**F**	**F**	**T F**	**T**	**T F**
F	F	T	T	T	F	T	F	F T	F	T F
F	F	F	F	T	F	T	F	T F	T	T F

4.a. First assume that { 𝒫 } is truth-functionally inconsistent. Then, since 𝒫 is the only member of { 𝒫 }, there is no truth-value assignment on which 𝒫 is true; so 𝒫 is false on every truth-value assignment. But then ~𝒫 is true on every truth-value assignment, and so ~𝒫 is truth-functionally true.

c. No. For example, 'A' and '~A' are both truth-functionally indeterminate, but {A, ~A} is truth-functionally inconsistent.

3.5E

1.a. Truth-functionally valid

A	H	J	A	⊃↓	(H	&	J)	J	≡↓	H	~J↓	~A↓
T	T	T	T	T	T	T	T	T	T	T	F T	F T
T	T	F	T	F	T	F	F	F	F	T	T F	F T
T	F	T	T	F	F	F	T	T	F	F	F T	F T
T	F	F	T	F	F	F	F	F	T	F	T F	F T
F	T	T	F	T	T	T	T	T	T	T	F T	T F
F	T	F	F	T	T	F	F	F	F	T	T F	T F
F	F	T	F	T	F	F	T	T	F	F	F T	T F
F	F	F	F	T	F	F	F	F	T	F	T F	T F

c. Truth-functionally valid

A D G	(D ≡ ~G) &↓ G	(G ∨ [(A ⊃ D) & A]) ⊃↓ ~D	G ⊃↓ ~D
T T T	T F F T F T	T T T T T T T F F T	T F F T
T T F	T T T F F F	F T T T T T T F F T	F T F T
T F T	F T F T T T	T T T F F F T T T F	T T T F
T F F	F F T F F F	F F T F F F T T T F	F T T F
F T T	T F F T F T	T T F T T F F F F T	T F F T
F T F	T T T F F F	F F F T T F F T F T	F T F T
F F T	F T F T T T	T T F T F F F T T F	T T T F
F F F	F F T F F F	F F F T F F F T T F	F T T F

e. Truth-functionally valid

C	D	E	(C	⊃	D)	⊃↓	(D	⊃	E)	D↓	C	⊃↓	E
T	T	T	T	T	T	T	T	T	T	T	T	T	T
T	T	F	T	T	T	F	T	F	F	T	T	F	F
T	F	T	T	F	F	T	F	T	T	F	T	T	T
T	F	F	T	F	F	T	F	T	F	F	T	F	F
F	T	T	F	T	T	T	T	T	T	T	F	T	T
F	T	F	F	T	T	F	T	F	F	T	F	T	F
F	F	T	F	T	F	T	F	T	T	F	F	T	T
F	F	F	F	T	F	T	F	T	F	F	F	T	F

g. Truth-functionally valid

```
            ↓                                    ↓
G  H | (G  ≡  H)  ∨  (~G  ≡  H)    (~G  ≡  ~H)  ∨  ~(G  ≡H)

T  T |  T  T  T   T   FT  F  T      FT  T  FT   T   FT T  T
T  F |  T  F  F   T   FT  T  F      FT  F  TF   T   TT F  F
F  T |  F  F  T   T   TF  T  T      TF  F  FT   T   TF F  T
F  F |  F  T  F   T   TF  F  F      TF  T  TF   T   FF T  F
```

i. Truth-functionally invalid

```
          ↓                          ↓                   ↓
F   G | ~~F  ⊃  ~~G      ~G  ⊃  ~F       G  ⊃  F

T   T | TFT  T  TFT      FT  T  FT       T  T  T
T   F | TFT  F  FTF      TF  F  FT       F  T  T
F   T | FTF  T  TFT      FT  T  TF       T  F  F
F   F | FTF  T  FTF      TF  T  TF       F  T  F
```

2.a. Truth-functionally valid

```
              ↓                            ↓                      ↓
J  M | (J  ∨  M)  ⊃  ~(J  &  M)    M  ≡  (M  ⊃  J)    M  ⊃  J

T  T |  T  T  T   F   FT  T  T      T  T  T  T  T      T  T  T
T  F |  T  T  F   T   TT  F  F      F  F  F  T  T      F  T  T
F  T |  F  T  T   T   TF  F  T      T  F  T  F  F      T  F  F
F  F |  F  F  F   T   TF  F  F      F  F  F  T  F      F  T  F
```

c. Truth-functionally valid

```
          ↓                       ↓                  ↓
A  B | A  ⊃  ~ A      (B  ⊃  A)  ⊃  B      A  ≡  ~ B

T  T | T  F  F T      T  T  T   T  T        T  F  F T
T  F | T  F  F T      F  T  T   F  F        T  T  T F
F  T | F  T  T F      T  F  F   T  T        F  T  F T
F  F | F  T  T F      F  T  F   F  F        F  F  T F
```

e. Truth-functionally invalid

```
              ↓                                    ↓             ↓
A B C|A  &  ~ [(B  &  C)  ≡  (C  ⊃  A)]    B  ⊃  ~B      ~C  ⊃  C

T F F|T  T  T   F  F  F   F  F  T  T        F  T  T F     T  F  F F
```

3.a. Truth-functionally valid

B	C	(B	&	C)	↓⊃	(B	∨	C)
T	T	T	T	T	T	T	T	T
T	F	T	F	F	T	T	T	F
F	T	F	F	T	T	F	T	T
F	F	F	F	F	T	F	F	F

c. Truth-functionally invalid

J	T	([(J	⊃	T)	⊃	J]	&	[(T	⊃	J)	⊃	T])	↓⊃	(~J	∨	~T)
T	T	T	T	T	T	T	T	T	T	T	T	T	F	F T	F	F T

e. Truth-functionally invalid

B	C	D	[(B	&	C)	&	(B	∨	D)]	↓⊃	D
T	T	F	T	T	T	T	T	T	F	F	F

4.a. Truth-functionally invalid

S: 'Stern' means the same as 'star'.
N: 'Nacht' means the same as 'day'.

N	S	N	↓⊃	S	↓~N	↓~S
T	T	T	T	T	F T	F T
T	F	T	F	F	F T	T F
F	T	F	T	T	T F	F T
F	F	F	T	F	T F	T F

c. Truth-functionally valid

S: September has thirty days.
A: April has thirty days.
N: November has thirty days.
F: February has forty days.
M: May has thirty days.

A	F	M	N	S	S	&	(A	&	N)	(A	≡	~	M)	&	(N	⊃	M)	F
T	T	T	T	T	T	T	T	T	T	T	F	F	T	F	T	T	T	T
T	T	T	T	F	F	F	T	T	T	T	F	F	T	F	T	T	T	T
T	T	T	F	T	T	F	T	F	F	T	F	F	T	F	F	T	T	T
T	T	T	F	F	F	F	T	F	F	T	F	F	T	F	F	T	T	T
T	T	F	T	T	T	T	T	T	T	T	T	T	F	F	T	F	F	T
T	T	F	T	F	F	F	T	T	T	T	T	T	F	F	T	F	F	T
T	T	F	F	T	T	F	T	F	F	T	T	T	F	T	F	T	F	T
T	T	F	F	F	F	F	T	F	F	T	T	T	F	T	F	T	F	T
T	F	T	T	T	T	T	T	T	T	T	F	F	T	F	T	T	T	F
T	F	T	T	F	F	F	T	T	T	T	F	F	T	F	T	T	T	F
T	F	T	F	T	T	F	T	F	F	T	F	F	T	F	F	T	T	F
T	F	T	F	F	F	F	T	F	F	T	F	F	T	F	F	T	T	F
T	F	F	T	T	T	T	T	T	T	T	T	T	F	F	T	F	F	F
T	F	F	T	F	F	F	T	T	T	T	T	T	F	F	T	F	F	F
T	F	F	F	T	T	F	T	F	F	T	T	T	F	T	F	T	F	F
T	F	F	F	F	F	F	T	F	F	T	T	T	F	T	F	T	F	F
F	T	T	T	T	T	F	F	F	T	F	T	F	T	T	T	T	T	T
F	T	T	T	F	F	F	F	F	T	F	T	F	T	T	T	T	T	T
F	T	T	F	T	T	F	F	F	F	F	T	F	T	T	F	T	T	T
F	T	T	F	F	F	F	F	F	F	F	T	F	T	T	F	T	T	T
F	T	F	T	T	T	F	F	F	T	F	F	T	F	F	T	F	F	T
F	T	F	T	F	F	F	F	F	T	F	F	T	F	F	T	F	F	T
F	T	F	F	T	T	F	F	F	F	F	F	T	F	F	F	T	F	T
F	T	F	F	F	F	F	F	F	F	F	F	T	F	F	F	T	F	T
F	F	T	T	T	T	F	F	F	T	F	T	F	T	T	T	T	T	F
F	F	T	T	F	F	F	F	F	T	F	T	F	T	T	T	T	T	F
F	F	T	F	T	T	F	F	F	F	F	T	F	T	T	F	T	T	F
F	F	T	F	F	F	F	F	F	F	F	T	F	T	T	F	T	T	F
F	F	F	T	T	T	F	F	F	T	F	F	T	F	F	T	F	F	F
F	F	F	T	F	F	F	F	F	T	F	F	T	F	F	T	F	F	F
F	F	F	F	T	T	F	F	F	F	F	F	T	F	F	F	T	F	F
F	F	F	F	F	F	F	F	F	F	F	F	T	F	F	F	T	F	F

e. Truth-functionally valid

D: Computers can have desires.
E: Computers can have emotions.
T: Computers can think.

| | | | | ↓ | | | ↓ | | | ↓ | | ↓ |
D	E	T	T	≡	E	E	⊃	D	D	⊃	~T	~T
T	T	T	T	T	T	T	T	T	T	F	F T	F T
T	T	F	F	F	T	T	T	T	T	T	T F	T F
T	F	T	T	F	F	F	T	T	T	F	F T	F T
T	F	F	F	T	F	F	T	T	T	T	T F	T F
F	T	T	T	T	T	T	F	F	F	T	F T	F T
F	T	F	F	F	T	T	F	F	F	T	T F	T F
F	F	T	T	F	F	F	T	F	F	T	F T	F T
F	F	F	F	T	F	F	T	F	F	T	T F	T F

5.a. Suppose that the argument is truth-functionally valid. Then there is no truth-value assignment on which $\mathscr{P}_1, \ldots, \mathscr{P}_n$ are all true and $\mathscr{Q}$ is false. But, by the characteristic truth-table for '&', the iterated conjunction $(\ldots(\mathscr{P}_1 \mathbin{\&} \mathscr{P}_2) \mathbin{\&} \ldots \mathscr{P}_n)$ has the truth-value **T** on a truth-value assignment if and only if all of $\mathscr{P}_1, \ldots, \mathscr{P}_n$ have the truth-value **T** on that assignment. So, on our assumption, there is no truth-value assignment on which the antecedent of $(\ldots(\mathscr{P}_1 \mathbin{\&} \mathscr{P}_2) \mathbin{\&} \ldots \mathbin{\&} \mathscr{P}_n) \supset \mathscr{Q}$ has the truth-value **T** and the consequent has the truth-value **F**. It follows that there is no truth-value assignment on which the corresponding material conditional is false, so it is truth-functionally true.

Assume that $(\ldots(\mathscr{P}_1 \mathbin{\&} \mathscr{P}_2) \mathbin{\&} \ldots \mathbin{\&} \mathscr{P}_n) \supset \mathscr{Q}$ is truth-functionally true. Then there is no truth-value assignment on which the antecedent is true and the consequent false. But the iterated conjunction is true if and only if the sentences $\mathscr{P}_1, \ldots, \mathscr{P}_n$ are all true. So there is no truth-value assignment on which $\mathscr{P}_1, \ldots, \mathscr{P}_n$ are all true and $\mathscr{Q}$ is false; hence the argument is truth-functionally valid.

c. No. For example, $\{A \supset B\} \vDash$ '$\sim A \lor B$'. But $\{A \supset B\}$ does not entail '$\sim A$', nor does it entail 'B'.

3.6E

1.a. If $\{\sim\mathscr{P}\}$ is truth-functionally inconsistent, then there is no truth-value assignment on which $\sim\mathscr{P}$ is true (since $\sim\mathscr{P}$ is the only member of its unit set). But then $\sim\mathscr{P}$ is false on every truth-value assignment, so $\mathscr{P}$ is true on every truth-value assignment and is truth-functionally true.

c. If $\Gamma \cup \{\sim\mathscr{P}\}$ is truth-functionally inconsistent, then there is no truth-value assignment on which every member of $\Gamma \cup \{\sim\mathscr{P}\}$ is true. But $\sim\mathscr{P}$ is true on a truth-value assignment if and only if $\mathscr{P}$ is false on that assignment. Hence there is no truth-value assignment on which every member of Γ is true and $\mathscr{P}$ is false. Hence $\Gamma \vDash \mathscr{P}$.

2.a. $\mathcal{P}$ is truth-functionally true if and only if the set $\{\sim\mathcal{P}\}$ is truth-functionally inconsistent. But $\{\sim\mathcal{P}\}$ is the same set as $\varnothing \cup \{\sim\mathcal{P}\}$. So $\mathcal{P}$ is truth-functionally true if and only if $\varnothing \cup \{\sim\mathcal{P}\}$ is truth-functionally inconsistent. But we have already seen, by previous results, that $\varnothing \cup \{\sim\mathcal{P}\}$ is truth-functionally inconsistent if and only if $\varnothing \vDash \mathcal{P}$. Hence $\mathcal{P}$ is truth-functionally true if and only if $\varnothing \vDash \mathcal{P}$.

c. Assume that Γ is truth-functionally inconsistent. Then there is no truth-value assignment on which every member of Γ is true. Let $\mathcal{P}$ be an *arbitrarily* selected sentence of *SL*. Then there is no truth-value assignment on which every member of Γ is true and $\mathcal{P}$ false, since there is no truth-value assignment on which every member of Γ is true. Hence $\Gamma \vDash \mathcal{P}$.

3.a. Let Γ be a truth-functionally consistent set. Then there is at least one truth-value assignment on which every member of Γ is true. But $\mathcal{P}$ is also true on such an assignment, since a truth-functionally true sentence is true on every truth-value assignment. Hence on at least one truth-value assignment every member of $\Gamma \cup \{\mathcal{P}\}$ is true; so the set is truth-functionally consistent.

4.a. $\mathcal{P}$ is either true or false on each truth-value assignment. On any assignment on which $\mathcal{P}$ is true, $\mathcal{Q}$ is true (because $\{\mathcal{P}\} \vDash \mathcal{Q}$) and so $\mathcal{Q} \vee \mathcal{R}$ is true. On any assignment on which $\mathcal{P}$ is false, $\sim\mathcal{P}$ is true, $\mathcal{R}$ is therefore also true (because $\{\sim\mathcal{P}\} \vDash \mathcal{R}$), and so $\mathcal{Q} \vee \mathcal{R}$ is true as well. Either way, then, $\mathcal{Q} \vee \mathcal{R}$ is true—so the sentence is truth-functionally true.

c. Assume that every member of $\Gamma \cup \Gamma'$ is true on some truth-value assignment. Then every member of Γ is true, and so $\mathcal{P}$ is true (because $\Gamma \vDash \mathcal{P}$). Every member of Γ' is also true, and so $\mathcal{Q}$ is true (because $\Gamma' \vDash \mathcal{Q}$). Therefore $\mathcal{P} \& \mathcal{Q}$ is true. So $\Gamma \cup \Gamma' \vDash \mathcal{P} \& \mathcal{Q}$.

CHAPTER FOUR

4.2E

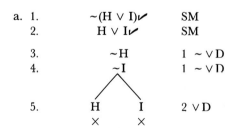

a.	1.	~(H ∨ I)✔	SM
	2.	H ∨ I✔	SM
	3.	~H	1 ~∨D
	4.	~I	1 ~∨D
	5.	H I	2 ∨D
		× ×	

Since the truth-tree is closed, the set is truth-functionally inconsistent.

c. 1.   ~(H ∨ I)✔   SM
   2.   H ∨ ~I✔   SM

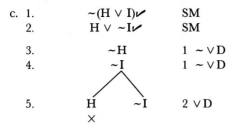

   3.   ~H   1 ~∨ D
   4.   ~I   1 ~∨ D

   5.   H   ~I   2 ∨ D
          ×

Since the truth-tree has at least one completed open branch, the set is truth-functionally consistent. The recoverable fragment is

   H   I

   F   F

e. 1.   A & (B & C)✔   SM
   2.   ~(A & (B & C))✔   SM

   3.   A   1 & D
   4.   B & C✔   1 & D
   5.   B   4 & D
   6.   C   4 & D

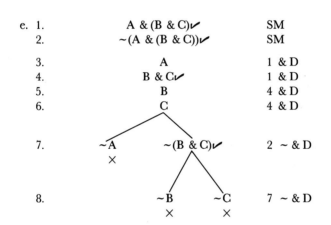

   7.   ~A   ~(B & C)✔   2 ~ & D
        ×

   8.   ~B   ~C   7 ~ & D
        ×   ×

Since the truth-tree is closed, the set is truth-functionally inconsistent.

g. 1.   ~C ∨ (A & B)✔   SM
   2.   C   SM
   3.   ~(A & B)✔   SM

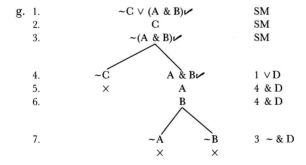

   4.   ~C   A & B✔   1 ∨ D
   5.   ×   A   4 & D
   6.   B   4 & D

   7.   ~A   ~B   3 ~ & D
        ×   ×

Since the truth-tree is closed, the set is truth-functionally inconsistent.

i. 1.   (~F & ~G) & ((G ∨ ~I) & (I ∨ ~H))✔   SM

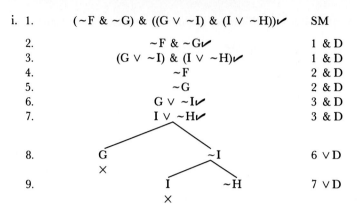

Since the truth-tree has at least one completed open branch, the set is truth-functionally consistent. The recoverable fragment is

F	G	H	I
F	**F**	**F**	**F**

k. 1.   (F ∨ ~G) & ((G ∨ ~I) & (I ∨ ~H))✔   SM

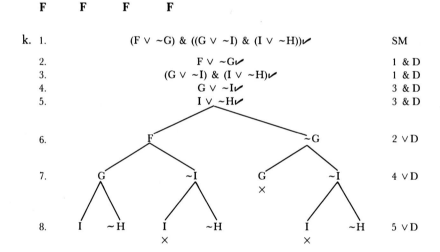

Since the truth-tree has at least one completed open branch, the set is truth-functionally consistent. The recoverable fragments are

F	G	H	I
T	T	T	T
T	T	F	T
T	T	F	F
T	F	F	F
F	F	F	F

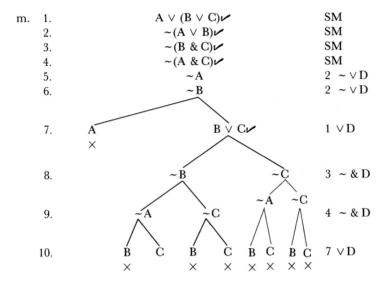

m. 1. A ∨ (B ∨ C)✔   SM
    2. ~(A ∨ B)✔   SM
    3. ~(B & C)✔   SM
    4. ~(A & C)✔   SM
    5. ~A   2 ~∨D
    6. ~B   2 ~∨D
    7. A   B ∨ C✔   1 ∨D
    8.   ~B   ~C   3 ~ & D
    9.   ~A   ~C   ~A ~C 4 ~ & D
    10. B C B C B C B C 7 ∨D

Since the truth-tree has at least one completed open branch, the set is truth-functionally consistent. The recoverable fragment is

A	B	C
F	F	T

4.3E

a. 1. ~(A ⊃ B)✔   SM
    2. ~(B ⊃ A)✔   SM
    3. A   1 ~⊃ D
    4. ~B   1 ~⊃ D
    5. B   2 ~⊃ D
    6. ~A   2 ~⊃ D
                ×

Since the truth-tree is closed, the set is truth-functionally inconsistent.

c. 1.　　　　~((A ⊃ ~B) ⊃ (B ⊃ A))✔　　SM
　　2.　　　　　~(~A ⊃ ~B)✔　　　　　　SM

　　3.　　　　　　A ⊃ ~B✔　　　　　1 ~⊃ D
　　4.　　　　　　~(B ⊃ A)✔　　　　1 ~⊃ D
　　5.　　　　　　　~A　　　　　　　2 ~⊃ D
　　6.　　　　　　　~~B✔　　　　　　2 ~⊃ D
　　7.　　　　　　　　B　　　　　　　4 ~⊃ D
　　8.　　　　　　　~A　　　　　　　4 ~⊃ D
　　9.　　　　　　　　B　　　　　　　6 ~~D

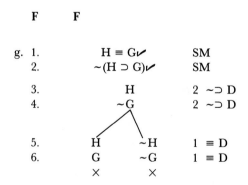

　　10.　　　~A　　　　　~B　　　　3 ⊃ D
　　　　　　　　　　　　　×

Since the truth-tree has at least one completed open branch, the set is truth-functionally consistent. The recoverable fragment is

　　A　　B

　　F　　T

e. 1.　　　　　H ≡ G✔　　　　　SM
　　2.　　　　　　~G　　　　　　SM

　　3.　　　H　　　~H　　　1 ≡ D
　　4.　　　G　　　~G　　　1 ≡ D
　　　　　　×

Since the truth-tree has at least one completed open branch, the set is truth-functionally consistent. The recoverable fragment is

　　H　　G

　　F　　F

g. 1.　　　　　H ≡ G✔　　　　　SM
　　2.　　　　　~(H ⊃ G)✔　　　SM

　　3.　　　　　　H　　　　　2 ~⊃ D
　　4.　　　　　　~G　　　　2 ~⊃ D

　　5.　　　H　　　~H　　　1 ≡ D
　　6.　　　G　　　~G　　　1 ≡ D
　　　　　　×　　　×

Since the truth-tree is closed, the set is truth-functionally inconsistent.

i.
1.   H ≡ G✔   SM
2.   G ≡ I✔   SM
3.   ~(H ⊃ I)✔   SM

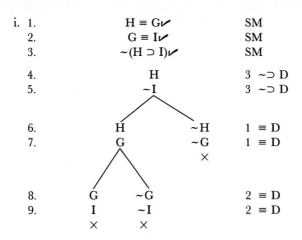

4.   H   3   ~⊃ D
5.   ~I   3   ~⊃ D

6.   H   ~H   1   ≡ D
7.   G   ~G   1   ≡ D
              ×

8.   G   ~G   2   ≡ D
9.   I   ~I   2   ≡ D
   ×   ×

Since the truth-tree is closed, the set is truth-functionally inconsistent.

k.
1.   A ≡ (~B ≡ C)✔   SM
2.   ~A ⊃ (B ⊃ ~C)✔   SM
3.   ~(A ⊃ ~C)✔   SM

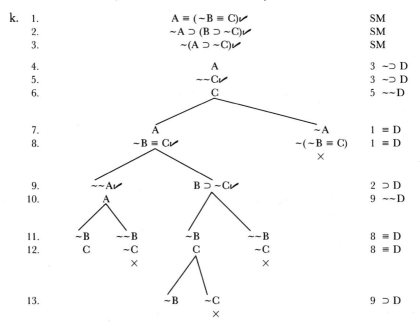

4.   A   3   ~⊃ D
5.   ~~C✔   3   ~⊃ D
6.   C   5   ~~D

7.   A   ~A   1   ≡ D
8.   ~B ≡ C✔   ~(~B ≡ C)   1   ≡ D
                          ×

9.   ~~A✔   B ⊃ ~C✔   2   ⊃ D
10.   A   9   ~~D

11.   ~B   ~~B   ~B   ~~B   8   ≡ D
12.   C   ~C   C   ~C   8   ≡ D
         ×   ×

13.   ~B   ~C   9   ⊃ D
                  ×

Since the truth-tree has at least one completed open branch, the set is truth-functionally consistent. The recoverable fragment is

A	B	C
T	F	T

m.

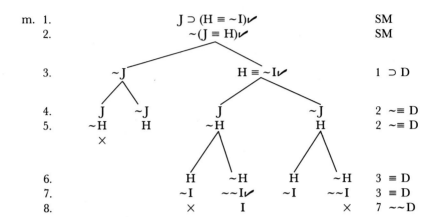

1.	J ⊃ (H ≡ ~I)✔	SM
2.	~(J ≡ H)✔	SM
3.	~J H ≡ ~I✔	1 ⊃ D
4.	J ~J J ~J	2 ~≡ D
5.	~H H ~H H	2 ~≡ D
	X	
6.	H ~H H ~H	3 ≡ D
7.	~I ~~I✔ ~I ~~I	3 ≡ D
8.	X I X	7 ~~D

Since the truth-tree has at least one completed open branch, the set is truth-functionally consistent. The recoverable fragments are

H	I	J
T	T	F
T	F	F
F	T	T

4.4E

1.a.

1.	H ∨ G✔	SM
2.	~G & ~H✔	SM
3.	~G	2 & D
4.	~H	2 & D
5.	H G	1 ∨ D
	X X	

Since the truth-tree is closed, the set is truth-functionally inconsistent.

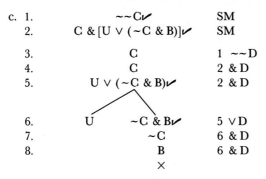

c. 1.   ~~C✔   SM
2.   C & [U ∨ (~C & B)]✔   SM

3.   C   1   ~~D
4.   C   2 & D
5.   U ∨ (~C & B)✔   2 & D

6.   U   ~C & B✔   5 ∨ D
7.   ~C   6 & D
8.   B   6 & D
           ✕

Since the truth-tree has at least one completed open branch, the set is truth-functionally consistent. The recoverable fragments are

B	C	U
F	T	T
T	T	T

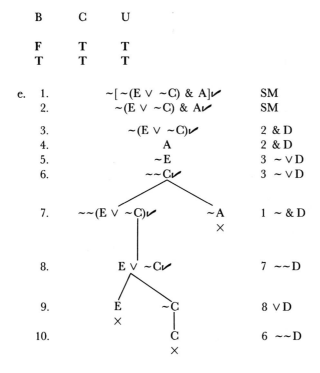

e. 1.   ~[~(E ∨ ~C) & A]✔   SM
2.   ~(E ∨ ~C) & A✔   SM

3.   ~(E ∨ ~C)✔   2 & D
4.   A   2 & D
5.   ~E   3   ~ ∨ D
6.   ~~C✔   3   ~ ∨ D

7.   ~~(E ∨ ~C)✔   ~A   1   ~ & D
                     ✕

8.   E ∨ ~C✔   7   ~~D

9.   E   ~C   8 ∨ D
      ✕
10.   C   6   ~~D
        ✕

Since the truth-tree is closed, the set is truth-functionally inconsistent.

g.

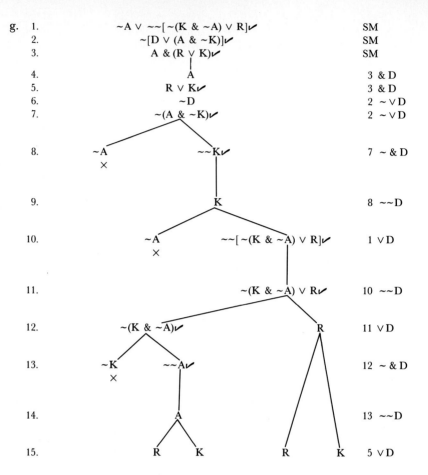

1.	~A ∨ ~~[~(K & ~A) ∨ R]✔		SM
2.	~[D ∨ (A & ~K)]✔		SM
3.	A & (R ∨ K)✔		SM
4.	A		3 & D
5.	R ∨ K✔		3 & D
6.	~D		2 ~∨ D
7.	~(A & ~K)✔		2 ~∨ D
8.	~A ~~K✔		7 ~& D
9.	K		8 ~~D
10.	~A ~~[~(K & ~A) ∨ R]✔		1 ∨ D
11.	~(K & ~A) ∨ R✔		10 ~~D
12.	~(K & ~A)✔ R		11 ∨ D
13.	~K ~~A✔		12 ~& D
14.	A		13 ~~D
15.	R K R K		5 ∨ D

Since the truth-tree has at least one completed open branch, the set is truth-functionally consistent. The recoverable fragments are

A	D	K	R
T	F	T	T
T	F	T	F

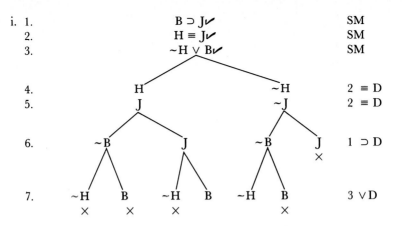

i.
1. B ⊃ J✔   SM
2. H ≡ J✔   SM
3. ~H ∨ B✔   SM
4. H   ~H   2 ≡ D
5. J   ~J   2 ≡ D
6. ~B   J   ~B   J   1 ⊃ D
7. ~H   B   ~H   B   ~H   B   3 ∨ D

Since the truth-tree has at least one completed open branch, the set is truth-functionally consistent. The recoverable fragments are

B	H	J
T	T	T
F	F	F

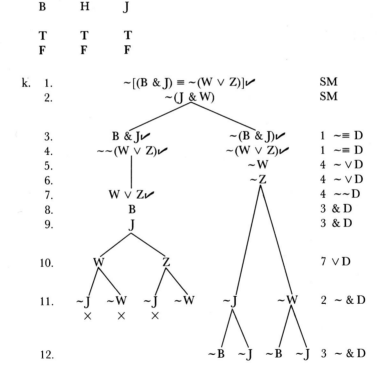

k.
1. ~[(B & J) ≡ ~(W ∨ Z)]✔   SM
2. ~(J & W)   SM
3. B & J✔   ~(B & J)✔   1 ~≡ D
4. ~~(W ∨ Z)✔   ~(W ∨ Z)✔   1 ~≡ D
5.   ~W   4 ~∨ D
6.   ~Z   4 ~∨ D
7. W ∨ Z✔   4 ~~D
8. B   3 & D
9. J   3 & D
10. W   Z   7 ∨ D
11. ~J   ~W   ~J   ~W   ~J   ~W   2 ~ & D
12.   ~B   ~J   ~B   ~J   3 ~ & D

Since the truth-tree has at least one completed open branch, the set is truth-functionally consistent. The recoverable fragments are

B	J	W	Z
T	T	F	T
T	F	F	F
F	T	F	F
F	F	F	F

2.a. True. Truth-trees test for consistency. An open branch shows that the set is consistent, because it yields at least one truth-value assignment on which all the members of the set being tested are true.

c. True. If a set has an open truth-tree, then we can recover from that tree a truth-value assignment on which every member of the set is true. And a set is, by definition, consistent if and only if there is at least one truth-value assignment on which all its members are true.

e. True. If all the branches are closed, there is no truth-value assignment on which all the members of the set being tested are true, and if there is no such assignment, that set is truth-functionally inconsistent.

g. False. The number of branches on a completed tree and the number of distinct atomic components of the members of the set being tested are not related.

i. False. Closed branches represent unsuccessful attempts to find truth-value assignments on which all the members of the set being tested are true. No fragments of truth-value assignments are recoverable from them; hence they do not yield assignments on which all the members of the set being tested are false.

k. False. The truth-tree for {A ⊃ B, A} has a closed branch.

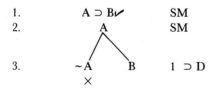

1.	A ⊃ B✔	SM
2.	A	SM
3.	~A B	1 ⊃ D
	×	

3.a.

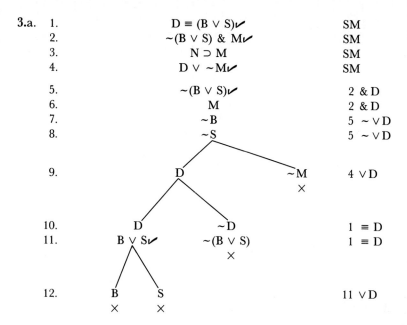

1.	D ≡ (B ∨ S)✔		SM
2.	~(B ∨ S) & M✔		SM
3.	N ⊃ M		SM
4.	D ∨ ~M✔		SM
5.	~(B ∨ S)✔		2 & D
6.	M		2 & D
7.	~B		5 ~∨D
8.	~S		5 ~∨D
9.	D ~M		4 ∨D
	✗		
10.	D ~D		1 ≡ D
11.	B ∨ S✔ ~(B ∨ S)		1 ≡ D
	✗		
12.	B S		11 ∨D
	✗ ✗		

The truth-tree closes so the set is truth-functionally inconsistent.

c.

1.	$[(B \lor M) \lor G] \mathbin{\&} \sim[(B \mathbin{\&} M) \mathbin{\&} G]$✔	SM
2.	$(B \supset I) \mathbin{\&} (\sim I \supset \sim G)$✔	SM
3.	$[U \supset (B \lor M)] \mathbin{\&} \sim M$✔	SM
4.	$U \mathbin{\&} \sim I$✔	SM
5.	U	4 & D
6.	$\sim I$	4 & D
7.	$U \supset (B \lor M)$	3 & D
8.	$\sim M$	3 & D
9.	$B \supset I$✔	2 & D
10.	$\sim I \supset \sim G$✔	2 & D
11.	$(B \lor M) \lor G$✔	1 & D
12.	$\sim[(B \mathbin{\&} M) \mathbin{\&} G]$	1 & D

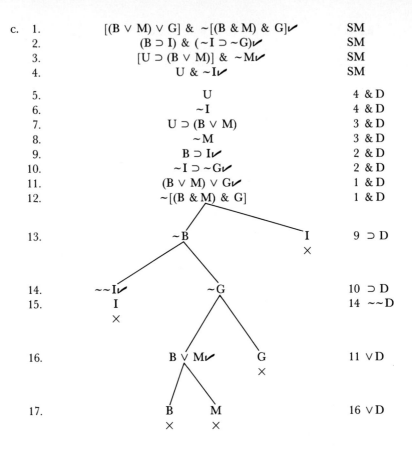

13.	$\sim B \qquad\qquad I$	9 ⊃ D
14.	$\sim\sim I$✔ $\qquad$ $\sim G$	10 ⊃ D
15.	I	14 $\sim\sim$ D
16.	$B \lor M$✔ $\qquad$ G	11 ∨ D
17.	$B \qquad M$	16 ∨ D

Since the truth-tree is closed, the set is truth-functionally inconsistent.

4.5E

1a.

1.	$M \mathbin{\&} \sim M$✔	SM
2.	M	1 & D
3.	$\sim M$	1 & D

Since the truth-tree is closed, the sentence we are testing is truth-functionally false.

c. 1.   ~M ∨ ~M✔   SM

2.   ~M   ~M   1 ∨ D

1.   ~(~M ∨ ~M)✔   SM
2.   ~~M✔   1 ~∨D
3.   ~~M✔   1 ~∨D
4.   M   2 ~~D
5.   M   3 ~~D

Since neither the tree for ' ~M ∨ ~M' nor the tree for ' ~(~M ∨ ~M)' is closed, ' ~M ∨ ~M' is truth-functionally indeterminate.

e. 1.   (C ⊃ R) & [(C ⊃ ~R) & ~(~C ∨ R)]✔   SM
2.   C ⊃ R✔   1 & D
3.   (C ⊃ ~R) & ~(~C ∨ R)✔   1 & D
4.   C ⊃ ~R   3 & D
5.   ~(~C ∨ R)✔   3 & D
6.   ~~C✔   5 ~∨D
7.   ~R   5 ~∨D
8.   C   6 ~~D

9.   ~C   R   2 ⊃ D
     ×   ×

Since the truth-tree is closed, the sentence we are testing is truth-functionally false.

g. 1.   (~A ≡ ~Z) & (A & ~Z)✔   SM
2.   ~A ≡ ~Z✔   1 & D
3.   A & ~Z✔   1 & D
4.   A   3 & D
5.   ~Z   3 & D

6.   ~A   ~~A   2 ≡ D
7.   ~Z   ~~Z✔   2 ≡ D
     ×
8.   Z   7 ~~D
         ×

Since the truth-tree is closed, the sentence we are testing is truth-functionally false.

i. 1.   (A ∨ B) & ~(A ∨ B)✔   SM

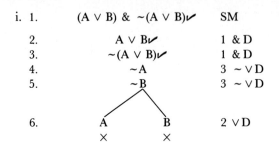

2.   A ∨ B✔   1 & D
3.   ~(A ∨ B)✔   1 & D
4.   ~A   3 ~ ∨ D
5.   ~B   3 ~ ∨ D

6.   A   B   2 ∨ D
          ×   ×

The tree is closed, so the sentence is truth-functionally false.

k. 1.   (A ∨ B) ≡ ~(A ∨ B)✔   SM

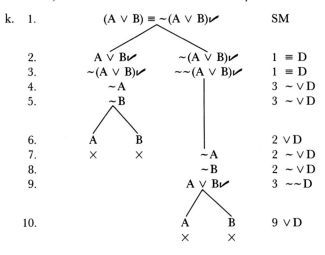

2.   A ∨ B✔   ~(A ∨ B)✔   1 ≡ D
3. ~(A ∨ B)✔   ~~(A ∨ B)✔ 1 ≡ D
4.   ~A   3 ~ ∨ D
5.   ~B   3 ~ ∨ D

6.   A   B   2 ∨ D
7.   ×   ×   ~A   2 ~ ∨ D
8.   ~B   2 ~ ∨ D
9.   A ∨ B✔   3 ~~ D

10.   A   B   9 ∨ D
                ×   ×

The tree is closed, so the sentence is truth-functionally false.

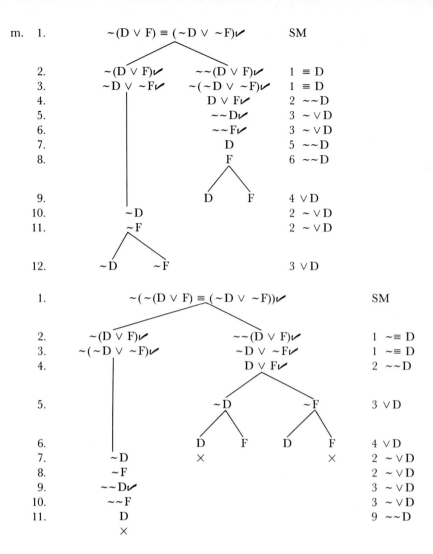

m. 1.   ~(D ∨ F) ≡ (~D ∨ ~F)✔   SM

2.   ~(D ∨ F)✔   ~~(D ∨ F)✔   1 ≡ D
3.   ~D ∨ ~F✔   ~(~D ∨ ~F)✔   1 ≡ D
4.   D ∨ F✔   2 ~~D
5.   ~~D✔   3 ~∨ D
6.   ~~F✔   3 ~∨ D
7.   D   5 ~~D
8.   F   6 ~~D

9.   D   F   4 ∨ D
10.   ~D   2 ~∨ D
11.   ~F   2 ~∨ D

12.   ~D   ~F   3 ∨ D

1.   ~(~(D ∨ F) ≡ (~D ∨ ~F))✔   SM

2.   ~(D ∨ F)✔   ~~(D ∨ F)✔   1 ~≡ D
3.   ~(~D ∨ ~F)✔   ~D ∨ ~F✔   1 ~≡ D
4.   D ∨ F✔   2 ~~D

5.   ~D   ~F   3 ∨ D

6.   D   F   D   F   4 ∨ D
7.   ~D   ×   ×   2 ~∨ D
8.   ~F   2 ~∨ D
9.   ~~D✔   3 ~∨ D
10.   ~~F   3 ~∨ D
11.   D   9 ~~D
       ×

Neither the tree for the sentence nor the tree for its negation is closed. Therefore the sentence is truth-functionally indeterminate.

2.a.

1.	~[(B ⊃ L) ∨ (L ⊃ B)]✔	SM
2.	~(B ⊃ L)✔	1 ~∨ D
3.	~(L ⊃ B)✔	1 ~∨ D
4.	B	2 ~⊃ D
5.	~L	2 ~⊃ D
6.	L	3 ~⊃ D
7.	~B	3 ~⊃ D
	✕	

Since the truth-tree for the negation of the given sentence is closed, the given sentence is truth-functionally true.

c.

1.	~[(A ≡ K) ⊃ (A ∨ K)]✔	SM
2.	A ≡ K✔	1 ~⊃ D
3.	~(A ∨ K)✔	1 ~⊃ D
4.	~A	3 ~∨ D
5.	~K	3 ~∨ D

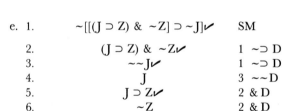

6.	A　　　　~A	2 ≡ D
7.	K　　　　~K	2 ≡ D
	✕	

Since the truth-tree for the negation of the given sentence is not closed, the given sentence is not truth-functionally true. The recoverable fragment is

A	K
F	F

e.

1.	~[[(J ⊃ Z) & ~Z] ⊃ ~J]✔	SM
2.	(J ⊃ Z) & ~Z✔	1 ~⊃ D
3.	~~J✔	1 ~⊃ D
4.	J	3 ~~D
5.	J ⊃ Z✔	2 & D
6.	~Z	2 & D

| 7. | ~J　　　　Z | 5 ⊃ D |
| | ✕　　　　✕ | |

Since the truth-tree for the negation of the given sentence is closed, the given sentence is truth-functionally true.

g. 1.   ~[(B ⊃ (M ⊃ H)) ≡ [(B ⊃ M) ⊃ (B ⊃ H)]]✔   SM

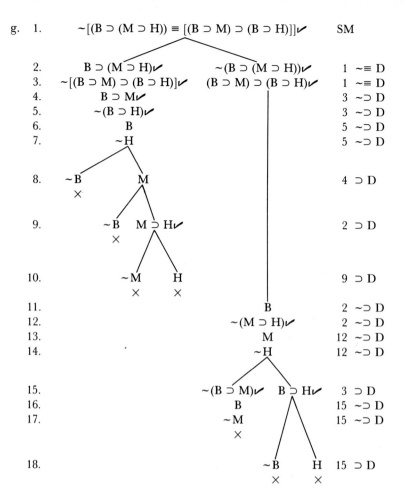

2.   B ⊃ (M ⊃ H)✔   ~(B ⊃ (M ⊃ H))✔   1   ~≡ D
3.   ~[(B ⊃ M) ⊃ (B ⊃ H)]✔   (B ⊃ M) ⊃ (B ⊃ H)✔   1   ~≡ D
4.   B ⊃ M✔   3   ~⊃ D
5.   ~(B ⊃ H)✔   3   ~⊃ D
6.   B   5   ~⊃ D
7.   ~H   5   ~⊃ D

8.   ~B   M   4   ⊃ D
      ×

9.   ~B   M ⊃ H✔   2   ⊃ D
        ×

10.   ~M   H   9   ⊃ D
        ×   ×

11.   B   2   ~⊃ D
12.   ~(M ⊃ H)✔   2   ~⊃ D
13.   M   12   ~⊃ D
14.   ·   ~H   12   ~⊃ D

15.   ~(B ⊃ M)✔   B ⊃ H✔   3   ⊃ D
16.   B   15   ~⊃ D
17.   ~M   15   ~⊃ D
             ×

18.   ~B   H   15   ⊃ D
                      ×   ×

Since the truth-tree for the negation of the given sentence is closed, the given sentence is truth-functionally true.

i. 1.   ~((A & ~B) ⊃ ~(A ∨ B))✔   SM

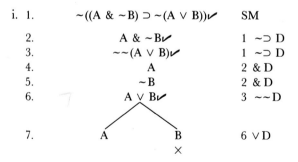

2.   A & ~B✔   1   ~⊃ D
3.   ~~(A ∨ B)✔   1   ~⊃ D
4.   A   2   & D
5.   ~B   2   & D
6.   A ∨ B✔   3   ~~ D

7.   A   B   6   ∨ D
            ×

The tree for the negation of the sentence is not closed. Therefore the sentence is not truth-functionally true. The recoverable fragment is

A   B

T   F

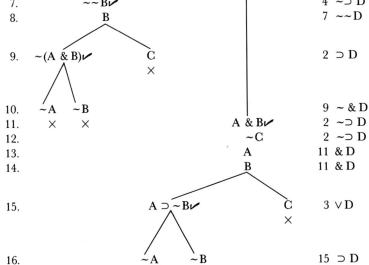

k. 1.   ~(((A & B) ⊃ C) ≡ ((A ⊃ ~B) ∨ C))✔   SM

2.   (A & B) ⊃ C✔   ~((A & B) ⊃ C)✔   1 ~≡ D
3.   ~((A ⊃ ~B) ∨ C)✔   (A ⊃ ~B) ∨ C✔   1 ~≡ D
4.   ~(A ⊃ ~B)✔   3 ~∨ D
5.   ~C   3 ~∨ D
6.   A   4 ~⊃ D
7.   ~~B✔   4 ~⊃ D
8.   B   7 ~~D

9. ~(A & B)✔   C   2 ⊃ D
                            ×

10. ~A ~B   9 ~& D
11. ×   ×   A & B✔   2 ~⊃ D
12.   ~C   2 ~⊃ D
13.   A   11 & D
14.   B   11 & D

15.   A ⊃ ~B✔   C   3 ∨ D
                                   ×

16.   ~A   ~B   15 ⊃ D
             ×   ×

The tree for the negation of the sentence is closed. Therefore the sentence is truth-functionally true.

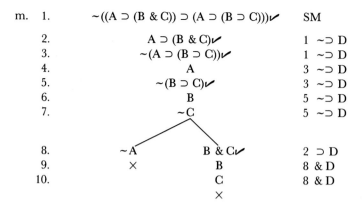

m. 1.   ~((A ⊃ (B & C)) ⊃ (A ⊃ (B ⊃ C)))✔   SM

    2.   A ⊃ (B & C)✔   1 ~⊃ D
    3.   ~(A ⊃ (B ⊃ C))✔   1 ~⊃ D
    4.   A   3 ~⊃ D
    5.   ~(B ⊃ C)✔   3 ~⊃ D
    6.   B   5 ~⊃ D
    7.   ~C   5 ~⊃ D

    8.   ~A   B & C✔   2 ⊃ D
    9.   ×   B   8 & D
    10.   C   8 & D
                                        ×

The tree for the negation of the sentence is closed. Therefore the sentence is truth-functionally true.

o. 1.   ~(((A & B) ⊃ C) ≡ (A ⊃ (B ⊃ C)))✔   SM

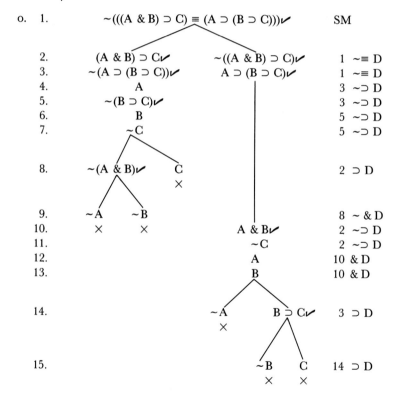

    2.   (A & B) ⊃ C✔   ~((A & B) ⊃ C)✔   1 ~≡ D
    3.   ~(A ⊃ (B ⊃ C))✔   A ⊃ (B ⊃ C)✔   1 ~≡ D
    4.   A   3 ~⊃ D
    5.   ~(B ⊃ C)✔   3 ~⊃ D
    6.   B   5 ~⊃ D
    7.   ~C   5 ~⊃ D

    8.   ~(A & B)✔   C   2 ⊃ D
                         ×

    9.   ~A   ~B   8 ~ & D
    10.   ×   ×   A & B✔   2 ~⊃ D
    11.   ~C   2 ~⊃ D
    12.   A   10 & D
    13.   B   10 & D

    14.   ~A   B ⊃ C✔   3 ⊃ D
                       ×

    15.   ~B   C   14 ⊃ D
                            ×   ×

The tree for the negation of the sentence is closed. Therefore the sentence is truth-functionally true.

3.a. 1.   ~(~A ⊃ A)✔   SM

2.   ~A   1 ~⊃ D
3.   ~A   1 ~⊃ D

The tree for the sentence does not close. Therefore the sentence is not truth-functionally false. The recoverable fragment is

    A

    F

Since only one of the two relevant fragments is recoverable, the sentence is not truth-functionally true. Therefore it is truth-functionally indeterminate.

    c. 1.   (A ≡ ~A) ⊃ ~(A ≡ ~A)✔   SM

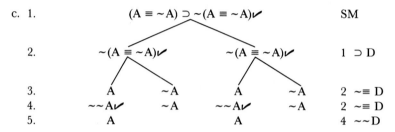

        2.   ~(A ≡ ~A)✔   ~(A ≡ ~A)✔   1 ⊃ D

        3.   A   ~A   A   ~A   2 ~≡ D
        4.   ~~A✔   ~A   ~~A✔   ~A   2 ~≡ D
        5.   A   A   4 ~~D

The tree for the sentence does not close. Therefore the sentence is not truth-functionally false. The recoverable fragments are

    A

    T
    F

Since both the two relevant fragments are recoverable, the sentence is truth-functionally true.

    e. 1.   (~B & ~D) ∨ ~(B ∨ D)✔   SM

        2.   ~B & ~D✔   ~(B ∨ D)✔   1 ∨ D
        3.   ~B   2 & D
        4.   ~D   2 & D
        5.   ~B   2 ~∨ D
        6.   ~D   2 ~∨ D

The tree for the sentence does not close. Therefore the sentence is not truth-functionally false. The recoverable fragment is

B   D

F   F

Since only one of the four relevant fragments is recoverable, the sentence is not truth-functionally true. Therefore it is truth-functionally indeterminate.

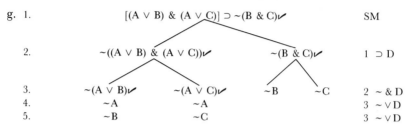

g. 1.   [(A ∨ B) & (A ∨ C)] ⊃ ~(B & C)✔   SM

2.   ~((A ∨ B) & (A ∨ C))✔   ~(B & C)✔   1 ⊃ D

3.   ~(A ∨ B)✔   ~(A ∨ C)✔   ~B   ~C   2 ~ & D

4.   ~A   ~A   3 ~ ∨ D

5.   ~B   ~C   3 ~ ∨ D

The tree for the sentence does not close. Therefore the sentence is not truth-functionally false. The recoverable fragments are

A	B	C
F	F	T
F	F	F
F	T	F
T	F	T
T	F	F
T	T	F

Since only six of the eight relevant fragments are recoverable, the sentence is not truth-functionally true. Therefore it is truth-functionally indeterminate.

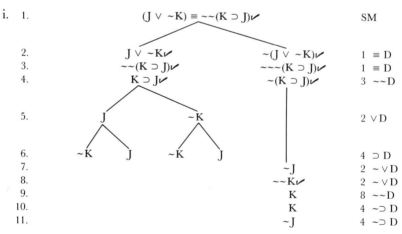

i. 1.   (J ∨ ~K) ≡ ~~(K ⊃ J)✔   SM

2.   J ∨ ~K✔   ~(J ∨ ~K)✔   1 ≡ D

3.   ~~(K ⊃ J)✔   ~~~(K ⊃ J)✔   1 ≡ D

4.   K ⊃ J✔   ~(K ⊃ J)✔   3 ~~D

5.   J   ~K   2 ∨ D

6. ~K J ~K J   4 ⊃ D

7.   ~J   2 ~ ∨ D

8.   ~~K✔   2 ~ ∨ D

9.   K   8 ~~D

10.   K   4 ~⊃ D

11.   ~J   4 ~⊃ D

The tree for the sentence does not close. Therefore the sentence is not truth-functionally false. The recoverable fragments are

J	K
T	F
T	T
F	T
F	F

Since all four of the four relevant fragments are recoverable, the sentence is truth-functionally true.

4.a. False. A tree or a truth-functionally true sentence can have some open and some closed branches '(H ∨ ~H) ∨ (~H & H)' is clearly truth-functionally true, inasmuch as its left disjunct is truth-functionally true. Yet the tree for this sentence has two open branches and one closed branch.

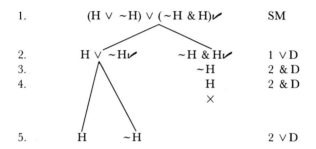

1.	(H ∨ ~H) ∨ (~H & H)✔	SM
2.	H ∨ ~H✔ ~H & H✔	1 ∨D
3.	~H	2 &D
4.	H	2 &D
	×	
5.	H ~H	2 ∨D

    c. False. Many truth-functionally indeterminate sentences have completed trees all of whose branches are open. A simple example is

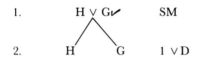

| 1. | H ∨ G✔ | SM |
| 2. | H   G | 1 ∨D |

    e. False. Some such unit sets will have open trees; for example { 𝒫 ∨ 𝒬 } will, but not all such unit sets need have open trees. For example, { 𝒫 & 𝒬 } will have a closed tree if 𝒫 is 'H & G' and 𝒬 is ' ~H & K'.

1.	(H & G) & (~H & K)✔	SM
2.	H & G✔	1 &D
3.	~H & K✔	1 &D
4.	H	2 &D
5.	G	2 &D
6.	~H	3 &D
7.	K	3 &D
	×	

4.6E

1.a.

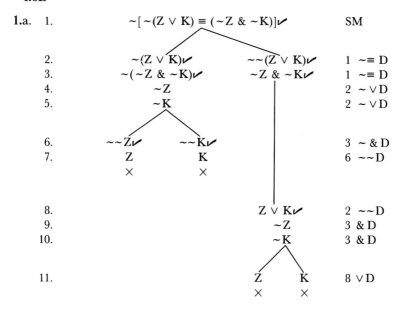

1.   ~[~(Z ∨ K) ≡ (~Z & ~K)]✔   SM

2.   ~(Z ∨ K)✔   ~~(Z ∨ K)✔   1   ~≡ D
3.   ~(~Z & ~K)✔   ~Z & ~K✔   1   ~≡ D
4.   ~Z   2   ~∨ D
5.   ~K   2   ~∨ D

6.   ~~Z✔   ~~K✔   3   ~& D
7.   Z   K   6   ~~D
      ×   ×

8.   Z ∨ K✔   2   ~~D
9.   ~Z   3 & D
10.   ~K   3 & D

11.   Z   K   8 ∨ D
                      ×   ×

Our truth-tree for the negation of the biconditional of the sentences we are testing, ' ~(Z ∨ K)' and ' ~Z & ~K', is closed. Therefore that negation is truth-functionally false, the biconditional it is a negation of is truth-functional true, and the sentences we are testing are truth-functionally equivalent.

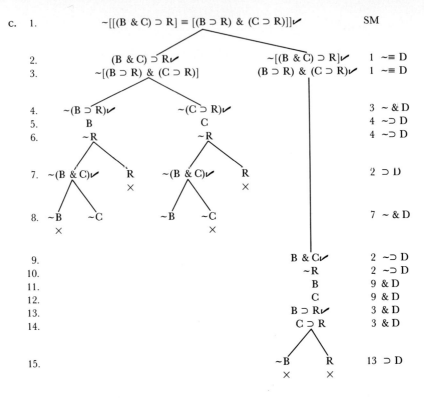

c. 1.   ~[[(B & C) ⊃ R] ≡ [(B ⊃ R) & (C ⊃ R)]]✔   SM

2.   (B & C) ⊃ R✔   ~[(B & C) ⊃ R]✔   1 ~≡ D
3.   ~[(B ⊃ R) & (C ⊃ R)]   (B ⊃ R) & (C ⊃ R)✔   1 ~≡ D

4.   ~(B ⊃ R)✔   ~(C ⊃ R)✔   3 ~ & D
5.   B   C   4 ~⊃ D
6.   ~R   ~R   4 ~⊃ D

7.   ~(B & C)✔   R   ~(B & C)✔   R   2 ⊃ D
                   ✕   ✕

8. ~B   ~C   ~B   ~C   7 ~ & D
   ✕   ✕

9.   B & C✔   2 ~⊃ D
10.   ~R   2 ~⊃ D
11.   B   9 & D
12.   C   9 & D
13.   B ⊃ R✔   3 & D
14.   C ⊃ R   3 & D

15.   ~B   R   13 ⊃ D
                         ✕   ✕

Since our truth-tree for the negation of the biconditional of the sentences we are testing is open, those sentences are not truth-functionally equivalent. The recoverable fragments are

B	C	R
T	F	F
F	T	F

e. 1.

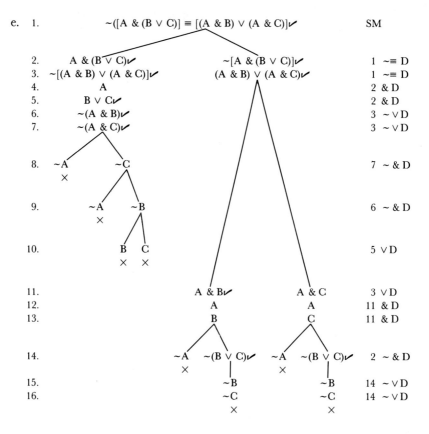

1.	~([A & (B ∨ C)] ≡ [(A & B) ∨ (A & C)]✔	SM
2.	A & (B ∨ C)✔	~[A & (B ∨ C)]✔	1 ~≡ D
3.	~[(A & B) ∨ (A & C)]✔	(A & B) ∨ (A & C)✔	1 ~≡ D
4.	A	2 & D
5.	B ∨ C✔	2 & D
6.	~(A & B)✔	3 ~∨ D
7.	~(A & C)✔	3 ~∨ D
8.	~A ~C	7 ~ & D
9.	~A ~B	6 ~ & D
10.	B C	5 ∨ D
11.	A & B✔ A & C	3 ∨ D
12.	A A	11 & D
13.	B C	11 & D
14.	~A ~(B ∨ C)✔ ~A ~(B ∨ C)✔	2 ~ & D
15.	~B ~B	14 ~∨ D
16.	~C ~C	14 ~∨ D

Since our truth-tree for the negation of the biconditional of the sentences we are testing is closed, those sentences are truth-functionally equivalent.

g. 1.   ~[(D ⊃ (L ⊃ M)) ≡ ((D ⊃ L) ⊃ M)]✔   SM

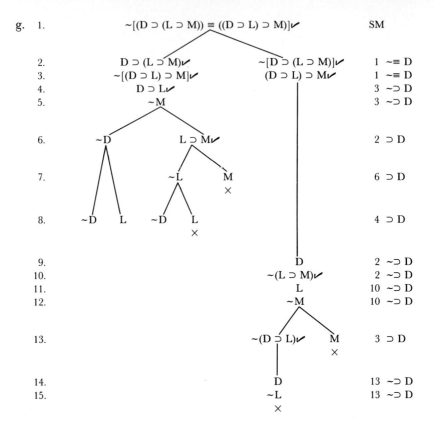

2.   D ⊃ (L ⊃ M)✔   ~[D ⊃ (L ⊃ M)]✔   1 ~≡ D
3.   ~[(D ⊃ L) ⊃ M]✔   (D ⊃ L) ⊃ M✔   1 ~≡ D
4.   D ⊃ L✔   3 ~⊃ D
5.   ~M   3 ~⊃ D

6.   ~D   L ⊃ M✔   2 ⊃ D

7.   ~L   M   6 ⊃ D
                               ×

8. ~D   L   ~D   L   4 ⊃ D
            ×

9.   D   2 ~⊃ D
10.   ~(L ⊃ M)✔   2 ~⊃ D
11.   L   10 ~⊃ D
12.   ~M   10 ~⊃ D

13.   ~(D ⊃ L)✔   M   3 ⊃ D
                                                  ×

14.   D   13 ~⊃ D
15.   ~L   13 ~⊃ D
                                        ×

Since our truth-tree for the negation of the biconditional of the sentences we are testing is open, those sentences are not truth-functionally equivalent. The recoverable fragments are

D	L	M
F	T	F
F	F	F

2.a. True. If *𝒫* and *𝒬* are truth-functionally equivalent, their biconditional is truth-functionally true. And all truth-functionally true sentences have open trees.

c. False. The tree for the set {*𝒫*, *𝒬*} may close, for *𝒫* and *𝒬* may both be truth-functionally false. Remember that all truth-functionally false sentences are truth-functionally equivalent and a set composed of one or more truth-functionally false sentences will have a closed tree.

4.7E

1.a.

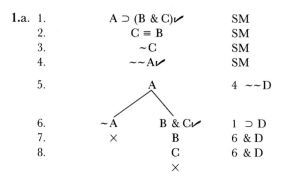

1.	A ⊃ (B & C)✔	SM
2.	C ≡ B	SM
3.	~C	SM
4.	~~A✔	SM
5.	A	4 ~~D
6.	~A B & C✔	1 ⊃ D
7.	× B	6 & D
8.	C	6 & D
	×	

Our tree is closed, so the set {A ⊃ (B & C), C ≡ B, ~C} does truth-functionally entail '~A'.

c.

1.	~(A ≡ B)✔	SM
2.	~A	SM
3.	~B	SM
4.	~(C & ~C)	SM
5.	A ~A	1 ~≡ D
6.	~B B	1 ~≡ D
	× ×	

Our tree is closed, so the set {~(A ≡ B), ~A, ~B} does truth-functionally entail 'C & ~C'.

e.

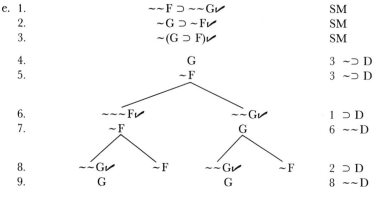

1.	~~F ⊃ ~~G✔	SM
2.	~G ⊃ ~F✔	SM
3.	~(G ⊃ F)✔	SM
4.	G	3 ~⊃ D
5.	~F	3 ~⊃ D
6.	~~~F✔ ~~G✔	1 ⊃ D
7.	~F G	6 ~~D
8.	~~G✔ ~F ~~G✔ ~F	2 ⊃ D
9.	G G	8 ~~D

Our truth-tree is open, so the set {~~F ⊃ ~G, ~G ⊃ ~F} does not truth-functionally entail 'G ⊃ F'. The relevant fragment of the recoverable truth-value assignments is

    F   G

    F   **T**

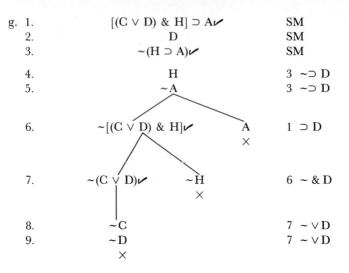

g. 1.   [(C ∨ D) & H] ⊃ A✔   SM
   2.   D   SM
   3.   ~(H ⊃ A)✔   SM

   4.   H   3 ~⊃ D
   5.   ~A   3 ~⊃ D

Our truth-tree is closed, so the given set does truth-functionally entail 'H ⊃ A'.

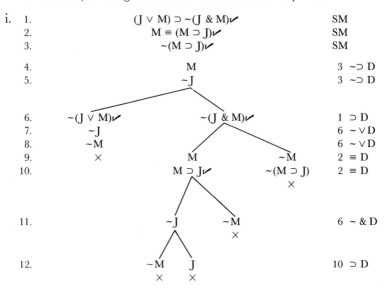

i. 1.   (J ∨ M) ⊃ ~(J & M)✔   SM
   2.   M ≡ (M ⊃ J)✔   SM
   3.   ~(M ⊃ J)✔   SM

The tree is closed, so the set {(J ∨ M) ⊃ ~(J & M), M ≡ (M ⊃ J)} does truth-functionally entail 'M ⊃ J'.

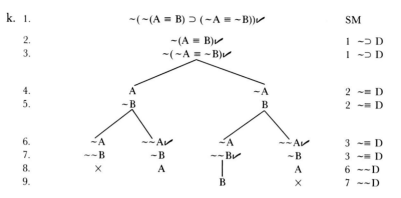

k. 1.   ~(~(A ≡ B) ⊃ (~A ≡ ~B))✔   SM
   2.   ~(A ≡ B)✔   1 ~⊃ D
   3.   ~(~A ≡ ~B)✔   1 ~⊃ D

   4.   A   ~A   2 ~≡ D
   5.   ~B   B   2 ~≡ D

   6. ~A   ~~A✔   ~A   ~~A✔   3 ~≡ D
   7. ~~B   ~B   ~~B✔   ~B   3 ~≡ D
   8. ×   A   A   6 ~~D
   9.   B   ×   7 ~~D

Our truth-tree is open, so the empty set does not truth-functionally entail '~(A ≡ B) ⊃ (~A ≡ ~B)'. The relevant fragments of the recoverable truth-value assignments are

A	B
T	F
F	T

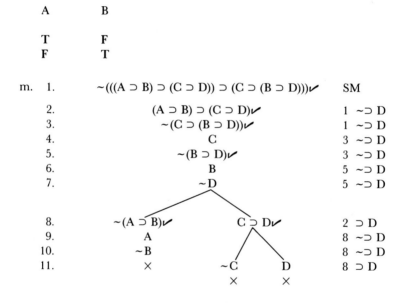

m. 1.   ~(((A ⊃ B) ⊃ (C ⊃ D)) ⊃ (C ⊃ (B ⊃ D)))✔   SM
  2.   (A ⊃ B) ⊃ (C ⊃ D)✔   1 ~⊃ D
  3.   ~(C ⊃ (B ⊃ D))✔   1 ~⊃ D
  4.   C   3 ~⊃ D
  5.   ~(B ⊃ D)✔   3 ~⊃ D
  6.   B   5 ~⊃ D
  7.   ~D   5 ~⊃ D

  8.   ~(A ⊃ B)✔   C ⊃ D✔   2 ⊃ D
  9.   A   8 ~⊃ D
 10. ~B   8 ~⊃ D
 11. ×   ~C   D   8 ⊃ D
          ×   ×

The tree is closed, so the empty set does truth-functionally entail '[(A ⊃ B) ⊃ (C ⊃ D)] ⊃ [C ⊃ (B ⊃ D)]'.

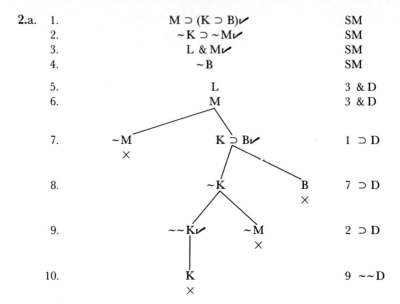

2.a.

1.	M ⊃ (K ⊃ B)✔		SM
2.	~K ⊃ ~M✔		SM
3.	L & M✔		SM
4.	~B		SM
5.	L		3 & D
6.	M		3 & D
7.	~M / K ⊃ B✔		1 ⊃ D
	×		
8.	~K	B	7 ⊃ D
		×	
9.	~~K✔	~M	2 ⊃ D
		×	
10.	K		9 ~~D
	×		

Our truth-tree for the premises and the negation of the conclusion of the argument we are testing is closed. Therefore there is no truth-value assignment on which the premises and the negation of the conclusion are all true, hence no assignment on which the premises are true and the conclusion false. So the argument is truth-functionally valid.

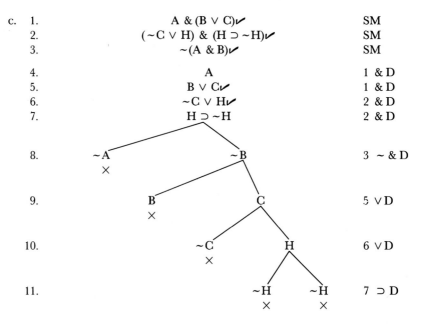

c.

1.	A & (B ∨ C)✔		SM
2.	(~C ∨ H) & (H ⊃ ~H)✔		SM
3.	~(A & B)✔		SM
4.	A		1 & D
5.	B ∨ C✔		1 & D
6.	~C ∨ H✔		2 & D
7.	H ⊃ ~H		2 & D
8.	~A / ~B		3 ~ & D
	×		
9.	B	C	5 ∨ D
	×		
10.	~C	H	6 ∨ D
	×		
11.		~H / ~H	7 ⊃ D
		× ×	

Our truth-tree for the premises and the negation of the conclusion of the argument we are testing is closed. Therefore the argument is truth-functionally valid.

e.

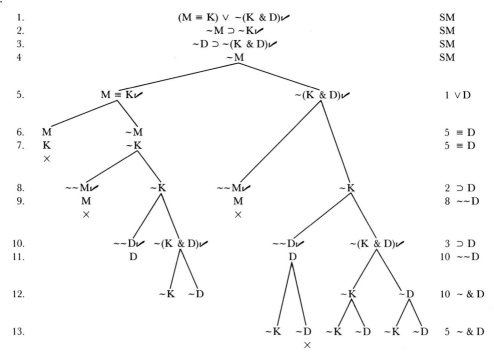

1.	(M ≡ K) ∨ ~(K & D)✔	SM
2.	~M ⊃ ~K✔	SM
3.	~D ⊃ ~(K & D)✔	SM
4	~M	SM
5.	M ≡ K✔ ~(K & D)✔	1 ∨ D
6.	M ~M	5 ≡ D
7.	K ~K	5 ≡ D
8.	~~M✔ ~K ~~M✔ ~K	2 ⊃ D
9.	M M	8 ~~D
10.	~~D✔ ~(K & D)✔ ~~D✔ ~(K & D)✔	3 ⊃ D
11.	D D	10 ~~D
12.	~K ~D ~K ~D	10 ~ & D
13.	~K ~D ~K ~D ~K ~D	5 ~ & D

Our truth-tree for the premises and the negation of the conclusion of the argument we are testing is open. Therefore that argument is truth-functionally invalid. The recoverable fragments are

D	K	M
T	F	F
F	F	F

g. 1. B & (H ∨ Z)✔   SM
   2. ~Z ⊃ K✔   SM
   3. (B ≡ Z) ⊃ ~Z✔   SM
   4. ~K   SM
   5. ~(M & N)   SM

   6. B   1 & D
   7. H ∨ Z   1 & D

   8. ~~Z✔   K   2 ⊃ D
                     ×

   9. Z   8 ~~D

   10. ~(B ≡ Z)✔   ~Z   3 ⊃ D
                      ×

   11. B   ~B   10 ~≡ D
   12. ~Z   Z   10 ~≡ D
       ×   ×

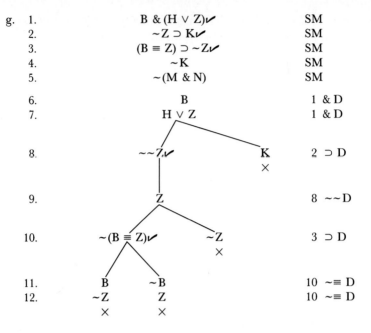

Our truth-tree for the premises and the negation of the conclusion of the argument we are testing is closed. Therefore that argument is truth-functionally valid. Notice that our tree closed before we decomposed the negation of the conclusion. Thus the premises of the argument form a truth-functionally inconsistent set, and therefore those premises and any conclusion will constitute a truth-functionally valid argument, even where the conclusion has no atomic components in common with the premises.

i. 1. A & (B ⊃ C)✔   SM
   2. ~((A & C) ∨ (A & ~B))✔   SM

   3. A   1 & D
   4. B ⊃ C✔   1 & D
   5. ~(A & C)✔   2 ~∨ D
   6. ~(A & ~B)✔   2 ~∨ D

   7.   ~B   C   4 ⊃ D

   8. ~A   ~C   ~A   ~C   5 ~ & D
       ×   ×   ×

   9.   ~A   ~~B✔   6 ~ & D
   10.   ×   B   9 ~~D
              ×

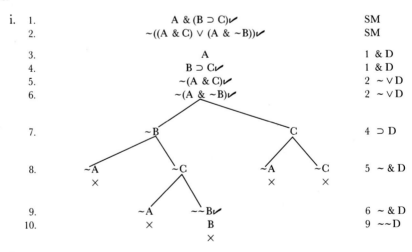

Our truth-tree for the premise and the negation of the conclusion is closed. Therefore the argument is truth-functionally valid.

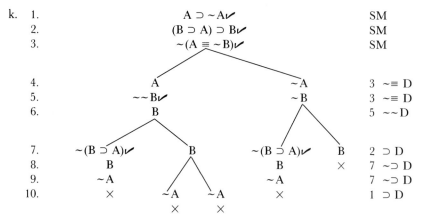

k.
1.   A ⊃ ~A✔   SM
2.   (B ⊃ A) ⊃ B✔   SM
3.   ~(A ≡ ~B)✔   SM

4.   A   ~A   3 ~≡ D
5.   ~~B✔   ~B   3 ~≡ D
6.   B   5 ~~D

7. ~(B ⊃ A)✔   B   ~(B ⊃ A)✔   B   2 ⊃ D
8.   B   B   ×   7 ~⊃ D
9.   ~A   ~A   7 ~⊃ D
10.   ×   ~A   ~A   ×   1 ⊃ D
      ×   ×

Our truth-tree for the premise and the negation of the conclusion is closed. Therefore the argument is truth-functionally valid.

3.a. In symbolizing the argument we use the following abbreviations:

C: Members of Congress claim to be sympathetic to senior citizens.
M: More money will be collected through social security taxes.
S: The social security system will succeed.
T: Many senior citizens will be in trouble.

Here is our tree for the premises and the negation of the conclusion:

1.   S ≡ M✔   SM
2.   S ∨ T   SM
3.   C & ~M✔   SM
4.   ~~S✔   SM

5.   S   4 ~~D
6.   C   3 & D
7.   ~M   3 & D

8.   S   ~S   1 ≡ D
9.   M   ~M   1 ≡ D
   ×   ×

Since our truth-tree is closed, the argument is truth-functionally valid.

c. In symbolizing the argument we use the following abbreviations:

A: The President acts quickly.
C: The President is pressured by senior citizens.
D: Senior citizens will be delighted.
H: The President is pressured by members of the House.
M: The President is pressured by members of the Senate.
S: The social security system will be saved.

Here is our tree for the premises and the negation of the conclusion.

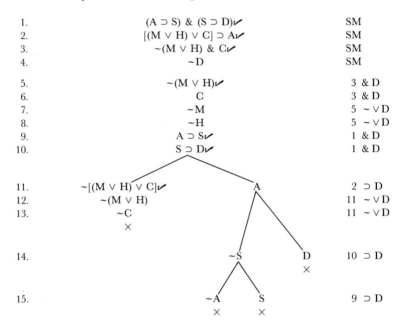

1.	(A ⊃ S) & (S ⊃ D)✔	SM
2.	[(M ∨ H) ∨ C] ⊃ A✔	SM
3.	~(M ∨ H) & C✔	SM
4.	~D	SM
5.	~(M ∨ H)✔	3 & D
6.	C	3 & D
7.	~M	5 ~∨ D
8.	~H	5 ~∨ D
9.	A ⊃ S✔	1 & D
10.	S ⊃ D✔	1 & D
11.	~[(M ∨ H) ∨ C]✔ A	2 ⊃ D
12.	~(M ∨ H)	11 ~∨ D
13.	~C	11 ~∨ D
	×	
14.	~S D	10 ⊃ D
	×	
15.	~A S	9 ⊃ D
	× ×	

Since our tree is closed, the argument is truth-functionally valid.

e. In symbolizing the argument we use the following abbreviations:

H: The House of Representatives will pass the bill.
S: The Senate will pass the bill.
T: The President will be pleased.
V: The voters will be pleased.
W: All the members of the White House will be happy.

Here is our tree for the premises and the negation of the conclusion.

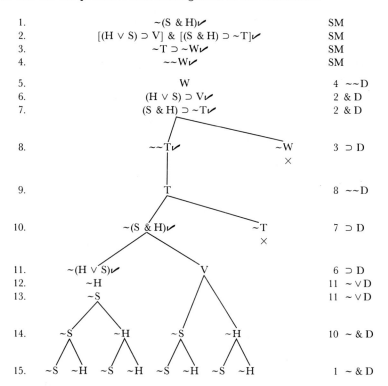

1.	~(S & H)✔	SM
2.	[(H ∨ S) ⊃ V] & [(S & H) ⊃ ~T]✔	SM
3.	~T ⊃ ~W✔	SM
4.	~~W✔	SM
5.	W	4 ~~D
6.	(H ∨ S) ⊃ V✔	2 & D
7.	(S & H) ⊃ ~T✔	2 & D
8.	~~T✔ ~W	3 ⊃ D
	×	
9.	T	8 ~~D
10.	~(S & H)✔ ~T	7 ⊃ D
	×	
11.	~(H ∨ S)✔ V	6 ⊃ D
12.	~H	11 ~∨D
13.	~S	11 ~∨D
14.	~S ~H ~S ~H	10 ~ & D
15.	~S ~H ~S ~H ~S ~H ~S ~H	1 ~ & D

Since our truth-tree is open, the argument is truth-functionally invalid. The recoverable fragments are

H	S	T	W	V
T	F	T	T	T
F	T	T	T	T
F	F	T	T	T
F	F	T	T	F

5. The needed rules are

The tree or the negation of the biconditional of the given sentences is

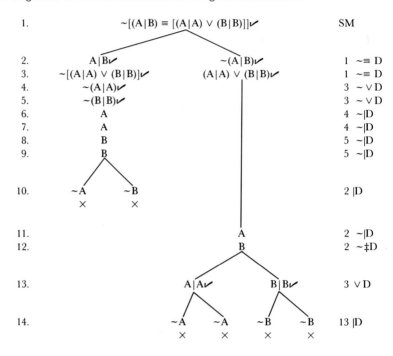

1.   ~[(A|B) ≡ [(A|A) ∨ (B|B)]]✔   SM

2.   A|B✔   ~(A|B)✔   1   ~≡ D
3.   ~[(A|A) ∨ (B|B)]✔   (A|A) ∨ (B|B)✔   1   ~≡ D
4.   ~(A|A)✔   3   ~∨ D
5.   ~(B|B)✔   3   ~∨ D
6.   A   4   ~|D
7.   A   4   ~|D
8.   B   5   ~|D
9.   B   5   ~|D

10.   ~A   ~B   2 |D
    ×   ×

11.   A   2   ~|D
12.   B   2   ~‡D

13.   A|A✔   B|B✔   3 ∨ D

14.   ~A   ~A   ~B   ~B   13 |D
    ×   ×   ×   ×

Since our tree closes, the sentences we are testing are truth-functionally equivalent.

CHAPTER FIVE

5.1.1E

a. Derive: Q & R

1	R & Q	Assumption
2	Q	1 & E
3	R	1 & E
4	Q & R	2, 3 & I

c. Derive: K

1	S & [~T & (K & ~F)]	Assumption
2	~T & (K & ~F)	1 & E
3	K & ~F	2 & E
4	K	3 & E

e. Derive: [(J ⊃ T) & ~R] & (~U ∨ G)

1	N & ~R	Assumption
2	K & (J ⊃ T)	Assumption
3	(~U ∨ G) & ~J	Assumption
4	J ⊃ T	2 & E
5	~R	1 & E
6	~U ∨ G	3 & E
7	(J ⊃ T) & ~R	4, 5 & I
8	[(J ⊃ T) & ~R] & (~U ∨ G)	6, 7 & I

5.1.2E

a. Derive: U

1	H ⊃ U	Assumption
2	S & H	Assumption
3	H	2 & E
4	U	1, 3 ⊃ E

c. Derive: J ⊃ T

1	J ⊃ (S & T)	Assumption
2	J	Assumption
3	S & T	1, 2 ⊃ E
4	T	3 & E
5	J ⊃ T	2-4 ⊃ I

e. Derive: (S & B) ⊃ ~N

1	S ⊃ (L & ~N)	Assumption
2	S & B	Assumption
3	S	2 & E
4	L & ~N	1, 3 ⊃ E
5	~N	4 & E
6	(S & B) ⊃ ~N	2-5 ⊃ I

5.1.3E

a. Derive: ~G

1	(G ⊃ I) & ~I	Assumption
2	G	Assumption
3	G ⊃ I	1 & E
4	I	2, 3 ⊃ E
5	~I	1 & E
6	~G	2-5 ~I

c. Derive: ~~R

1	~R ⊃ A	Assumption
2	~R ⊃ ~A	Assumption
3	~R	Assumption
4	A	1, 3 ⊃ E
5	~A	2, 3 ⊃ E
6	~~R	3-5 ~I

e. Derive: P

1	(~P ⊃ ~L) & (~L ⊃ L)	Assumption
2	~P	Assumption
3	~P ⊃ ~L	1 & E
4	~L	2, 3 ⊃ E
5	~L ⊃ L	1 & E
6	L	4, 5 ⊃ E
7	P	2-6 ~E

5.1.4E

a. Derive: B ∨ (K ∨ G)

1	K	Assumption
2	K ∨ G	1 ∨I
3	B ∨ (K ∨ G)	2 ∨I

c. Derive: D

1	D ∨ D	Assumption
2	D	Assumption
3	D	2 R
4	D	1, 2-3, 2-3 ∨ E

e. Derive: X

1	~E ∨ X	Assumption
2	~E ⊃ X	Assumption
3	~E	Assumption
4	X	2, 3 ⊃ E
5	X	Assumption
6	X	5 R
7	X	1, 3-4, 5-6 ∨ E

5.1.5E

a. Derive: Q

1	K ≡ (~E & Q)	Assumption
2	K	Assumption
3	~E & Q	1, 2 ≡ E
4	Q	3 & E

c. Derive: S & ~A

1	(S ≡ ~I) & N	Assumption
2	(N ≡ ~I) & ~A	Assumption
3	~A	2 & E
4	N ≡ ~I	2 & E
5	N	1 & E
6	~I	4, 5 ≡ E
7	S ≡ ~I	1 & E
8	S	6, 7 ≡ E
9	S & ~A	3, 8 & I

e. Derive: (E ≡ O) & (O ≡ E)

```
1 | (E ⊃ T) & (T ⊃ O)                    Assumption
2 | O ⊃ E                                Assumption
  |_____
3 |   | E                                Assumption
  |   |_____
4 |   | E ⊃ T                            1 & E
5 |   | T                                3, 4 ⊃ E
6 |   | T ⊃ O                            1 & E
7 |   | O                                5, 6 ⊃ E
8 |   | O                                Assumption
  |   |_____
9 |   | E                                2, 8 ⊃ E
10| E ≡ O                                3-7, 8-9 ≡ I
11| O ≡ E                                3-7, 8-9 ≡ I
12| (E ≡ O) & (O ≡ E)                    10, 11 & I
```

2.a. Derive: (A & C) ∨ (B & C)

```
1 | (A ∨ B) & C                          Assumption
  |_____
2 | A ∨ B                                1 & E
3 | C                                    1 & E
4 |   | A                                Assumption
  |   |_____
5 |   | A & C                            3, 4 & I
6 |   | (A & C) ∨ (B & C)                5 ∨ I
  |
7 |   | B                                Assumption
  |   |_____
8 |   | B & C                            3, 7 & I
9 |   | (A & C) ∨ (B & C)                8 ∨ I
10| (A & C) ∨ (B & C)                    2, 4-6, 7-9 ∨ E
```

c. Derive: ∼B

```
1 | B ⊃ (A & ∼B)                         Assumption
  |_____
2 |   | B                                Assumption
  |   |_____
3 |   | A & ∼B                           1, 2 ⊃ E
4 |   | ∼B                               3 & E
5 |   | B                                2 R
6 | ∼B                                   2-5 ∼I
```

e. Derive: C ⊃ (~A & B)

1	~D	Assumption
2	C ⊃ (A ≡ B)	Assumption
3	(D ∨ B) ⊃ ~A	Assumption
4	(A ≡ B) ⊃ (D & E)	Assumption
5	~B ⊃ D	Assumption
6	C	Assumption
7	A ≡ B	2, 6 ⊃ E
8	D & E	7, 4 ⊃ E
9	D	8 & E
10	D ∨ B	9 ∨ I
11	~A	3, 10 ⊃ E
12	~B	Assumption
13	D	5, 12 ⊃ E
14	~D	1 R
15	B	12-14 ~E
16	~A & B	11, 15 & I
17	C ⊃ (~A & B)	6-16 ⊃ I

g. Derive: A ≡ B

1	~A & ~B	Assumption
2	A	Assumption
3	~B	Assumption
4	~A	1 & E
5	A	2 R
6	B	3-5 ~E
7	B	Assumption
8	~A	Assumption
9	B	7 R
10	~B	1 & E
11	A	8-10 ~E
12	A ≡ B	2-6, 7-11 ≡ I

5.4E

1. Derivability

a. Derive: H & (K ⊃ J)

1	(Z ≡ R) & H	Assumption
2	(K ⊃ J) & ~~Y	Assumption
3	D ∨ B	Assumption
4	H	1 & E
5	K ⊃ J	2 & E
6	H & (K ⊃ J)	4, 5 & I

c. Derive: A ⊃ B

1	A ≡ (A ⊃ B)	Assumption
2	A	Assumption
3	A ⊃ B	1, 2 ≡ E
4	B	2, 3 ⊃ E
5	A ⊃ B	2-4 ⊃ I

e. Derive: ~G

1	B & F	Assumption
2	~(B & G)	Assumption
3	G	Assumption
4	B	1 & E
5	B & G	4, 3 & I
6	~(B & G)	2 R
7	~G	3-6 ~I

2. Validity

a. Derive: L ∨ P

1	~(L & E)	Assumption
2	~(L & E) ≡ P	Assumption
3	P	1, 2 ≡ E
4	L ∨ P	3 ∨ E

c. Derive: R ⊃ T

1	R ⊃ S	Assumption
2	S ⊃ T	Assumption
3	R	Assumption
4	S	1, 3 ⊃ E
5	T	2, 4 ⊃ E
6	R ⊃ T	3-6 ⊃ I

e. Derive: ~(A & D)

1	A ⊃ (B & C)	Assumption
2	~C	Assumption
3	A & D	Assumption
4	A	3 & E
5	B & C	1, 4 ⊃ E
6	C	5 & E
7	~C	2 R
8	~(A & D)	3-7 ~I

g. Derive: A ≡ C

1	A ≡ B	Assumption
2	B ≡ C	Assumption
3	A	Assumption
4	B	1, 3 ≡ E
5	C	4, 2 ≡ E
6	C	Assumption
7	B	6, 2 ≡ E
8	A	7, 1 ≡ E
9	A ≡ C	3-5, 6-8 ≡ I

i. Derive: F & G

1	F ≡ G	Assumption
2	F ∨ G	Assumption
3	F	Assumption
4	F	3 R
5	G	Assumption
6	F	5, 1 ≡ E
7	F	2, 3-4, 5-6 ∨ E
8	G	1, 7 ≡ E
9	F & G	7, 8 & I

3. Theorems

a. Derive: A ⊃ (A ∨ B)

1	A	Assumption
2	A ∨ B	1 ∨ I
3	A ⊃ (A ∨ B)	1-2 ⊃ I

c. Derive: (A ≡ B) ⊃ (A ⊃ B)

1	A ≡ B	Assumption
2	A	Assumption
3	B	1, 2 ≡ E
4	A ⊃ B	2-3 ⊃ I
5	(A ≡ B) ⊃ (A ⊃ B)	1-4 ⊃ I

e. Derive: (A ⊃ B) ⊃ [(C ⊃ A) ⊃ (C ⊃ B)]

1	A ⊃ B	Assumption
2	C ⊃ A	Assumption
3	C	Assumption
4	A	2, 3 ⊃ E
5	B	1, 4 ⊃ E
6	C ⊃ B	3-5 ⊃ I
7	(C ⊃ A) ⊃ (C ⊃ B)	2-6 ⊃ I
8	(A ⊃ B) ⊃ [(C ⊃ A) ⊃ (C ⊃ B)]	1-7 ⊃ I

g. Derive: [(A ⊃ B) & ~B] ⊃ ~A

1		(A ⊃ B) & ~B	Assumption
2		A ⊃ B	1 & E
3		A	Assumption
4		B	2, 3 ⊃ E
5		~B	1 & E
6		~A	3-5 ~I
7	[(A ⊃ B) & ~B] ⊃ ~A	1-6 ⊃ I

i. Derive: A ⊃ [B ⊃ (A ⊃ B)]

1		A	Assumption
2		B	Assumption
3		A	Assumption
4		B	2 R
5		A ⊃ B	3-4 ⊃ I
6		B ⊃ (A ⊃ B)	2-5 ⊃ I
7	A ⊃ [B ⊃ (A ⊃ B)]	1-6 ⊃ I

k. Derive: (A ⊃ B) ⊃ [~B ⊃ ~(A & D)]

1		A ⊃ B	Assumption
2		~B	Assumption
3		A & D	Assumption
4		A	3 & E
5		B	1, 4 ⊃ E
6		~B	2 R
7		~(A & D)	3-6 ~I
8		~B ⊃ ~(A & D)	2-7 ⊃ I
9	(A ⊃ B) ⊃ [~B ⊃ ~(A & D)]	1-8 ⊃ I

4. Equivalence

a. Derive: (A ∨ ~~B) & C

| 1 | (A ∨ ~~B) & C | Assumption |
| 2 | (A ∨ ~~B) & C | 1 R |

Derive: (A ∨ ~~B) & C

1	(A ∨ ~~B) & C	Assumption
2	(A ∨ ~~B) & C	1 R

c. Derive: ~~A

1	A	Assumption
2	~A	Assumption
3	A	1 R
4	~A	2 R
5	~~A	2-4 ~I

Derive: A

1	~~A	Assumption
2	~A	Assumption
3	~~A	1 R
4	~A	2 R
5	A	2-4 ~E

e. Derive: ~B ⊃ ~A

1	A ⊃ B	Assumption
2	~B	Assumption
3	A	Assumption
4	B	1, 3 ⊃ E
5	~B	2 R
6	~A	3-5 ~I
7	~B ⊃ ~A	2-6 ⊃ I

Derive: A ⊃ B

1	~B ⊃ ~A	Assumption
2	A	Assumption
3	~B	Assumption
4	~A	1, 3 ⊃ E
5	A	2 R
6	B	3-5 ~E
7	A ⊃ B	2-6 ⊃ I

5. Inconsistency

a.

1	A ≡ ~ (A ≡ A)	Assumption
2	A	Assumption
3	~(A ≡ A)	1, 2 ≡ E
4	A	Assumption
5	A	4 R
6	A ≡ A	4-5, 4-5 ≡ I

c.

1	M ⊃ (K ⊃ B)	Assumption
2	~K ⊃ ~M	Assumption
3	(L & M) & ~B	Assumption
4	L & M	3 & E
5	M	4 & E
6	K ⊃ B	5, 1 ⊃ E
7	~K	Assumption
8	~M	7, 2 ⊃ E
9	M	4 & E
10	K	7-9 ~E
11	B	6, 10 ⊃ E
12	~B	3 & E

e.

1	~(Y ≡ A)	Assumption
2	~Y	Assumption
3	~A	Assumption
4	Y	Assumption
5	~A	Assumption
6	~Y	2 R
7	Y	4 R
8	A	5-7 ~E
9	A	Assumption
10	~Y	Assumption
11	A	9 R
12	~A	3 R
13	Y	10-12 ~E
14	Y ≡ A	4-8, 9-13 ≡ I
15	~(Y ≡ A)	1 R

g. 1 | (~C ⊃ ~D) & (C ⊃ D)   Assumption
   2 | D ⊃ ~C   Assumption
   3 | ~(B & ~D)   Assumption
   4 | B ≡ (~C ∨ D)   Assumption
   ─────────────────────
   5 | | D   Assumption
        ─────────
   6 | | ~C   2, 5 ⊃ E
   7 | | ~C ⊃ ~D   1 & E
   8 | | ~D   6, 7 ⊃ E
   9 | | D   5 R
  10 | ~D   5-9 ~I
  11 | | ~D   Assumption
        ─────────
  12 | | C ⊃ D   1 & E
  13 | | | C   Assumption
              ─────
  14 | | | D   12, 13 ⊃ E
  15 | | | ~D   11 R
  16 | | ~C   13-15 ~I
  17 | | ~C ∨ D   16 ∨ I
  18 | | B   4, 17 ≡ E
  19 | | B & ~D   18, 11 & I
  20 | | ~(B & ~D)   3 R
  21 | D   11-20 ~E

6. Derivability

a. Derive: ~Q ⊃ ~P

   1 | P ⊃ Q   Assumption
   2 | | ~Q   Assumption
        ─────────
   3 | | | P   Assumption
              ─────
   4 | | | Q   1, 3 ⊃ E
   5 | | | ~Q   2 R
   6 | | ~P   3-5 ~I
   7 | ~Q ⊃ ~P   2-6 ⊃ I

c. Derive: H ≡ M

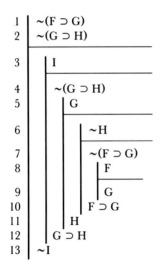

1	H ⊃ M		Assumption
2	~H ⊃ ~M		Assumption
3		H	Assumption
4		M	1, 3 ⊃ E
5		M	Assumption
6		~H	Assumption
7		~M	2, 6 ⊃ E
8		M	5 R
9		H	6-8 ~E
10	H ≡ M		3-4, 5-9 ≡ I

e. Derive: ~I

1	~(F ⊃ G)		Assumption
2	~(G ⊃ H)		Assumption
3		I	Assumption
4		~(G ⊃ H)	2 R
5		G	Assumption
6		~H	Assumption
7		~(F ⊃ G)	1 R
8		F	Assumption
9		G	5 R
10		F ⊃ G	8-9 ⊃ I
11		H	6-10 ~E
12		G ⊃ H	5-11 ⊃ I
13	~I		3-12 ~I

g. Derive: $\sim A \equiv B$

1	$\sim(A \equiv B)$	Assumption
2	$\sim A$	Assumption
3	$\sim B$	Assumption
4	A	Assumption
5	$\sim B$	Assumption
6	$\sim A$	2 R
7	A	4 R
8	B	5-7 $\sim$ E
9	B	Assumption
10	$\sim A$	Assumption
11	B	9 R
12	$\sim B$	3 R
13	A	10-12 $\sim$ E
14	$A \equiv B$	4-8, 9-13 $\equiv$ I
15	$\sim(A \equiv B)$	1 R
16	B	3-15 $\sim$ E
17	B	Assumption
18	A	Assumption
19	A	Assumption
20	B	17 R
21	B	Assumption
22	A	18 R
23	$A \equiv B$	19-20, 21-22 $\equiv$ I
24	$\sim(A \equiv B)$	1 R
25	$\sim A$	18-24 $\sim$ I
26	$\sim A \equiv B$	2-16, 17-25 $\equiv$ I

7. Validity

a. Derive: H

1	(H & I) ∨ (H & S)	Assumption
2	H & I	Assumption
3	H	2 & E
4	H & S	Assumption
5	H	4 & E
6	H	1, 2-3, 4-5 ∨ E

c. Derive: J ≡ ~C

1	B ≡ ~B	Assumption
2	~(J ≡ ~C)	Assumption
3	B	Assumption
4	~B	1, 3 ≡ E
5	B	3 R
6	~B	3-5 ~I
7	B	1, 6 ≡ E
8	J ≡ ~C	2-7 ~E

e. Derive: (H & I) ⊃ J

1	(~H ∨ J) ∨ K	Assumption
2	K ⊃ ~I	Assumption
3	H & I	Assumption
4	~H ∨ J	Assumption
5	~H	Assumption
6	~J	Assumption
7	H	3 & E
8	~H	5 R
9	J	6-8 ~E
10	J	Assumption
11	J	10 R
12	J	4, 5-9, 10-11 ∨ E
13	K	Assumption
14	~J	Assumption
15	I	3 & E
16	~I	2, 13 ⊃ E
17	J	14-16 ~E
18	J	1, 4-12, 13-17 ∨ I
19	(H & I) ⊃ J	3-18 ⊃ I

g. Derive: E ∨ F

1	(A ∨ B) & ~C	Assumption
2	~C ⊃ (D & ~A)	Assumption
3	B ⊃ (A ∨ E)	Assumption
4	~C	1 & E
5	D & ~A	2, 4 ⊃ E
6	A ∨ B	1 & E
7	A	Assumption
8	~B	Assumption
9	A	7 R
10	~A	5 & E
11	B	8-10 ~E
12	B	Assumption
13	B	12 R
14	B	6, 7-11, 12-13 ∨ E
15	A ∨ E	14, 3 ⊃ E
16	A	Assumption
17	~E	Assumption
18	A	16 R
19	~A	5 & E
20	E	17-19 ~E
21	E	Assumption
22	E	21 R
23	E	15, 16-20, 21-22 ∨ E
24	E ∨ F	23 ∨ I

8. Theorems

a. Derive: ~[(A & B) & ~(A & B)]

1	(A & B) & ~(A & B)	Assumption
2	A & B	1 & E
3	~(A & B)	1 & E
4	~[(A & B) & ~(A & B)]	1-3 ~I

c. Derive: $(A \equiv \sim A) \supset \sim(A \equiv \sim A)$

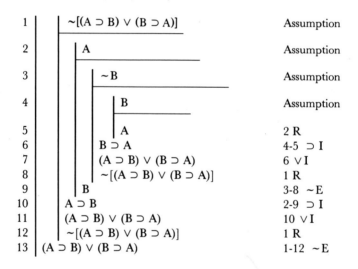

1	$A \equiv \sim A$	Assumption
2	A	Assumption
3	$\sim A$	1, 2 $\equiv$ E
4	A	2 R
5	$\sim A$	2-4 $\sim$I
6	$\sim A$	Assumption
7	A	1, 6 $\equiv$ E
8	$\sim A$	6 R
9	A	6-8 $\sim$E
10	$\sim(A \equiv \sim A)$	1-9 $\sim$I
11	$A \equiv \sim A$	Assumption
12	$\sim(A \equiv \sim A)$	10 R
13	$(A \equiv \sim A) \supset \sim(A \equiv A)$	11-12 $\supset$ I

e. Derive: $(A \supset B) \lor (B \supset A)$

1	$\sim[(A \supset B) \lor (B \supset A)]$	Assumption
2	A	Assumption
3	$\sim B$	Assumption
4	B	Assumption
5	A	2 R
6	$B \supset A$	4-5 $\supset$ I
7	$(A \supset B) \lor (B \supset A)$	6 $\lor$ I
8	$\sim[(A \supset B) \lor (B \supset A)]$	1 R
9	B	3-8 $\sim$E
10	$A \supset B$	2-9 $\supset$ I
11	$(A \supset B) \lor (B \supset A)$	10 $\lor$ I
12	$\sim[(A \supset B) \lor (B \supset A)]$	1 R
13	$(A \supset B) \lor (B \supset A)$	1-12 $\sim$E

g. Derive: [A ⊃ (B ⊃ C)] ≡ [(A ⊃ B) ⊃ (A ⊃ C)]

1	A ⊃ (B ⊃ C)	Assumption
2	A ⊃ B	Assumption
3	A	Assumption
4	B	2, 3 ⊃ E
5	B ⊃ C	1, 3 ⊃ E
6	C	4, 5 ⊃ E
7	A ⊃ C	3-6 ⊃ I
8	(A ⊃ B) ⊃ (A ⊃ C)	2-7 ⊃ I
9	(A ⊃ B) ⊃ (A ⊃ C)	Assumption
10	A	Assumption
11	B	Assumption
12	A	Assumption
13	B	11 R
14	A ⊃ B	12-13 ⊃ I
15	A ⊃ C	9, 14 ⊃ E
16	C	10, 15 ⊃ E
17	B ⊃ C	11-16 ⊃ I
18	A ⊃ (B ⊃ C)	10-17 ⊃ I
19	[A ⊃ (B ⊃ C)] ≡ [(A ⊃ B) ⊃ (A ⊃ C)]	1-8, 9-18 ≡ I

i. Derive: [(A ≡ B) ⊃ C] ⊃ [~(A & B) ∨ C]

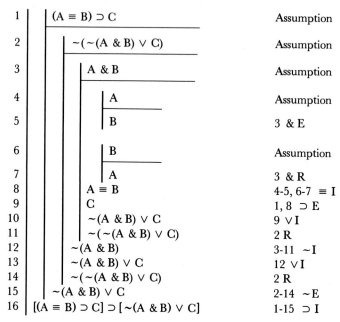

1	(A ≡ B) ⊃ C	Assumption
2	~(~(A & B) ∨ C)	Assumption
3	A & B	Assumption
4	A	Assumption
5	B	3 & E
6	B	Assumption
7	A	3 & R
8	A ≡ B	4-5, 6-7 ≡ I
9	C	1, 8 ⊃ E
10	~(A & B) ∨ C	9 ∨ I
11	~(~(A & B) ∨ C)	2 R
12	~(A & B)	3-11 ~I
13	~(A & B) ∨ C	12 ∨ I
14	~(~(A & B) ∨ C)	2 R
15	~(A & B) ∨ C	2-14 ~E
16	[(A ≡ B) ⊃ C] ⊃ [~(A & B) ∨ C]	1-15 ⊃ I

9. Equivalence

a. Derive: A ⊃ B

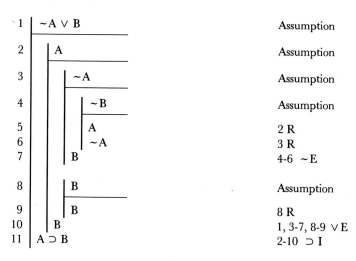

1	~A ∨ B	Assumption
2	A	Assumption
3	~A	Assumption
4	~B	Assumption
5	A	2 R
6	~A	3 R
7	B	4-6 ~E
8	B	Assumption
9	B	8 R
10	B	1, 3-7, 8-9 ∨ E
11	A ⊃ B	2-10 ⊃ I

Derive: ~A ∨ B

1	A ⊃ B	Assumption
2	~(~A ∨ B)	Assumption
3	~A	Assumption
4	~A ∨ B	3 ∨I
5	~(~A ∨ B)	2 R
6	A	3-5 ~E
7	B	1, 6 ⊃ E
8	~A ∨ B	7 ∨I
9	~(~A ∨ B)	2 R
10	~A ∨ B	2-9 ~E

c. Derive: A & ~B

1	~(A ⊃ B)	Assumption
2	~A	Assumption
3	A	Assumption
4	~B	Assumption
5	~A	2 R
6	A	3 R
7	B	4-6 ~E
8	A ⊃ B	3-7 ⊃ I
9	~(A ⊃ B)	1 R
10	A	2-9 ~E
11	B	Assumption
12	A	Assumption
13	B	11 R
14	A ⊃ B	12-13 ⊃ I
15	~(A ⊃ B)	1 R
16	~B	11-15 ~I
17	A & ~B	10, 16 & I

Derive: ~(A ⊃ B)

1	A & ~B	Assumption
2	A ⊃ B	Assumption
3	A	1 & E
4	B	2, 3 ⊃ E
5	~B	1 & E
6	~(A ⊃ B)	2-5 ~I

e. Derive: (A & B) ∨ (~A & ~B)

1	A ≡ B	Assumption
2	~[(A & B) ∨ (~A & ~B)]	Assumption
3	A	Assumption
4	B	1, 3 ≡ E
5	A & B	3, 4 & I
6	(A & B) ∨ (~A & ~B)	5 ∨ I
7	~[(A & B) ∨ (~A & ~B)]	2 R
8	~A	3-7 ~I
9	B	Assumption
10	A	1, 9 ≡ E
11	~A	8 R
12	~B	9-11 ~I
13	~A & ~B	8, 12 & I
14	(A & B) ∨ (~A & ~B)	13 ∨ I
15	~[(A & B) ∨ (~A & ~B)]	2 R
16	(A & B) ∨ (~A & ~B)	2-15 ~E

Derive: A ≡ B

1	(A & B) ∨ (~A & ~B)			Assumption
2		A & B		Assumption
3			A	Assumption
4			B	2 & E
5			B	Assumption
6			A	2 & E
7		A ≡ B		3-4, 5-6 ≡ I
8		~A & ~B		Assumption
9			A	Assumption
10				~B	Assumption
11				A	9 R
12				~A	8 & E
13			B	10-12 ~E
14			B	Assumption
15				~A	Assumption
16				B	14 R
17				~B	8 & E
18			A	15-17 ~E
19		A ≡ B		9-13, 14-18 ≡ I
20	A ≡ B			1, 2-7, 8-19 ∨ E

10. Inconsistency

a. 1	(A ⊃ B) & (A ⊃ ~B)		Assumption
2	(C ⊃ A) & (~C ⊃ A)		Assumption
3	A ⊃ B		1 & E
4	A ⊃ ~B		1 & E
5		C	Assumption
6		C ⊃ A	2 & E
7		A	5, 6 ⊃ E
8		B	3, 7 ⊃ E
9		~B	4, 7 ⊃ E
10	~ C		5-9 ~I
11	~C ⊃ A		2 & E
12	A		10, 11 ⊃ E
13	B		3, 12 ⊃ E
14	~B		4, 12 ⊃ E

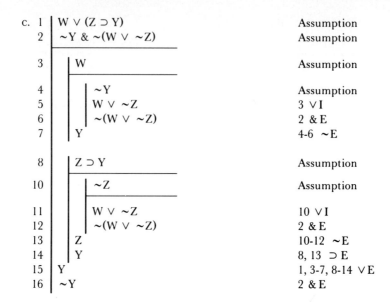

c.
1	W ∨ (Z ⊃ Y)	Assumption
2	~Y & ~(W ∨ ~Z)	Assumption
3	W	Assumption
4	~Y	Assumption
5	W ∨ ~Z	3 ∨ I
6	~(W ∨ ~Z)	2 & E
7	Y	4-6 ~E
8	Z ⊃ Y	Assumption
10	~Z	Assumption
11	W ∨ ~Z	10 ∨ I
12	~(W ∨ ~Z)	2 & E
13	Z	10-12 ~E
14	Y	8, 13 ⊃ E
15	Y	1, 3-7, 8-14 ∨ E
16	~Y	2 & E

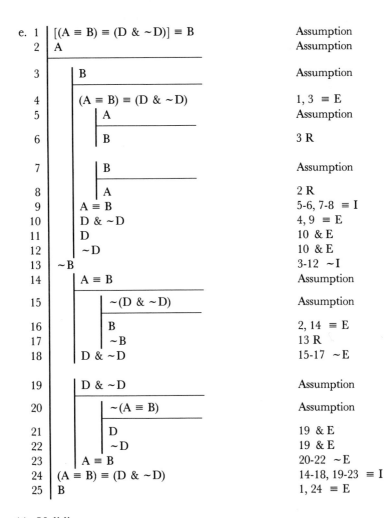

e.
1	$[(A \equiv B) \equiv (D \mathbin{\&} \sim D)] \equiv B$	Assumption
2	A	Assumption
3	B	Assumption
4	$(A \equiv B) \equiv (D \mathbin{\&} \sim D)$	$1, 3 \equiv E$
5	A	Assumption
6	B	3 R
7	B	Assumption
8	A	2 R
9	$A \equiv B$	$5\text{-}6, 7\text{-}8 \equiv I$
10	$D \mathbin{\&} \sim D$	$4, 9 \equiv E$
11	D	10 & E
12	$\sim D$	10 & E
13	$\sim B$	$3\text{-}12 \sim I$
14	$A \equiv B$	Assumption
15	$\sim(D \mathbin{\&} \sim D)$	Assumption
16	B	$2, 14 \equiv E$
17	$\sim B$	13 R
18	$D \mathbin{\&} \sim D$	$15\text{-}17 \sim E$
19	$D \mathbin{\&} \sim D$	Assumption
20	$\sim(A \equiv B)$	Assumption
21	D	19 & E
22	$\sim D$	19 & E
23	$A \equiv B$	$20\text{-}22 \sim E$
24	$(A \equiv B) \equiv (D \mathbin{\&} \sim D)$	$14\text{-}18, 19\text{-}23 \equiv I$
25	B	$1, 24 \equiv E$

11. Validity

a. Derive: M

1	S & F	Assumption
2	$F \supset B$	Assumption
3	$(B \mathbin{\&} \sim M) \supset \sim S$	Assumption
4	$\sim M$	Assumption
5	F	1 & E
6	B	$2, 5 \supset E$
7	$B \mathbin{\&} \sim M$	6, 4 & I
8	$\sim S$	$3, 7 \supset E$
9	S	1 & E
10	M	$4\text{-}9 \sim E$

c. Derive: ~J

1	(C ⊃ ~R) & (R ⊃ L)	Assumption
2	C ≡ (C ∨ L)	Assumption
3	J ⊃ R	Assumption
4	⎢ J	Assumption
5	⎢ R	3, 4 ⊃ E
6	⎢ R ⊃ L	1 & E
7	⎢ L	5, 6 ⊃ E
8	⎢ C ∨ L	7 ∨ I
9	⎢ C	2, 8 ≡ E
10	⎢ C ⊃ ~R	1 & E
11	⎢ ~R	9, 10 ⊃ E
12	~J	4-11 ~I

e. Derive: ~M

1	~(R ∨ W)	Assumption
2	(R ≡ M) ∨ [(M ∨ G) ⊃ (W ≡ M)]	Assumption
3	⎢ M	Assumption
4	⎢ ⎢ R ≡ M	Assumption
5	⎢ ⎢ R	3, 4 ≡ E
6	⎢ ⎢ R ∨ W	5 ∨ I
7	⎢ ⎢ (M ∨ G) ⊃ (W ≡ M)	Assumption
8	⎢ ⎢ M ∨ G	3 ∨ I
9	⎢ ⎢ W ≡ M	7, 8 ⊃ E
10	⎢ ⎢ W·	3, 9 ≡ E
11	⎢ ⎢ R ∨ W	10 ∨ I
12	⎢ R ∨ W	2, 4-6, 7-11 ∨ E
13	⎢ ~(R ∨ W)	1 R
14	~M	3-13 ~I

g. Derive: H ⊃ J

1	(H & T) ⊃ J	Assumption
2	(M ⊃ D) & (M ∨ D)	Assumption
3	~T ≡ (~D & M)	Assumption
4	H	Assumption
5	~J	Assumption
6	T	Assumption
7	H & T	4, 6 & I
8	J	1, 7 ⊃ E
9	~J	5 R
10	~T	6-9 ~I
11	~D & M	3, 10 ≡ E
12	M ⊃ D	2 & E
13	M	11 & E
14	D	12, 13 ⊃ E
15	~D	11 & E
16	J	5-15 ~E
17	H ⊃ J	4-16 ⊃ I

i. Derive: L ⊃ T

1	L ⊃ (C ∨ T)	Assumption
2	(~L ∨ B) & (~B ∨ ~C)	Assumption
3	L	Assumption
4	C ∨ T	1, 3 ⊃ E
5	C	Assumption
6	~B ∨ ~C	2 & E
7	~B	Assumption
8	~L ∨ B	2 & E
9	~L	Assumption
10	~T	Assumption
11	L	3 R
12	~L	9 R
13	T	10-12 ~E
14	B	Assumption
15	~T	Assumption
16	B	14 R
17	~B	7 R
18	T	15-17 ~E
19	T	8, 9-13, 14-18 ∨ E
20	~C	Assumption
21	~T	Assumption
22	~C	20 R
23	C	5 R
24	T	21-23 ~E
25	T	6, 7-19, 20-24 ∨ E
26	T	Assumption
27	T	26 R
28	T	4, 5-25, 26-27 ∨ E
29	L ⊃ T	3-28 ⊃ I

12. Inconsistency

a.

1	(M ⊃ B) & (B ⊃ P)	Assumption
2	M & ~P	Assumption
3	M	2 & E
4	M ⊃ B	1 & E
5	B	3, 4 ⊃ E
6	B ⊃ P	1 & E
7	P	5, 6 ⊃ E
8	~P	2 & E

c.

1	B ⊃ I	Assumption
2	(~B & ~I) ⊃ C	Assumption
3	~C & ~I	Assumption
4	B	Assumption
5	I	1, 4 ⊃ E
6	~I	3 & E
7	~B	4-6 ~ I
8	~I	3 & E
9	~B & ~I	7, 8 & I
10	C	2, 9 ⊃ E
11	~C	3 & E

e.

1	M ∨ (F ⊃ T)	Assumption
2	N ≡ ~T	Assumption
3	(F & N) & ~M	Assumption
4	M	Assumption
5	M	4 R
6	F ⊃ T	Assumption
7	~M	Assumption
8	F & N	3 R
9	F	8 & E
10	T	6, 9 ⊃ E
11	N	8 & E
12	~T	2, 11 ≡ E
13	M	7-12 ~E
14	M	1, 4-5, 6-13 ∨ E
15	~M	3 & E

13.a. We would not want to include this derivation rule because it is not truth-preserving. A sentence of *SL* of the form $\mathscr{P} \vee \mathscr{Q}$ can be true while $\mathscr{P}$ is false.

c. Suppose we are on line n of a derivation and a sentence $\mathcal{P}$ occurs on an earlier accessible line i. $\mathcal{P}$ can be derived without using the rule Reiteration as follows:

$$
\begin{array}{ll}
i & \mathcal{P} \\
\\
n & \mathcal{P} \& \mathcal{P} \quad i, i \,\&\, \mathrm{I} \\
n+1 & \mathcal{P} \qquad\quad n \,\&\, \mathrm{E}
\end{array}
$$

e. Suppose an argument of *SL* has $\sim\!\mathcal{P}$ among its premises, where $\mathcal{P}$ is a theorem in *SD*. Consider a derivation that has the premises of the argument as its only primary assumptions and that has the negation of the conclusion as an auxiliary assumption immediately after the primary assumptions. Within the subderivation that has the negation of the conclusion as its assumption, $\sim\!\mathcal{P}$ can be derived by Reiteration, for $\sim\!\mathcal{P}$ occurs as one of the primary assumptions. Since $\mathcal{P}$ is a theorem in *SD*, it can also be derived within the subderivation without introducing any new assumptions that are not discharged. Consequently, Negation Elimination can be applied to discharge the negation of the conclusion yielding the (unnegated) conclusion. The conclusion is derivable from the set of premises; hence the argument is valid in *SD*.

14.a. Assume that some argument of *SL* is valid in *SD*. Then, by definition, the conclusion is derivable in *SD* from the set consisting of only premises. By the result (*), the conclusion is truth-functionally entailed by that set. So the argument is truth-functionally valid. Assume that some argument of *SL* is truth-functionally valid. Then the conclusion is truth-functionally entailed by the set consisting of the premises. By (*), the conclusion is derivable in *SD* from that set. So the argument is valid in *SD*.

c. Assume that sentences $\mathcal{P}$ and $\mathcal{Q}$ of *SL* are equivalent in *SD*. Then $\{\mathcal{P}\} \vdash \mathcal{Q}$ and $\{\mathcal{Q}\} \vdash \mathcal{P}$. By (*), it follows that $\{\mathcal{P}\} \vDash \mathcal{Q}$ and $\{\mathcal{Q}\} \vDash \mathcal{P}$. By Exercise 5.b of 3.5E, $\mathcal{P}$ and $\mathcal{Q}$ are truth-functionally equivalent. Assume that sentences $\mathcal{P}$ and $\mathcal{Q}$ of *SL* are truth-functionally equivalent. By Exercise 5.b of 3.5E, $\{\mathcal{P}\} \vDash \mathcal{Q}$ and $\{\mathcal{Q}\} \vDash \mathcal{P}$. By (*), then, $\{\mathcal{P}\} \vdash \mathcal{Q}$, and $\{\mathcal{Q}\} \vDash \mathcal{P}$. So $\mathcal{P}$ and $\mathcal{Q}$ are equivalent in *SD*.

5.5E

1. Derivability

a. Derive: $\sim\!\mathrm{D}$

1	$\mathrm{D} \supset \mathrm{E}$	Assumption
2	$\mathrm{E} \supset (\mathrm{Z} \,\&\, \mathrm{W})$	Assumption
3	$\sim\!\mathrm{Z} \lor \sim\!\mathrm{W}$	Assumption
4	$\sim\!(\mathrm{Z} \,\&\, \mathrm{W})$	3 DeM
5	$\sim\!\mathrm{E}$	2, 4 MT
6	$\sim\!\mathrm{D}$	1, 5 MT

c. Derive: K

1	(W ⊃ S) & ~M	Assumption
2	(~W ⊃ H) ∨ M	Assumption
3	(~S ⊃ H) ⊃ K	Assumption
4	W ⊃ S	1 & E
5	~S ⊃ ~W	4 Trans
6	~M	1 & E
7	~W ⊃ H	2, 6 DS
8	~S ⊃ H	5, 7 HS
9	K	3, 8 ⊃ E

e. Derive: C

1	(M ∨ B) ∨ (C ∨ G)	Assumption
2	~B & (~G & ~M)	Assumption
3	~B	2 & E
4	(B ∨ M) ∨ (C ∨ G)	1 Com
5	B ∨ [M ∨ (C ∨ G)]	4 Assoc
6	M ∨ (C ∨ G)	3, 5 DS
7	~G & ~M	2 & E
8	~G	7 & E
9	(M ∨ C) ∨ G	6 Assoc
10	M ∨ C	8, 9 DS
11	~M	7 & E
12	C	10, 11 DS

2. Validity

a. Derive: Y ≡ Z

1	~Y ⊃ ~Z	Assumption
2	~Z ⊃ ~X	Assumption
3	~X ⊃ ~Y	Assumption
4	Y	Assumption
5	~Z ⊃ ~Y	2, 3 HS
6	Y ⊃ Z	5 Trans
7	Z	4, 6 ⊃ E
8	Z	Assumption
9	Z ⊃ Y	1 Trans
10	Y	8, 9 ⊃ E
11	Y ≡ Z	4-7, 8-10 ≡ I

c. Derive: I ⊃ ~D

1	(F & G) ∨ (H & ~I)	Assumption
2	I ⊃ ~(F & D)	Assumption
3	⎸ I	Assumption
4	⎸ ~(F & D)	2, 3 ⊃ E
5	⎸ ~F ∨ ~D	4 DeM
6	⎸ ~~I	3 DN
7	⎸ ~H ∨ ~~I	6 ∨I
8	⎸ ~(H & ~I)	7 DeM
9	⎸ F & G	1, 8 DS
10	⎸ F	9 & E
11	⎸ ~~F	10 DN
12	⎸ ~D	5, 11 DS
13	I ⊃ ~D	3-12 ⊃ I

e. Derive: I ∨ H

1	F ⊃ (G ⊃ H)	Assumption
2	~I ⊃ (F ∨ H)	Assumption
3	F ⊃ G	Assumption
4	⎸ ~I	Assumption
5	⎸ F ∨ H	2, 4 ⊃ E
6	⎸ ⎸ ~H	Assumption
7	⎸ ⎸ F	5, 6 DS
8	⎸ ⎸ G	3, 7 ⊃ E
9	⎸ ⎸ G ⊃ H	1, 7 ⊃ E
10	⎸ ⎸ ~G	6, 9 MT
11	⎸ H	6-10 ~E
12	~I ⊃ H	4-11 ⊃ I
13	~~I ∨ H	12 Impl
14	I ∨ H	13 DN

g. Derive: X ≡ Y

1	[(X & Z) & Y] ∨ (~X ⊃ ~Y)	Assumption
2	X ⊃ Z	Assumption
3	Z ⊃ Y	Assumption
4	X	Assumption
5	Z	2, 4 ⊃ E
6	Y	3, 5 ⊃ E
7	Y	Assumption
8	(X & Z) & Y	Assumption
9	X & Z	8 & E
10	X	9 & E
11	~X ⊃ ~Y	Assumption
12	Y ⊃ X	11 Trans
13	X	7, 12 ⊃ E
14	X	1, 8-10, 11-13 ∨ E
15	X ≡ Y	4-6, 7-14 ≡ I

3. Theorems

a. Derive: A ∨ ~A

1	~(A ∨ ~A)	Assumption
2	~A & ~~A	1 DeM
3	~A	2 & E
4	~~A	2 & E
5	A ∨ ~A	1-4 ~E

c. Derive: A ∨ [(~A ∨ B) & (~A ∨ C)]

1	~A	Assumption
2	~A ∨ (B & C)	1 ∨I
3	(~A ∨ B) & (~A ∨ C)	2 Dist
4	~A ⊃ [(~A ∨ B) & (~A ∨ C)]	1-3 ⊃ I
5	~~A ∨ [(~A ∨ B) & (~A ∨ C)]	4 Impl
6	A ∨ [(~A ∨ B) & (~A ∨ C)]	5 DN

e. Derive: $[A \supset (B \mathbin{\&} C)] \equiv [(\sim B \vee \sim C) \supset \sim A]$

1	$A \supset (B \mathbin{\&} C)$	Assumption
2	$\sim(B \mathbin{\&} C) \supset \sim A$	1 Trans
3	$(\sim B \vee \sim C) \supset \sim A$	2 DeM
4	$(\sim B \vee \sim C) \supset \sim A$	Assumption
5	$\sim(B \mathbin{\&} C) \supset \sim A$	4 DeM
6	$A \supset (B \mathbin{\&} C)$	5 Trans
7	$[A \supset (B \mathbin{\&} C)] \equiv [(\sim B \vee \sim C) \supset \sim A]$	1-3, 4-6 $\equiv$ I

g. Derive: $[A \supset (B \equiv C)] \equiv (A \supset [(\sim B \vee C) \mathbin{\&} (\sim C \vee B)])$

1	$A \supset (B \equiv C)$	Assumption
2	$A \supset [(B \supset C) \mathbin{\&} (C \supset B)]$	1 Equiv
3	$A \supset [(\sim B \vee C) \mathbin{\&} (C \supset B)]$	2 Impl
4	$A \supset [(\sim B \vee C) \mathbin{\&} (\sim C \vee B)]$	3 Impl
5	$A \supset [(\sim B \vee C) \mathbin{\&} (\sim C \vee B)]$	Assumption
6	$A \supset [(B \supset C) \mathbin{\&} (\sim C \vee B)]$	5 Impl
7	$A \supset [(B \supset C) \mathbin{\&} (C \supset B)]$	6 Impl
8	$A \supset (B \equiv C)$	7 Equiv
9	$[A \supset (B \equiv C)] \equiv (A \supset [(\sim B \vee C) \mathbin{\&} (\sim C \vee B)])$	1-4, 5-8 $\equiv$ I

i. Derive: $[\sim A \supset (\sim B \supset C)] \supset [(A \vee B) \vee (\sim\sim B \vee C)]$

1	$\sim A \supset (\sim B \supset C)$	Assumption
2	$\sim\sim A \vee (\sim B \supset C)$	1 Impl
3	$\sim\sim A \vee (\sim\sim B \vee C)$	2 Impl
4	$A \vee (\sim\sim B \vee C)$	3 DN
5	$A \vee [(\sim\sim B \vee \sim\sim B) \vee C]$	4 Idem
6	$A \vee [\sim\sim B \vee (\sim\sim B \vee C)]$	5 Assoc
7	$(A \vee \sim\sim B) \vee (\sim\sim B \vee C)$	6 Assoc
8	$(A \vee B) \vee (\sim\sim B \vee C)$	7 DN
9	$[\sim A \supset (\sim B \supset C)] \supset [(A \vee B) \vee (\sim\sim B \vee C)]$	1-8 $\supset$ I

4. Equivalence

a. Derive: $\sim(\sim A \mathbin{\&} \sim B)$

1	$A \vee B$	Assumption
2	$\sim\sim A \vee B$	1 DN
3	$\sim\sim A \vee \sim\sim B$	2 DN
4	$\sim(\sim A \mathbin{\&} \sim B)$	3 DeM

Derive: A ∨ B

1	~(~A & ~B)	Assumption
2	~~A ∨ ~~B	1 DeM
3	A ∨ ~~B	2 DN
4	A ∨ B	3 DN

c. Derive: ~(A ⊃ C) ⊃ ~B

1	(A & B) ⊃ C	Assumption
2	(B & A) ⊃ C	1 Com
3	B ⊃ (A ⊃ C)	2 Exp
4	~(A ⊃ C) ⊃ ~B	3 Trans

Derive: (A & B) ⊃ C

1	~(A ⊃ C) ⊃ ~B	Assumption
2	B ⊃ (A ⊃ C)	1 Trans
3	(B & A) ⊃ C	2 Exp
4	(A & B) ⊃ C	3 Com

e. Derive: A ∨ (~B ≡ ~C)

1	A ∨ (B ≡ C)	Assumption
2	A ∨ [(B ⊃ C) & (C ⊃ B)]	1 Equiv
3	A ∨ [(~C ⊃ ~B) & (C ⊃ B)]	2 Trans
4	A ∨ [(~C ⊃ ~B) & (~B ⊃ ~C)]	3 Trans
5	A ∨ [(~B ⊃ ~C) & (~C ⊃ ~B)]	4 Com
6	A ∨ (~B ≡ ~C)	5 Equiv

Derive: A ∨ (B ≡ C)

1	A ∨ (~B ≡ ~C)	Assumption
2	A ∨ [(~B ⊃ ~C) & (~C ⊃ ~B)]	1 Equiv
3	A ∨ [(C ⊃ B) & (~C ⊃ ~B)]	2 Trans
4	A ∨ [(C ⊃ B) & (B ⊃ C)]	3 Trans
5	A ∨ [(B ⊃ C) & (C ⊃ B)]	4 Com
6	A ∨ (B ≡ C)	5 Equiv

5. Inconsistency

a. 1 $[(E \& F) \lor \sim\sim G] \supset M$ Assumption
   2 $\sim[[(G \lor E) \& (F \lor G)] \supset (M \& M)]$ Assumption

   3 $\sim([(G \lor E) \& (F \lor G)] \supset M)$ 2 Idem
   4 $\sim([G \lor E) \& (G \lor F)] \supset M)$ 3 Com
   5 $\sim([G \lor (E \& F)] \supset M)$ 4 Dist
   6 $\sim([(E \& F) \lor G] \supset M)$ 5 Com
   7 $\sim([(E \& F) \lor \sim\sim G] \supset M)$ 6 DN

c. 1 $M \& L$ Assumption
   2 $[L \& (M \& \sim S)] \supset K$ Assumption
   3 $\sim K \lor \sim S$ Assumption
   4 $\sim(K \equiv \sim S)$ Assumption

   5 $K \supset \sim S$ 3 Impl
   6 $[(L \& M) \& \sim S] \supset K$ 2 Assoc
   7 $(L \& M) \supset (\sim S \supset K)$ 6 Exp
   8 $L \& M$ 1 Com
   9 $\sim S \supset K$ 7, 8 $\supset$ E
   10 $(K \supset \sim S) \& (\sim S \supset K)$ 5, 9 & I
   11 $K \equiv \sim S$ 10 Equiv

e. 1 $\sim[W \& (Z \lor Y)]$ Assumption
   2 $(Z \supset Y) \supset Z$ Assumption
   3 $(Y \supset Z) \supset W$ Assumption

   4 $\sim W \lor \sim(Z \lor Y)$ 1 DeM
   5 $\quad \sim Z$ Assumption

   6 $\quad \sim(Z \supset Y)$ 2, 5 MT
   7 $\quad \sim(\sim Z \lor Y)$ 6 Impl
   8 $\quad \sim\sim Z \& \sim Y$ 7 DeM
   9 $\quad \sim\sim Z$ 8 & E
   10 $\quad \sim Z$ 5 R
   11 Z 5-10 $\sim$ E
   12 $Z \lor Y$ 11 $\lor$ I
   13 $\sim\sim(Z \lor Y)$ 12 DN
   14 $\sim W$ 4, 13 DS
   15 $\sim(Y \supset Z)$ 3, 14 MT
   16 $\sim(\sim Y \lor Z)$ 15 Impl
   17 $\sim\sim Y \& \sim Z$ 16 DeM
   18 $\sim Z$ 17 & E

6. Validity

a. Derive: ~B

1	(R ⊃ C) ∨ (B ⊃ C)	Assumption
2	~(E & A) ⊃ ~(R ⊃ C)	Assumption
3	~E & ~C	Assumption
4	~E	3 & E
5	~E ∨ ~A	4 ∨ I
6	~(E & A)	5 DeM
7	~(R ⊃ C)	2, 6 ⊃ E
8	B ⊃ C	1, 7 DS
9	~C	3 & E
10	~B	8, 9 MT

c. Derive: ~W ⊃ ~A

1	A ⊃ [W ∨ ~(C ∨ R)]	Assumption
2	~R ⊃ C	Assumption
3	~W	Assumption
4	A	Assumption
5	W ∨ ~(C ∨ R)	1, 4 ⊃ E
6	~(C ∨ R)	3, 5 DS
7	~~R ∨ C	2 Impl
8	R ∨ C	7 DN
9	C ∨ R	8 Com
10	~A	4-9 ~I
11	~W ⊃ ~A	3-10 ⊃ I

e. Derive: J ⊃ ~(E ∨ ~M)

1	~(J & ~H)	Assumption
2	~H ∨ M	Assumption
3	E ⊃ ~M	Assumption
4	J	Assumption
5	~J ∨ ~~H	1 DeM
6	~~J	4 DN
7	~~H	5, 6 DS
8	M	2, 7 DS
9	~~M	8 DN
10	~E	3, 9 MT
11	~E & ~~M	10, 9 & I
12	~(E ∨ ~M)	11 DeM
13	J ⊃ ~(E ∨ ~M)	4-12 ⊃ I

g. Derive: ~A ⊃ [H ⊃ (F & D)]

1	(H & ~S) ⊃ A	Assumption
2	~D ⊃ ~S	Assumption
3	~S ∨ C	Assumption
4	C ⊃ F	Assumption
5	~A	Assumption
6	H	Assumption
7	H ⊃ (~S ⊃ A)	1 Exp
8	~S ⊃ A	6, 7 ⊃ E
9	~~S	5, 8 MT
10	C	3, 9 DS
11	F	4, 10 ⊃ E
12	~~D	2, 9 MT
13	D	12 DN
14	F & D	11, 13 & I
15	H ⊃ (F & D)	6-14 ⊃ I
16	~A ⊃ [H ⊃ (F & D)]	5-15 ⊃ I

7. Inconsistency

a.

1	B ∨ ~C	Assumption
2	(L ⊃ ~G) ⊃ C	Assumption
3	(G ≡ ~B) & (~L ⊃ ~B)	Assumption
4	~L	Assumption
5	~L ∨ ~G	4 ∨I
6	L ⊃ ~G	5 Impl
7	C	2, 6 ⊃ E
8	~L ⊃ ~B	3 & E
9	~B	4, 8 ⊃ E
10	~C	1, 9 DS

8.a. The rules of replacement are two-way rules. If we can derive $\mathscr{Q}$ from $\mathscr{P}$ by using only these rules, we can derive $\mathscr{P}$ from $\mathscr{Q}$ by using the rules in reverse order.

c. Suppose that before a current line n of a derivation, an accessible line i contains a sentence of the form $\mathscr{P} \supset \mathscr{Q}$. The sentence $\mathscr{P} \supset (\mathscr{P} \& \mathscr{Q})$ can be derived by using the following routine:

i	$\mathscr{P} \supset \mathscr{Q}$	
n	$\mathscr{P}$	Assumption
$n + 1$	$\mathscr{Q}$	$i, n \supset$ E
$n + 2$	$\mathscr{P} \& \mathscr{Q}$	$n, n + 1$ & E
$n + 3$	$\mathscr{P} \supset (\mathscr{P} \& \mathscr{Q})$	n-$n + 2 \supset$ I

CHAPTER SIX

6.1E

1.a. We shall prove that every sentence of *SL* that contains only binary connectives, if any, is true on every truth-value assignment on which all its atomic components are true. Hence every sentence of *SL* that contains only binary connectives is true on at least one truth-value assignment, and thus no such sentence can be truth-functionally false. We proceed by mathematical induction on the number of occurrences of connectives in such sentences. (Note that we need not consider *all* sentences of *SL* in our induction but only those with which the thesis is concerned.)

Basis clause: Every sentence with zero occurrences of a binary connective (and no occurrences of unary connectives) is true on every truth-value assignment on which all its atomic components are true.

Inductive step: If every sentence with *k* or fewer occurrences of binary connectives (and no occurrences of unary connectives) is true on every truth-value assignment on which all its atomic components are true, then every sentence with *k* + 1 occurrences of binary connectives (and no occurrences of unary connectives) is true on every truth-value assignment on which all its atomic components are true.

The proof of the basis clause is straightforward. A sentence with zero occurrences of a connective is an atomic sentence, and each atomic sentence is true on every truth-value assignment on which its atomic component (which is the sentence itself) is true.

The inductive step is also straightforward. Assume that the thesis holds for every sentence of *SL* with *k* or fewer occurrences of binary connectives and no unary connectives. Any sentence $\mathscr{P}$ with *k* + 1 occurrences of binary connectives and no unary connectives must be of one of the four forms $\mathscr{Q} \mathbin{\&} \mathscr{R}$, $\mathscr{Q} \vee \mathscr{R}$, $\mathscr{Q} \supset \mathscr{R}$, and $\mathscr{Q} \equiv \mathscr{R}$. In each case $\mathscr{Q}$ and $\mathscr{R}$ contain *k* or fewer occurrences of binary connectives, so the inductive hypothesis holds for both $\mathscr{Q}$ and $\mathscr{R}$. That is, both $\mathscr{Q}$ and $\mathscr{R}$ are true on every truth-value assignment on which all their atomic components are true. Since $\mathscr{P}$'s immediate components are $\mathscr{Q}$ and $\mathscr{R}$, its atomic components are just those of $\mathscr{Q}$ and $\mathscr{R}$. But conjunctions, disjunctions, conditionals, and biconditionals are true when both their immediate components are true. So $\mathscr{P}$ is also true on every truth-value assignment on which its atomic components are true, for both its immediate components are then true. This completes our proof. (Note that in this clause we ignored sentences of the form $\sim \mathscr{Q}$, for the thesis concerns only those sentences of *SL* that contain *no* occurrences of ' $\sim$ '.)

b. Every sentence $\mathscr{P}$ that contains no binary connectives either contains no connectives or contains at least one occurrence of ' $\sim$ '. We prove the thesis by mathematical induction on the number of occurrences of ' $\sim$ ' in such sentences. The first case consists of the atomic sentences of *SL*, since these contain zero occurrences of connectives.

Basis clause: Every atomic sentence is truth-functionally indeterminate.

Inductive step: If every sentence with k or fewer occurrences of ' $\sim$ ' (and no binary connectives) is truth-functionally indeterminate, then every sentence with $k + 1$ occurrences of ' $\sim$ ' (and no binary connectives) is truth-functionally indeterminate.

The basis clause is obvious.

The inductive step is also obvious. Suppose $\mathscr{P}$ contains $k + 1$ occurrences of ' $\sim$ ' and no binary connectives and that the thesis holds for every sentence with fewer than $k + 1$ occurrences of ' $\sim$ ' and no binary connectives. $\mathscr{P}$ is a sentence of the form $\sim \mathscr{Q}$, where $\mathscr{Q}$ contains k occurrences of ' $\sim$ '; hence, by the inductive hypothesis, $\mathscr{Q}$ is truth-functionally indeterminate. The negation of a truth-functionally indeterminate sentence is also truth-functionally indeterminate. Hence $\sim \mathscr{Q}$, that is, $\mathscr{P}$, is truth-functionally indeterminate. This completes the induction.

c. The induction is on the number of occurrences of connectives in $\mathscr{P}$. The thesis to be proved is

> If two truth-value assignments $\mathscr{A}'$ and $\mathscr{A}''$ assign the same truth-values to the atomic components of a sentence $\mathscr{P}$, then $\mathscr{P}$ has the same truth-value on $\mathscr{A}'$ and $\mathscr{A}''$.

Basis clause: The thesis holds for every sentence with zero occurrences of connectives.

Inductive step: If the thesis holds for every sentence with k or fewer occurrences of connectives, then the thesis holds for every sentence with $k + 1$ occurrences of connectives.

The basis clause is obvious. If $\mathscr{P}$ contains zero occurrences of connectives, then $\mathscr{P}$ is an atomic sentence and its own only atomic component. $\mathscr{P}$ must have the same truth-value on $\mathscr{A}'$ and $\mathscr{A}''$ because *ex hypothesi* it is assigned the same truth-value on each assignment.

To prove the inductive step, we let $\mathscr{P}$ be a sentence with $k + 1$ occurrences of connectives and assume that the thesis holds for every sentence containing k or fewer occurrences of connectives. Then $\mathscr{P}$ is of the form $\sim \mathscr{Q}$, $\mathscr{Q} \& \mathscr{R}$, $\mathscr{Q} \vee \mathscr{R}$, $\mathscr{Q} \supset \mathscr{R}$, or $\mathscr{Q} \equiv \mathscr{R}$. In each case the immediate component(s) of $\mathscr{P}$ contain k or fewer occurrences of connectives and hence fall under the inductive hypothesis. So each immediate component of $\mathscr{P}$ has the same truth-value on $\mathscr{A}'$ and $\mathscr{A}''$. $\mathscr{P}$ therefore has the same truth-value on $\mathscr{A}'$ and $\mathscr{A}''$, as determined by the characteristic truth-tables.

d. We prove the thesis by mathematical induction on the number of conjuncts in an iterated conjunction of sentences $\mathscr{P}_1, \ldots, \mathscr{P}_n$ of *SL*.

Basis clause: Every iterated conjunction of just one sentence of *SL* is true on a truth-value assignment if and only if that one sentence is true on that assignment.

Inductive step: If every iterated conjunction of k or fewer sentences of *SL* is true on a truth-value assignment if and only if each of those conjuncts is true on that assignment, then every iterated conjunction of $k + 1$ sentences of *SL* is true on a truth-value assignment if and only if each of those conjuncts is true on that assignment.

The basis clause is trivial.

To prove the inductive step, we assume that the thesis holds for iterated conjunctions of k or fewer sentences of SL. Let $\mathscr{P}$ be an iterated conjunction of $k + 1$ sentences. Then $\mathscr{P}$ is $\mathscr{Q}\,\&\,\mathscr{R}$, where $\mathscr{Q}$ is an iterated conjunction of k sentences. $\mathscr{P}$ is therefore an iterated conjunction of all the sentences of which $\mathscr{Q}$ is an iterated conjunction, and $\mathscr{R}$. By the inductive hypothesis, the thesis holds of $\mathscr{Q}$; that is, $\mathscr{Q}$ is true on a truth-value assignment if and only if the sentences of which $\mathscr{Q}$ is an iterated conjunction are true on that assignment. Hence, whenever all the sentences of which $\mathscr{P}$ is an iterated conjunction are true, both $\mathscr{Q}$ and $\mathscr{R}$ are true, and thus $\mathscr{P}$ is true as well. Whenever at least one of those sentences is false, either $\mathscr{Q}$ is false or $\mathscr{R}$ is false, making $\mathscr{P}$ false as well. Hence $\mathscr{P}$ is true on a truth-value assignment if and only if all the sentences of which it is an iterated conjunction are true on that assignment.

e. We proceed by mathematical induction on the number of occurrences of connectives in $\mathscr{P}$. The argument is

The thesis holds for every atomic sentence $\mathscr{P}$.

If the thesis holds for every sentence $\mathscr{P}$ with k or fewer occurrences of connectives, then it holds for every sentence $\mathscr{P}$ with $k + 1$ occurrences of connectives.

The thesis holds for every sentence $\mathscr{P}$ of SL.

The proof of the basis clause is fairly simple. If $\mathscr{P}$ is an atomic sentence and $\mathscr{Q}$ is a sentential component of $\mathscr{P}$, then $\mathscr{Q}$ must be identical with $\mathscr{P}$ (since each atomic sentence is its own only atomic component). For any sentence $\mathscr{Q}_1$, then, $[\mathscr{P}](\mathscr{Q}_1//\mathscr{Q})$ is simply the sentence $\mathscr{Q}_1$. Here it is trivial that if $\mathscr{Q}$ and $\mathscr{Q}_1$ are truth-functionally equivalent, so are $\mathscr{P}$ (which is just $\mathscr{Q}$) and $[\mathscr{P}](\mathscr{Q}_1//\mathscr{Q})$ (which is just $\mathscr{Q}_1$).

In proving the inductive step, the following result will be useful:
6.1.1. If $\mathscr{Q}$ and $\mathscr{Q}_1$ are truth-functionally equivalent and $\mathscr{R}$ and $\mathscr{R}_1$ are truth-functionally equivalent, then each of the following pairs are pairs of truth-functionally equivalent sentences:

$\sim\mathscr{Q}$	$\sim\mathscr{Q}_1$
$\mathscr{Q}\,\&\,\mathscr{R}$	$\mathscr{Q}_1\,\&\,\mathscr{R}_1$
$\mathscr{Q}\lor\mathscr{R}$	$\mathscr{Q}_1\lor\mathscr{R}_1$
$\mathscr{Q}\supset\mathscr{R}$	$\mathscr{Q}_1\supset\mathscr{R}_1$
$\mathscr{Q}\equiv\mathscr{R}$	$\mathscr{Q}_1\equiv\mathscr{R}_1$

Proof: The truth-value of a molecular sentence is wholly determined by the truth-values of its immediate components. Hence, if there is a truth-value assignment on which some sentence in the left-hand column has a truth-value different from that of its partner in the right-hand column, then on that assignment either $\mathscr{Q}$ and $\mathscr{Q}_1$ have different truth-values or $\mathscr{R}$ and $\mathscr{R}_1$ have different truth-values. But this is impossible because *ex hypothesi* $\mathcal{Q}$ and $\mathcal{Q}_1$ are truth-functionally equivalent and $\mathcal{R}$ and $\mathcal{R}_1$ are truth-functionally equivalent.

To prove the inductive step of the thesis, we assume the inductive hypothesis: that the thesis holds for every sentence with k or fewer occurrences of connectives. Let $\mathcal{P}$ be a sentence of *SL* with $k + 1$ occurrences of connectives, let $\mathcal{Q}$ be a sentential component of $\mathcal{P}$, let $\mathcal{Q}_1$ be a sentence that is truth-functionally equivalent to $\mathcal{Q}$, and let $[\mathcal{P}](\mathcal{Q}_1//\mathcal{Q})$ be a sentence that results from replacing one or more occurrence of $\mathcal{Q}$ in $\mathcal{P}$ with $\mathcal{Q}_1$. Suppose, first, that $\mathcal{Q}$ is identical with $\mathcal{P}$. Then, by the reasoning in the proof of the basis clause, it follows trivially that $\mathcal{P}$ and $[\mathcal{P}](\mathcal{Q}_1//\mathcal{Q})$ are truth-functionally equivalent. Now suppose that $\mathcal{Q}$ is a sentential component of $\mathcal{P}$ that is *not* identical with $\mathcal{P}$ (in which case we say that $\mathcal{Q}$ is a *proper* sentential component of $\mathcal{P}$). Either $\mathcal{P}$ is of the form $\sim\mathcal{R}$ or $\mathcal{P}$ has a binary connective as its main connective and is of one of the four forms $\mathcal{R} \& \mathcal{S}$, $\mathcal{R} \vee \mathcal{S}$, $\mathcal{R} \supset \mathcal{S}$, and $\mathcal{R} \equiv \mathcal{S}$. We shall consider the two cases separately.

i. $\mathcal{P}$ is of the form $\sim\mathcal{R}$. Since $\mathcal{Q}$ is a proper sentential component of $\mathcal{P}$, $\mathcal{Q}$ must be a sentential component of $\mathcal{R}$. Hence $[\mathcal{P}](\mathcal{Q}_1//\mathcal{Q})$ is a sentence $\sim[\mathcal{R}](\mathcal{Q}_1//\mathcal{Q})$. But $\mathcal{R}$ has k occurrences of connectives, so, by the inductive hypothesis, $\mathcal{R}$ is truth-functionally equivalent to $[\mathcal{R}](\mathcal{Q}_1//\mathcal{Q})$. It follows from 6.1.1 that $\sim\mathcal{R}$ is truth-functionally equivalent to $\sim[\mathcal{R}](\mathcal{Q}_1//\mathcal{Q})$; that is, $\mathcal{P}$ is truth-functionally equivalent to $[\mathcal{P}](\mathcal{Q}_1//\mathcal{Q})$.

ii. $\mathcal{P}$ is of the form $\mathcal{R} \& \mathcal{S}$, $\mathcal{R} \vee \mathcal{S}$, $\mathcal{R} \supset \mathcal{S}$, or $\mathcal{R} \equiv \mathcal{S}$. Since $\mathcal{Q}$ is a proper component of $\mathcal{P}$, $[\mathcal{P}](\mathcal{Q}_1//\mathcal{Q})$ must be $\mathcal{P}$ with its left immediate component replaced by a sentence $[\mathcal{R}](\mathcal{Q}_1//\mathcal{Q})$, $\mathcal{P}$ with its right immediate component replaced with a sentence $[\mathcal{S}](\mathcal{Q}_1//\mathcal{Q})$, or $\mathcal{P}$ with both replacements made. Both $\mathcal{R}$ and $\mathcal{S}$ have fewer than $k + 1$ occurrences of connectives, and so the inductive hypothesis holds for both $\mathcal{R}$ and $\mathcal{S}$. Hence $\mathcal{R}$ is truth-functionally equivalent to $[\mathcal{R}](\mathcal{Q}_1//\mathcal{Q})$, and $\mathcal{S}$ is truth-functionally equivalent to $[\mathcal{S}](\mathcal{Q}_1//\mathcal{Q})$. And, of course, $\mathcal{R}$ is truth-functionally equivalent to $\mathcal{R}$ and $\mathcal{S}$ is truth-functionally equivalent to $\mathcal{S}$. Whatever replacements are made in $\mathcal{P}$, it follows by 6.1.1 that $\mathcal{P}$ is truth-functionally equivalent to $[\mathcal{P}](\mathcal{Q}_1//\mathcal{Q})$.

This completes the proof of the inductive step and thus the proof of our thesis.

2. An example of a sentence that contains only binary connectives and is truth-functionally true is 'A $\supset$ A'. An attempted proof would break down in the proof of the inductive step (since no atomic sentence is truth-functionally true, the basis clause will go through).

6.2E

1. Suppose that we have constructed, in accordance with the algorithm, a sentence for a row of a truth-function schema that defines a truth-function of n arguments. We proved in Exercise 1.d of Section 6.1E the result that an iterated conjunction $(\ldots(\mathscr{P}_1 \& \mathscr{P}_2) \& \ldots \& \mathscr{P}_n)$ is true on a truth-value assignment if and only if $\mathscr{P}_1, \ldots, \mathscr{P}_n$ are all true on that truth-value assignment. We have constructed the present iterated conjunction of atomic sentences and negations of atomic sentences in such a way that each conjunct is true when the atomic components have the truth-values represented in that row. Hence for that assignment the sentence constructed is true. For any other assignments to the atomic components of the sentence, at least one of the conjuncts is false; hence the conjunction is also false.

2.a. $(A \& \sim B) \lor (\sim A \& \sim B)$
   b. $A \& \sim A$
   d. $([(A \& B) \& C] \lor [(A \& B) \& \sim C]) \lor [(\sim A \& \sim B) \& C]$

3. Suppose that the table defines a truth-function of n arguments. We first construct an iterated disjunction of n disjuncts such that the ith disjunct is the negation of the ith atomic sentence of SL if the ith truth-value in the row is $\mathbf{T}$, and the ith disjunct is the ith atomic sentence of SL if the ith truth-value in the row is $\mathbf{F}$. Note that this iterated disjunction is *false* exactly when its atomic components have the truth-values displayed in that row. We then negate the iterated disjunction, to obtain a sentence that is *true* for those truth-values and false for all other truth-values that may be assigned to its atomic components.

4. To prove that $\{$ ' $\sim$ ', '$\&$'$\}$ is truth-functionally complete, it will suffice to show that for each sentence of SL containing only ' $\sim$ ', ' $\lor$ ', and '$\&$', there is a truth-functionally equivalent sentence of SL that contains the same atomic components and in which the only connectives are ' $\sim$ ' and '$\&$'. For it will then follow, from the fact that $\{$ ' $\sim$ ', ' $\lor$ ', '$\&$'$\}$ is truth-functionally complete, that $\{$ ' $\sim$ ', '$\&$'$\}$ is also truth-functionally complete. But every sentence of the form

$$\mathscr{P} \lor \mathscr{Q}$$

is truth-functionally equivalent to

$$\sim (\sim \mathscr{P} \& \sim \mathscr{Q})$$

So by repeated substitutions, we can obtain, from sentences containing ' $\sim$ ', ' $\lor$ ', and '$\&$', truth-functionally equivalent sentences that contain only ' $\sim$ ' and '$\&$'.

To show that $\{$ ' $\sim$ ', ' $\supset$ '$\}$ is truth-functionally complete, it suffices to point out that every sentence of the form

$$\mathscr{P} \& \mathscr{Q}$$

is truth-functionally equivalent to the corresponding sentence

$$\sim (\mathscr{P} \supset \sim \mathscr{Q})$$

and that every sentence of the form

$$\mathscr{P} \lor \mathscr{Q}$$

is truth-functionally equivalent to the corresponding sentence

$$\sim \mathscr{P} \supset \mathscr{Q}$$

For then we can find, for each sentence containing only ' ~ ', ' ∨ ', and '&', a truth-functionally equivalent sentence with the same atomic components containing only ' ~ ' and ' ⊃ '. It follows that {' ~ ', ' ⊃ '} is truth-functionally complete, since {' ~ ', ' ∨ ', '&'} is.

5. To show this, we need only note that the negation and disjunction truth-functions can be expressed using only the dagger.
The truth-table for 'A ↓ A' is

A	A	↓	A
T	T	F	T
F	F	T	F

The sentence 'A ↓ A' expresses the negation truth-function, for the column under the dagger is identical with the column to the right of the vertical line in the characteristic truth-table for negation.
The disjunction truth-function is expressed by '(A ↓ B) ↓ (A ↓ B)', as the following truth-table shows:

A	B	(A	↓	B)	↓	(A	↓	B)
T	T	T	F	T	T	T	F	T
T	F	T	F	F	T	T	F	F
F	T	F	F	T	T	F	F	T
F	F	F	T	F	F	F	T	F

This table shows that '(A ↓ B) ↓ (A ↓ B)' is true on every truth-value assignment on which at least one of 'A' and 'B' is true. Hence that sentence expresses the disjunction truth-function.
Thus any truth-function that is expressed by a sentence of *SL* containing only the connectives ' ~ ' and ' ∨ ' can be expressed by a sentence containing only ' ↓ ' as a connective. To form such a sentence, we convert the sentence of *SL* containing just ' ~ ' and ' ∨ ' that expresses the truth-function in question as follows. Repeatedly replace components of the form ~$\mathscr{P}$ with $\mathscr{P} ↓ \mathscr{P}$ and components of the form $\mathscr{P} \vee \mathscr{Q}$ with $(\mathscr{P} ↓ \mathscr{Q}) ↓ (\mathscr{P} ↓ \mathscr{Q})$ until a sentence containing ' ↓ ' as the only connective is obtained. Since {' ∨ ', ' ~ '} is truth-functionally complete, so is {' ↓ '}.

7. The set {' ~ '} is not truth-functionally complete because every sentence containing only ' ~ ' is truth-functionally indeterminate. Hence truth-functions expressed in *SL* by truth-functionally true sentences and truth-functions expressed in *SL* by truth-functionally false sentences cannot be expressed by a sentence that contains only ' ~ '.

The set {'&', 'V', ' ⊃ ', ' ≡ '} is not truth-functionally complete because no sentence that contains only binary connectives (if any) is truth-functionally false. Hence no truth-function that is expressed in *SL* by a truth-functionally false sentence can be expressed by a sentence containing only binary connectives of *SL*.

8. We shall prove by mathematical induction that in the truth-table for a sentence $\mathscr{P}$ containing only the connectives ' ~ ' and ' ≡ ' and two atomic components, the column under the main connective of $\mathscr{P}$ has an even number of T's and an even number of F's. For then we shall know that no sentence containing only those connectives can express, for example, the truth-function defined as follows (the material conditional truth-function):

T	T	T
T	F	F
F	T	T
F	F	T

In the induction remember that any sentence of *SL* that contains two atomic components will have a four-row truth-table. Our induction will proceed on the number of occurrences of connectives in $\mathscr{P}$. However, the first case, that considered in the basis clause, is the case where $\mathscr{P}$ contains *one* occurrence of a connective. This is because every sentence that contains zero occurrences of connectives is an atomic sentence and thus cannot contain more than one atomic component.

Basis clause: The thesis holds for every sentence of *SL* with exactly two atomic components and one occurrence of (one of) the connectives ' ~ ' and ' ≡ '.

In this case $\mathscr{P}$ cannot be of the form ~$\mathscr{Q}$, for if the initial ' ~ ' is the only connective in $\mathscr{P}$, then $\mathscr{Q}$ is atomic, and hence $\mathscr{P}$ does not contain two atomic components. So $\mathscr{P}$ is of the form $\mathscr{Q} \equiv \mathscr{R}$, where $\mathscr{Q}$ and $\mathscr{R}$ are atomic sentences. $\mathscr{Q} \equiv \mathscr{R}$ will have to be true on assignments that assign the same truth-values to $\mathscr{Q}$ and $\mathscr{R}$ and false on other assignments. Hence the thesis holds in this case.

Inductive step: If the thesis holds for every sentence of *SL* that contains k or fewer occurrences of the connectives ' ~ ' and ' ≡ ' (and no other connectives) and two atomic components, then the thesis holds for every sentence of *SL* that contains two atomic components and $k + 1$ occurrences of the connectives ' ~ ' and ' ≡ ' (and no other connectives).

Let $\mathscr{P}$ be a sentence of *SL* that contains exactly two atomic components and $k + 1$ occurrences of the connectives ' ~ ' and ' ≡ ' (and no other connectives). There are two cases to consider.

i. $\mathscr{P}$ is of the form ~$\mathscr{Q}$. Then $\mathscr{Q}$ falls under the inductive hypothesis; hence in the truth-table for $\mathscr{Q}$ the column under the main connective contains an even number of T's and an even number of F's. The column for the sentence ~$\mathscr{Q}$ will simply reverse the T's and F's, so it will also contain an even number of T's and an even number of F's.

ii. $\mathscr{P}$ is of the form $\mathscr{Q} \equiv \mathscr{R}$. Then $\mathscr{Q}$ and $\mathscr{R}$ each contain fewer occurrences of connectives. If, in addition, $\mathscr{Q}$ and $\mathscr{R}$ each contain both of the atomic components of $\mathscr{P}$, then they fall under the inductive hypothesis—$\mathscr{Q}$ has an even number of T's and an even number of F's in its truth-table column, and so does $\mathscr{R}$. On the other hand, if $\mathscr{Q}$ or $\mathscr{R}$ (or both) only contains one of the atomic components of $\mathscr{P}$ (e.g., if $\mathscr{P}$ is ' $\sim$A $\equiv$ (B $\equiv$ A)' then $\mathscr{Q}$ is 'A'), then $\mathscr{Q}$ or $\mathscr{R}$ (or both) fails to fall under the inductive hypothesis. However, in this case the component in question also has an even number of T's and an even number of F's in its column in the truth-table for $\mathscr{P}$. This is because (a) two rows assign T to the single atomic component of $\mathscr{Q}$ and, by the result in exercise 1.c, $\mathscr{Q}$ will have the same truth-value in these two rows; and (b) two rows assign F to the single atomic component of $\mathscr{Q}$ and so, by the same result, $\mathscr{Q}$ will have the same truth-value in these two rows.

We will now show that if $\mathscr{Q}$ and $\mathscr{R}$ each have an even number of T's and an even number of F's in their truth-table columns, then so must $\mathscr{P}$. Let us assume the contrary, that is, we shall suppose that $\mathscr{P}$ has an odd number of T's and an odd number of F's in its truth-table column. There are then two possibilities.

a. There are 3 T's and 1 F in $\mathscr{P}$'s truth-table column. Then in three rows of their truth-table columns, $\mathscr{Q}$ and $\mathscr{R}$ have the same truth-value, and in one row they have different truth-values. So either $\mathscr{Q}$ has one more T in its truth-table column than does $\mathscr{R}$, or vice versa. Either way, since the sum of an even number plus one is odd, it follows that either $\mathscr{Q}$ has an odd number of T's in its truth-table column or $\mathscr{R}$ has an odd number of T's in its truth-table column. This contradicts our inductive hypothesis, so we conclude that $\mathscr{P}$ cannot have 3 T's and 1 F in its truth-table column.

b. There are 3 F's and 1 T in $\mathscr{P}$'s truth-table column. By reasoning similar to (but more tedious than) that just given, it is easily shown that this is impossible, given the inductive hypothesis.

Therefore $\mathscr{P}$ must have an even number of T's and F's in its truth-table column.

9. First, a binary connective whose unit set is truth-functionally complete must be such that a sentence of which it is the main connective is false whenever all its immediate components are true. Otherwise, every sentence containing only that connective would be true whenever its atomic components were. And then, for example, the negation truth-function would not be expressible using that connective. Similar reasoning shows that the main column of the characteristic truth-table must contain T in the last row. Otherwise, no sentence containing that connective could be truth-functionally true.

Second, the column in the characteristic truth-table must contain an odd number of T's and an odd number of F's. For otherwise, as the induction in Exercise 7 shows, any sentence containing two atomic components and only this connective would have an even number of T's and an even number of F's in its truth-table column. The disjunction truth-function, for example, would then not be expressible.

Combining these two results, it is easily verified that there are only two possible characteristic truth-tables for a binary connective whose unit set is truth-functionally complete—that for ' ↓' and that for '|'.

6.3E

1.a. $\{A \supset B, C \supset D\}, \{A \supset B\}, \{C \supset D\},$ Ø
 b. $\{C \vee \sim D, \sim D \vee C, C \vee C\}, \{C \vee \sim D, \sim D \vee C\}, \{C \vee \sim D,$
$C \vee C\}, \{\sim D \vee C, C \vee C\}, \{C \vee \sim D\}, \{\sim D \vee C\}, \{C \vee C\},$ Ø
 c. $\{(B \ \& \ A) \equiv K\},$ Ø
 d. Ø

2.a, b, d, e.

4.a. To prove that SD^* is sound, it suffices to add a clause for the new rule to the induction in the proof of Metatheorem 6.2.

xiii. If $\mathcal{Q}_{k+1}$ at position $k + 1$ is justified by NBI, then $\mathcal{Q}_{k+1}$ is a negated biconditional.

$$
\begin{array}{c|l}
h & \mathcal{P} \\
j & \sim\mathcal{Q} \\
k+1 & \sim(\mathcal{P} \equiv \mathcal{Q}) \quad h, j \ \text{NBI}
\end{array}
$$

By the inductive hypothesis, $\Gamma_h \vDash \mathcal{P}$ and $\Gamma_j \vDash \sim\mathcal{Q}$. Since $\mathcal{P}$ and $\sim\mathcal{Q}$ are accessible at position $k + 1$, every member of Γ_h is a member of Γ_{k+1}, and every member of Γ_j is a member of Γ_{k+1}. Hence, by 6.3.1, $\Gamma_{k+1} \vDash \mathcal{P}$ and $\Gamma_{k+1} \vDash \sim\mathcal{Q}$. But $\sim(\mathcal{P} \equiv \mathcal{Q})$ is true whenever $\mathcal{P}$ and $\sim\mathcal{Q}$ are both true. So $\Gamma_{k+1} \vDash \sim(\mathcal{P} \equiv \mathcal{Q})$ as well.

c. To show that SD^* is not sound, it suffices to give an example of a derivation in SD^* of a sentence $\mathcal{P}$ from a set Γ of sentences such that $\mathcal{P}$ is *not* truth-functionally entailed by Γ. That is, we show that for some Γ and $\mathcal{P}$, $\Gamma \vdash \mathcal{P}$ in SD^*, but $\Gamma \nvDash \mathcal{P}$. Here is an example:

$$
\begin{array}{lll}
1 & A & \text{Assumption} \\
2 & A \vee B & \text{Assumption} \\
\\
3 & B & 1, 2 \ C \vee E
\end{array}
$$

It is easily verified that $\{A, A \vee B\}$ does not truth-functionally entail 'B'.

e. Yes. In proving Metatheorem 6.2, we showed that each rule of *SD* is truth-preserving. It follows that if every rule of *SD** is a rule of *SD*, then every rule of *SD** is truth-preserving. Of course, as we saw in Exercise 4.c, *adding* a rule will produce a system that is not sound if the rule is not truth-preserving.

5. No. In *SD* we can derive $\mathcal{Q}$ from a sentence $\mathcal{P}\ \&\ \mathcal{Q}$ by & E. But, if '&' had the suggested truth-table, then $\{\mathcal{P}\ \&\ \mathcal{Q}\}$ would *not* truth-functionally entail $\mathcal{Q}$, for (by the second row of the table) $\mathcal{P}\ \&\ \mathcal{Q}$ would be true when $\mathcal{P}$ is true and $\mathcal{Q}$ is false. Hence it would be the case that $\{\mathcal{P}\ \&\ \mathcal{Q}\} \vdash \mathcal{Q}$ in *SD* but not the case that $\{\mathcal{P}\ \&\ \mathcal{Q}\} \vDash \mathcal{Q}$.

6. To prove that *SD+* is sound for sentential logic, we must show that the rules of *SD+* that are not rules of *SD* are truth-preserving. (By Metatheorem 6.2, the rules of *SD* have been shown to be truth-preserving.) The three additional rules of inference in *SD+* are Modus Tollens, Hypothetical Syllogism, and Disjunctive Syllogism. We introduced each of these rules in Chapter Five as a *derived* rule. For example, we showed that Modus Tollens is eliminable, that anything that can be derived using this rule can be derived without it, using just the smaller set of rules in *SD*. It follows that each of these three rules is truth-preserving. For if use of one of these rules can lead from true sentences to false ones, then we can construct a derivation in *SD* (without using the derived rule) in which the sentence derived is not truth-functionally entailed by the set consisting of the undischarged assumptions. But Metatheorem 6.2 show that this is impossible. Hence each of the derived rules is truth-preserving.

All that remains to be shown, in proving that *SD+* is sound, is that the rules of replacement are also truth-preserving. We can incorporate this as a thirteenth case in the proof of the inductive step for Metatheorem 6.2:

xiii. If $\mathcal{Q}_{\ell+1}$ at position $\ell + 1$ is justified by a rule of replacement, then $\mathcal{Q}_{\ell+1}$ is derived as follows:

$$
\begin{array}{c|l}
h & \mathcal{P} \\
\ell+1 & [\mathcal{P}](\mathcal{Q}_1 //\mathcal{Q}) \quad h, \text{RR}
\end{array}
$$

where RR is some rule of replacement, sentence $\mathcal{P}$ at position h is accessible at position $\ell + 1$, and $[\mathcal{P}](\mathcal{Q}_1 //\mathcal{Q})$ is a sentence that is the result of replacing a component $\mathcal{Q}$ of $\mathcal{P}$ with a component $\mathcal{Q}_1$ in accordance with one of the rules of replacement. That the sentence $\mathcal{Q}$ is truth-functionally equivalent to $\mathcal{Q}_1$, no matter what the rule of replacement is, is easily verified. So, by Exercise 1.e of Section 6.1E, $[\mathcal{P}](\mathcal{Q}_1 //\mathcal{Q})$ is truth-functionally equivalent to $\mathcal{P}$. By the inductive hypothesis, $\Gamma_h \vDash \mathcal{P}$; and, since $\mathcal{P}$ at h is accessible at position $\ell + 1$, it follows that $\Gamma_{\ell+1} \vDash \mathcal{P}$. But $[\mathcal{P}](\mathcal{Q}_1 //\mathcal{Q})$ is true whenever $\mathcal{P}$ is true (since they are truth-functionally equivalent), so $\Gamma_{\ell+1} \vDash [\mathcal{P}](\mathcal{Q}_1 //\mathcal{Q})$; that is, $\Gamma_{\ell+1} \vDash \mathcal{Q}_{\ell+1}$.

6.4E

1.a. Assume that $\Gamma \vdash \mathcal{P}$ in *SD*. Then there is a derivation in *SD* of the following sort

$$
\begin{array}{c|l}
1 & \mathcal{P}_1 \\
2 & \mathcal{P}_2 \\
\cdot & \cdot \\
n & \mathcal{P}_n \\
\hline
\cdot & \cdot \\
m & \mathcal{P}
\end{array}
$$

(where $\mathcal{P}_1, \mathcal{P}_2, \ldots, \mathcal{P}_n$ are members of Γ). To show that $\Gamma \cup \{\sim\!\mathcal{P}\}$ is inconsistent in *SD*, we need only produce a derivation of some sentence $\mathcal{Q}$ and $\sim\!\mathcal{Q}$ from members of $\Gamma \cup \{\sim\!\mathcal{P}\}$. This is easy. Start with the derivation of $\mathcal{P}$ from Γ, and add $\sim\!\mathcal{P}$ as a new primary assumption at line $n + 1$, renumbering subsequent lines as is appropriate. As a new last line, enter $\sim\!\mathcal{P}$ by Reiteration. The result will be a derivation of the sort

$$
\begin{array}{c|ll}
1 & \mathcal{P}_1 \\
2 & \mathcal{P}_2 \\
\cdot & \cdot \\
n & \mathcal{P}_n \\
n + 1 & \sim\!\mathcal{P} \\
\hline
\cdot & \cdot \\
m + 1 & \mathcal{P} \\
m + 2 & \sim\!\mathcal{P} & n + 1 \text{ R}
\end{array}
$$

So if $\Gamma \vdash \mathcal{P}$, then $\Gamma \cup \{\sim\!\mathcal{P}\}$ is inconsistent in *SD*.

Now assume that $\Gamma \cup \{\sim\!\mathcal{P}\}$ is inconsistent in *SD*. Then there is a derivation in *SD* of the sort

$$
\begin{array}{c|l}
1 & \mathcal{P}_1 \\
2 & \mathcal{P}_2 \\
\cdot & \cdot \\
n & \mathcal{P}_n \\
n + 1 & \sim\!\mathcal{P} \\
\hline
\cdot & \cdot \\
m & \mathcal{Q} \\
\cdot & \cdot \\
p & \sim\!\mathcal{Q}
\end{array}
$$

(where $\mathcal{P}_1, \mathcal{P}_2, \ldots, \mathcal{P}_n$ are all members of Γ). To show that $\Gamma \vdash \mathcal{P}$, we need only produce a derivation in which the primary assumptions are members of Γ and the last line is $\mathscr{P}$. This is easy. Start with this derivation, but make $\sim\mathscr{P}$ an auxiliary assumption rather than a primary assumption. Enter $\mathscr{P}$ as a new last line, justified by Negation Elimination. The result will be a derivation of the sort

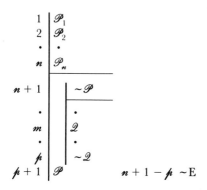

b. Assume $\Gamma \cup \{\mathscr{P}\}$ is inconsistent in SD. Then there is a derivation in SD of the sort

$$
\begin{array}{r|l}
1 & \mathscr{P}_1 \\
2 & \mathscr{P}_2 \\
\cdot & \cdot \\
n & \mathscr{P}_n \\
n+1 & \mathscr{P} \\[4pt]
\hline
\cdot & \cdot \\
m & \mathscr{Q} \\
\cdot & \cdot \\
p & \sim\mathscr{Q}
\end{array}
$$

(where $\mathscr{P}_1, \mathscr{P}_2, \dots, \mathscr{P}_n$ are members of Γ). But then there is also a derivation of the following sort

$$
\begin{array}{r|ll}
1 & \mathscr{P}_1 \\
2 & \mathscr{P}_2 \\
\cdot & \cdot \\
n & \mathscr{P}_n \\[4pt]
\hline
n+1 & \quad \mathscr{P} \\
& \quad \cdot \\
m & \quad \mathscr{Q} \\
p & \quad \sim\mathscr{Q} \\
p-1 & \sim\mathscr{P} \qquad n+1-p \;\;\sim\mathrm{I}
\end{array}
$$

This shows that if $\Gamma \cup \{\mathscr{P}\}$ is inconsistent in SD, then $\Gamma \vdash \sim\mathscr{P}$ in SD.

4. Since every rule of *SD* is a rule of *SD+* , every derivation in *SD* is a derivation in *SD+* . So if $\Gamma \vDash \mathcal{P}$, then $\Gamma \vdash \mathcal{P}$ in *SD*, by Metatheorem 6.3, and therefore $\Gamma \vdash \mathcal{P}$ in *SD+* . That is, *SD+* is complete for sentential logic.

7. a.Since we already know that *SD* is complete, we need only show that wherever Reiteration is used in a derivation in *SD*, it can be eliminated in favor of some combination of the remaining rules of *SD*. This has been proved in Exercise 13.c of Section 5.4E. Hence *SD** is complete as well.

8. We used the fact that Conjunction Elimination is a rule of *SD* in proving (b) for 6.4.7, where we showed that if a sentence $\mathcal{P} \,\&\, \mathcal{Q}$ is a member of a set Γ^* that is maximally consistent in *SD*, then both $\mathcal{P}$ and $\mathcal{Q}$ are members of Γ^*.

9. First assume that some set Γ is truth-functionally consistent. Then obviously every finite subset of Γ is truth-functionally consistent as well, for all members of a finite subset of Γ are members of Γ, hence all are true on at least one truth-value assignment.

Now assume that some set Γ is truth-functionally inconsistent. If Γ is finite, then obviously at least one finite subset of Γ (namely, Γ itself) is truth-functionally inconsistent. If Γ is infinite, then, by Lemma 6.1, Γ is inconsistent in *SD*, and, by 6.4.3, some finite subset Γ' of Γ is inconsistent in *SD*—that is, for some sentence $\mathcal{P}$, $\Gamma' \vdash \mathcal{P}$ and $\Gamma' \vdash {\sim}\mathcal{P}$. Hence, by Metatheorem 6.2, $\Gamma' \vDash \mathcal{P}$ and $\Gamma' \vDash {\sim}\mathcal{P}$, so (by 6.3.3) Γ' is truth-functionally inconsistent; hence not every finite subset of Γ is truth-functionally consistent.

CHAPTER SEVEN

7.1E

1.a. Bai
c. Bbn
e. Beh
g. (Aph & Ahn) & Ank
i. Aih ≡ Aip
k. ([Lap & Lbp) & (Lcp & Ldp)] & Lep) & ~([Bap ∨ Bbp) ∨ (Bcp ∨ Bdp)] ∨ Bep)
m. (Tda & Tdb) & (Tdc & Tde)
o. [~(Tab ∨ Tac) & ~(Tad ∨ Tae)] & [(Aab & Aac) & (Aad & Aah)]

2.a. (Ba & Ia) & ~Ra
  c. (Bd & Rd) & Id
  e. Ib ⊃ (Id & Ia)
  g. Lab & Dac
  i. ~(Lca ∨ Dca) & (Lcd & Dcd)
  k. Acb ≡ (Sbc & Rb)
  m. (Sdc & Sca) ⊃ Sda
  o. (Lcb & Lba) ⊃ (Dca & Sca)
  q. (Rd & ~Ra) & (~Rb & ~Rc)

3.a. One appropriate symbolization key is

  U.D.: Margaret, Todd, Charles, and Sarah
   Gx: x is good at skateboarding
   Lx: x likes skateboarding
   Hx: x wears headgear
   Kx: x wears kneepads
  Rxy: x is more reckless than y (at skateboarding)
  Sxy: x is more skillful than y (at skateboarding)
    c: Charles
    m: Margaret
    s: Sarah
    t: Todd

  (Lm & Lt) & ~(Gm ∨ Gt)
  Gc & ~Lc
  Gs & Ls
  [(Hm & Ht) & (Hc & Hs)] & [(Kc & Ks) & ~(Km ∨ Kt)]
  [(Rsm & Rst) & Rsc] & [(Scs & Scm) & Sct]

Note: It may be tempting to use a two-place predicate to symbolize being good at skateboarding, for example, 'Gxy', and another two-place predicate to symbolize liking skateboarding. So too we might use a two-place predicate ('Wxy') to symbolize both wearing headgear and wearing kneepads. Doing so would require including skateboarding, headgear, and kneepads in the universe of discourse. But things are now a little murky. Skateboarding is more of an activity than a thing (although activities are often the "topics of conversation" as when we say that some people like, e.g., hiking, skiing, and canoeing while others don't). And while we might include all headgear and kneepads in our universe of discourse, we do not know which ones the characters in our passage wear, so we would be hardpressed to name the favored items.

Moreover, here there is no need to invoke these two-place predicates, because we are not asked to investigate logical relations which can only be expressed with two-place predicates. The case would be different if the passage included the sentence 'If Sarah is good at anything she is good at sailing' and we were asked to show that it follows from the passage that Sarah is good at sailing. (On the revised scenario we are told that Sarah is good at skateboarding, *and* that if she is good at anything—she is, skateboarding—she is good at sailing. So she is good at sailing. Here we are treating skateboarding as *something*, something Sarah is good at. But we will leave these complexities until we have fully developed the language *PL*.)

7.2E

1.a. $(\forall z)Bz$
  c. $\sim(\exists x)Bx$
  e. $(\exists x)Bx \mathbin{\&} (\exists x)Rx$
  g. $(\exists z)Rz \supset (\exists z)Bz$
  i. $(\forall y)By \equiv \sim(\exists y)Ry$

2.a. $Pj \supset (\forall x)Px$
  c. $(\exists y)Py \supset (Pj \mathbin{\&} Pr)$
  e. $\sim Pr \supset \sim(\exists x)Px$
  g. $(Pj \supset Pr) \mathbin{\&} (Pr \supset (\forall x)Px)$
  i. $(\forall y)Sy \mathbin{\&} \sim(\forall y)Py$
  k. $(\forall x)Sx \supset (\exists y)Py$

7.3E

1.a. Formula and sentence.
  c. Formula and sentence.
  e. Formula and open sentence—the third occurrence of 'x' is free.
  g. Formula and sentence.
  i. Not a formula—a tilde can directly precede only a formula, and '$\exists$x' is not a formula; it is part of a quantifier.
  k. Not a formula—no variable for '$(\exists y)$' to bind.
  m. Formula and sentence.
  o. Formula and open sentence—the first occurrence of 'w' is free.

2. The main logical operator is given after each formula
  a. A sentence. The subformulas are

$(\exists x)(\forall y)Byx$	$(\exists x)$
$(\forall y)Byx$	$(\forall y)$
Byx	none

c. Not a sentence. The fourth occurrence of 'x' is free. The subformulas are

$(\forall x)(\sim Fx \,\&\, Gx) \equiv (Bg \supset Fx)$	$\equiv$
$(\forall x)(\sim Fx \,\&\, Gx)$	$(\forall x)$
$\sim Fx \,\&\, Gx$	$\&$
$\sim Fx$	$\sim$
Fx	none
Gx	none
$Bg \supset Fx$	$\supset$
Bg	none

e. A sentence. The subformulas are

$\sim(\exists x)Px \,\&\, Rab$	$\&$
$\sim(\exists x)Px$	$\sim$
$(\exists x)Px$	$(\exists x)$
Px	none
Rab	none

g. A sentence. The subformulas are

$\sim(\sim(\forall x)Fx \equiv (\exists w)\sim Gw) \supset Maa$	$\supset$
$\sim(\sim(\forall x)Fx \equiv (\exists w)\sim Gw)$	$\sim$
Maa	none
$\sim(\forall x)Fx \equiv (\exists w)\sim Gw$	$\equiv$
$\sim(\forall x)Fx$	$\sim$
$(\exists w)\sim Gw$	$(\exists w)$
$(\forall x)Fx$	$(\forall x)$
Fx	none
$\sim Gw$	$\sim$
Gw	none

i. A sentence. The subformulas are

$\sim\sim\sim(\exists x)(\forall z)(Gxaz \lor \sim Hazb)$	$\sim$
$\sim\sim(\exists x)(\forall z)(Gxaz \lor \sim Hazb)$	$\sim$
$\sim(\exists x)(\forall z)(Gxaz \lor \sim Hazb)$	$\sim$
$(\exists x)(\forall z)(Gxaz \lor \sim Hazb)$	$(\exists x)$
$(\forall z)(Gxaz \lor \sim Hazb)$	$(\forall z)$
$Gxaz \lor \sim Hazb$	$\lor$
$Gxaz$	none
$\sim Hazb$	$\sim$
$Hazb$	none

k. Not a sentence. The third and fourth occurrences of 'x' are free. The subformulas are

(∃x)Fx ⊃ (∀w)(~Gx ⊃ ~Hwx)	⊃
(∃x)Fx	(∃x)
(∀w)(~Gx ⊃ ~Hwx)	(∀w)
Fx	none
~Gx ⊃ ~Hwx	⊃
~Gx	~
~Hwx	~
Gx	none
Hwx	none

m. A sentence. The subformulas are

(H ∨ Fa) ≡ (∃z)(~Fz & Gza)	≡
H ∨ Fa	∨
(∃z)(~Fz & Gza)	(∃z)
H	none
Fa	none
~Fz & Gza	&
~Fz	~
Gza	none
Fz	none

3.a. Quantified sentence.
 c. Truth-functional compound.
 e. Truth-functional compound.
 g. Quantified sentence.
 i. Quantified sentence.
 k. Truth-functional compound.
 m. Truth-functional compound.
 o. Quantified sentence.
 q. Truth-functional compound.

4.a. Maa & Fa
 c. ~(Ca ≡ ~Ca)
 e. (Fa & ~Gb) ⊃ (Bab ∨ Bba)
 g. ~(∃z)Naz ≡ (∀w)(Mww & Naw)
 i. Fab ≡ Gba
 k. ~(∃y)(Hay & Hya)
 m. (∀y)[(Hay & Hya) ⊃ (∃z)Gza]

5.a. Not a substitution instance—parentheses should occur around 'Ray ⊃ Byy'.
 c. Not a substitution instance. The instantiating term must be a constant, not a variable.

e. Not a substitution instance. The instantiating term must be a constant, not a variable.

g. Not a substitution instance. The quantifier '(∀y)' has disappeared.

i. Not a substitution instance—only the initial quantifier is dropped in forming a substitution instance. The sentence 'Rab ⊃ Bbb' is a substitution instance of '(∀y)(Ray ⊃ Byy)'

6.a. A substitution instance.

c. Not a substitution instance—the same individual constant must be used as the instantiating constant *throughout* the formula.

e. Not a substitution instance—parentheses have been added, changing the scope of '(∀y)'.

g. Not a substitution instance—the variable 'y' has been replaced with 'w'.

7.4E

1.a. (∀y)(Py ⊃ Hy)
  c. (∃y)(Py & Hy)
  e. (∀z)[(Pz & Hz) ⊃ ~Iz]
  g. ~(∀w)[(Pw ∨ Iw) ⊃ Hw]
  i. (∀x)[(Ix & Hx) ⊃ Rx]
  k. (∃x)Ix ⊃ Ih
  m. (∃x)Ix ⊃ (∀y)(Ry ⊃ Iy)
  o. ~(∃x)[(Hx & Px) & Ix]
  q. (∀w)(Pw ⊃ Iw) ⊃ ~(∃y)(Py & Hy)
  s. (∀w)[Rw ⊃ ((Lw & Iw) & ~Hw)]

2.a. (∀x)(Ex ⊃ Yx)
  c. (∃y)(Ey & Yy) & ~(∀y)(Ey ⊃ Yy)
  e. (∃z)(Ez & Yz) ⊃ (∀x)(Lx ⊃ Yx)
  g. (∀w)[(Ew & Sw) ⊃ Yw]
  i. (∀w)[(Lw & Ew) ⊃ (Yw & Rw)]
  k. (∀x)[(Ex ∨ Lx) ⊃ (Yx ⊃ Rx)]
  m. ~(∃z)[(Pz & ~Rz) & Yz]
  o. (∀x)[(Ex & Sxx) ⊃ Yx]
  q. (∀x)([(Ex ∨ Lx) & (Rx ∨ Yx)] ⊃ Sxx)
  s. (∀z)([Yz & (Lz & Ez)] ⊃ Szz)

3.a. (∀z)(Lz ⊃ Az)
  c. (∀x)(Lx ⊃ Fx) & (∀x)(Tx ⊃ ~Fx)
  e. (∃y)[(Ly & Fy) & Cty]
  g. (∀x)[(Lx ∨ Tx) ⊃ Fx]
  i. (∃w)(Tw & Fw) & ~(∀y)(Ty ⊃ Fy)
  k. (∀z)[(Lz & Ctz) ⊃ (Az & ~Fz)]
  m. (∃x)(Lx & Fx) ⊃ (∀x)(Tx ⊃ Fx)
  o. ~Ft & Bt

4.a. $(\forall x)[Px \supset (Ux \ \& \ Ox)]$

  c. $(\forall z)[Az \supset \sim(Oz \lor Uz)]$

  e. $(\forall w)(Ow \equiv Uw)$

  g. $(\exists y)(Py \ \& \ Uy) \ \& \ (\forall y)[(Py \ \& \ Ay) \supset \sim Uy]$

  i. $(\exists z)[Pz \ \& \ (Oz \ \& \ Uz)] \ \& \ (\forall x)[Sx \supset (Ox \ \& \ Ux)]$

  k. $((\exists x)(Sx \ \& \ Ux) \ \& \ (\exists x)(Px \ \& \ Ux)) \ \& \ \sim(\exists x)(Ax \ \& \ Ux)$

5.a. An I-sentence and the corresponding O-sentence of *PL* can both be true. Consider the English sentences 'Some positive integers are even' and 'Some positive integers are not even'. Where the U.D. is positive integers, 'Ex' is interpreted as 'x is even', these can be symbolized as '$(\exists x)Ex$' and '$(\exists x) \sim Ex$', respectively, and both sentences of *PL* are true.

    An I-sentence and an O-sentence can also both be false. Consider 'Some snipes are fast' and 'Some snipes are not fast'. Where the U.D. is mammals, 'Sx' is interpreted as 'x is a snipe', and 'Fx' as 'x is fast', these become, respectively, '$(\exists x)(Sx \ \& \ Fx)$' and '$(\exists x)(Sx \ \& \ \sim Fx)$'. As it happens, there are no snipes, so both sentences are false. Note, however, that there cannot be an I-sentence and a corresponding O-sentence of the sorts $(\exists x)A$ and $(\exists x) \sim A$, where A is an atomic formula. For however A is interpreted, either there will be something which satisfies it, or there will not. In the first instance $(\exists x)A$ will be true, in the second $(\exists x) \sim A$.

7.5E

1.a. $(\exists y)[Sy \ \& \ (Cy \ \& \ Ly)]$

  c. $\sim(\forall w)[(Sw \ \& \ Lw) \supset Cw]$

  e. $\sim(\forall x)[(\exists y)(Sy \ \& \ Sxy) \supset Sx]$ [or] $\sim(\forall x)(\forall y)[(Sy \ \& \ Sxy) \supset Sx]$

  g. $\sim(\forall x)[(\exists y)[Sy \ \& \ (Dxy \lor Sxy)] \supset Sx]$ [or] $\sim(\forall x)(\forall y)[[Sy \ \& \ (Dxy \lor Sxy)] \supset Sx]$

  i. $(\forall z)[(Sz \ \& \ (\exists w)(Swz \lor Dwz)) \supset Lz]$

  k. $Sr \lor (\exists y)(Sy \ \& \ Dry)$

  m. $(Sr \ \& \ (\forall z)[(Dzr \lor Szr) \supset Sz]) \lor (Sj \ \& \ (\forall z)[(Dzj \lor Szj) \supset Sz])$

2.a. $(\forall x)[Ax \supset (\exists y)(Fy \ \& \ Exy)] \ \& \ (\forall x)[Fx \supset (\exists y)(Ay \ \& \ Exy)]$

  c. $\sim(\exists y)(Fy \ \& \ Eyp)$

  e. $\sim(\exists y)(Fy \ \& \ Eyp) \ \& \ (\exists y)(Cy \ \& \ Eyp)$

  g. $\sim(\exists w)(Aw \ \& \ Uw) \ \& \ (\exists w)(Aw \ \& \ Fw)$

  i. $(\exists w)[(Aw \ \& \ \sim Fw) \ \& \ (\forall y)[(Fy \ \& \ Ay) \supset Ewy]]$

  k. $(\exists z)[Fz \ \& \ (\forall y)(Ay \supset Dzy)] \ \& \ (\exists z)[Az \ \& \ (\forall y)(Fy \supset Dzy)]$

  m. $(\forall x)[(\forall y)Dxy \supset (Px \lor (Ax \lor Ox))]$

3.a. $(\forall x)[Px \supset (\exists y)(Syx \ \& \ Bxy)]$

  c. $(\forall w)[(Pw \ \& \ (\forall x)Bxw) \supset (\forall z)(Szw \supset Bwz)]$

  e. $(\forall x)(\forall y)[(Py \ \& \ Sxy) \supset Byx] \supset (\forall z)(Pz \supset Wz)$

  g. $(\forall x)(Px \supset (\forall y)[(Syx \ \& \ Bxy) \supset (\sim Uxy \ \& \ \sim Lyx)])$

  i. $(\exists w)[Pw \ \& \ (\forall y)(Py \supset Bwy)]$

  k. $(\forall x)((Px \ \& \ Ux) \supset [(\forall z)(Szx \supset Bxz) \lor (\forall z)(Szx \supset Gxz)])$

m. $(\forall x)(\forall y)([(Px \ \& \ Syx) \ \& \ (Bxy \ \& \ Byx)] \supset (Wx \ \& \ Wy))$

o. $(\exists x)[Px \ \& \ (\exists y)(Syx \ \& \ \sim Uxty)]$

q. $(\forall w)(\forall z)([(Pz \ \& \ Swz) \ \& \ \sim Lwz] \supset (\sim Uwz \ \& \ Bwz))$

4.a. Hildegard loves Manfred some of the time.

c. Manfred loves Hildegard some of the time, and he always loves Siegfried.

e. If Manfred ever loves himself, he does so whenever Hildegard loves him.

g. There is a person who is never loved.

i. There is a time at which someone loves everyone.

k. At every time someone loves everyone.

m. Nobody loves anybody all the time.

o. Everyone, at some time or other, loves him- or herself.

7.6E

1.a. $(\forall x)[(Wx \ \& \ \sim x = d) \supset Sx]$

c. $(\forall x)[(Wx \ \& \ \sim x = d) \supset [Sx \lor (\exists y)[Sy \ \& \ (Dxy \lor Sxy)]]]$

e. $[Sdj \ \& \ (\forall x)(Sxj \supset x = d)] \ \& \ \sim(\exists x)Dxj$

g. $(\exists x)[(Sxr \ \& \ Sxj) \ \& \ (\forall y)[(Syr \lor Syj) \supset y = x]]$

i. $(\exists x)(\exists y)[((Dxr \ \& \ Dyr) \ \& \ (Sx \ \& \ Sy)) \ \& \ \sim x = y]$

k. $(\exists x)[(Sxj \ \& \ Sx) \ \& \ (\forall y)(Syj \supset y = x)] \ \& \ (\exists x)(\exists y)(([(Sx \ \& \ Sy) \ \& \ (Dxj \ \& \ Dyj)] \ \& \ \sim x = y) \ \& \ (\forall z)[Dzj \supset (z = x \lor z = y)])$

2.a. Every positive integer is less than some positive integer [or] There is no largest positive integer.

c. There is a smallest positive integer.

e. The number 2 is even and prime, and it is the only positive integer which is both even and prime.

g. The product of any odd positive integers is itself odd.

i. The product of an odd positive integer and an even positive integer is even.

k. There is exactly one positive integer which prime, is greater than 5, and less than 9.

3.a. Symmetric only.

$(\forall x)(\forall y)(Nxy \supset Nyx)$

c. Neither reflexive nor symmetric nor transitive.

e. Symmetric and transitive.

$(\forall x)(\forall y)(Rxy \supset Ryx)$
$(\forall x)(\forall y)(\forall z)[(Rxy \ \& \ Ryz) \supset Rxz]$

g. Transitive and reflexive.

$(\forall x)(\forall y)(\forall z)[(Txy \ \& \ Tyz) \supset Txz]$
$(\forall x)Txx$ (U.D.: physical objects)

i. Symmetric and reflexive.

$(\forall x)(\forall y)(Exy \supset Eyx)$
$(\forall x)Exx$ (U.D.: people)

k. Symmetric, transitive, and reflexive.

$(\forall x)(\forall y)(Wxy \supset Wyx)$
$(\forall x)(\forall y)(\forall z)[(Wxy \ \& \ Wyz) \supset Wxz]$
$(\forall x)Wxx$ (U.D.: physical objects)

m. Transitive only.

$(\forall x)(\forall y)(\forall z)[(Axy \ \& \ Ayz) \supset Axz]$

o. Symmetric, transitive, and reflexive.

$(\forall x)(\forall y)(Lxy \supset Lyx)$
$(\forall x)(\forall y)(\forall z)[(Lxy \ \& \ Lyz) \supset Lxz]$
$(\forall x)Lxx$ (U.D.: people)

4.a. Sjc
   c. Sjc & $(\forall x)[(Sxc \ \& \ \sim x = j) \supset Ojx]$
   e. $(\exists x)[(Dxd \ \& \ (\forall y)[(Dyd \ \& \ \sim y = x) \supset Oxy]) \ \& \ Px]$
   g. Dcd & $(\forall x)[(Dxd \ \& \ \sim x = c) \supset Ocx]$
   i. $(\exists x)[(Sxh \ \& \ (\forall y)[(Syh \ \& \ \sim y = x) \supset Txy]) \ \& \ Mcx]$
   k. $(\exists x)[Bx \ \& \ (\forall y)(By \supset y = x)) \ \& \ (\exists w)((Mw \ \& \ (\forall z)(Mz \supset z = w)) \ \&$
x = w)]
   m. $(\exists x)[(Mxc \ \& \ (\forall y)(Myc \supset y = x)) \ \& \ (Bxj \ \& \ (\forall w)(Bwj \supset x = w))]$

CHAPTER EIGHT

8.1E

1.a. **F**
   c. **T**
   e. **F**
   g. **T**

2.a. **T**
   c. **T**
   e. **F**
   g. **F**

3.a. One interpretation is

U.D.: set of people
Nxy: x is the mother of y
   a: Jane Doe
   d: Jay Doe

c. One interpretation is

U.D.: set of U.S. cities
Lx: x is in California
Cxy: x is to the north of y
   h: San Francisco
   m: Los Angeles

e. One interpretation is

U.D.: set of positive integers
Mx: x is odd
Nx: x is even
   a: 1
   b: 2

4.a. One interpretation is

U.D.: set of positive integers
Cxy: x equals y squared
   r: 2
   s: 3

c. One interpretation is

U.D.: set of people
Lx: x is a lion
   i: Igor Stravinsky
   j: Jesse Winchester
   m: Margaret Mead

e. One interpretation is

U.D.: set of positive integers
Jx: x is even
   a: 1
   b: 2
   c: 3
   d: 4

5.a. One interpretation is

U.D.: set of people
Fxy: x is the mother of y
   a: Liza Minelli
   b: Judy Garland (Liza Minelli's mother)

On this interpretation, 'Fab ⊃ Fba' is true, and 'Fba ⊃ Fab' is false.

   c. One interpretation is

     U.D.: set of planets
     Cxyz: the orbit of x is between the orbit of y and the orbit of z
     Mx: x is inhabited by human life
       a: Earth
       p: Venus
       q: Pluto
       r: Mars

On this interpretation, ' ∼Ma ∨ Cpqr' is false, and 'Capq ∨ ∼Mr' is true.

   e. One interpretation is

     U.D.: set of positive integers
     Lxy: x is less than y
     Mxy: x equals y
       j: 1
       k: 1

On this interpretation the first sentence is true and the second false.

    6.a. Suppose that 'Ba' is true on some interpretation. Then 'Ba ∨ ∼Ba' is true on that interpretation. Suppose that 'Ba' is false on some interpretation. Then ' ∼Ba' is true on that interpretation, and so is 'Ba ∨ ∼Ba'. Since on any interpretation 'Ba' is either true or false, we have shown that 'Ba ∨ ∼Ba' is true on every interpretation.

    7.a. False. For consider any person w who is over forty years old. It is true that that person is over forty years old but false that some person is her own sister. So that person w is *not* such that <u>if</u> w is over forty years old <u>then</u> some person is her own sister.
    c. False. The sentence says that there is at least one person x such that every person y is either a child or a brother of x, which is obviously false.
    e. True. The antecedent, '(∃x)Cx', is true. At least one person is over forty years old. And the consequent, 'N ⊃ (∃y)By', is also true. 'N' is true, and '(∃y)By' is true.
    g. True. The antecedent, '(∀x)Bx', is false, so the conditional sentence is true.
    i. True. The sentence says that there is at least one person x such that either x is over forty years old or x and some person y are sisters and y is over forty years old. Both conditions are true.

    8.a. True. Every U.S. President held office after George Washington's first term. Note that for the sentence to be true, George Washington too must have held office after George Washington's first term of office. He did—he was in office for two terms.

c. True. George Washington was the first U.S. President, and at least one U.S. President y held office after Washington.

e. True. Each U.S. President y is such that if y is a U.S. citizen (which y is) then at least one U.S. President held office before or after y's first term.

g. False. Every U.S. President x held office after George Washington's first term, but, for any such President x, no non-U.S. citizen has held office before x (because every U.S. President *is* a U.S. citizen).

i. True (in 1989!). The sentence says that a disjunction is not the case and therefore that each of the disjuncts is false. The first disjunct is interpreted to be false, and the second disjunct, which says that there is a U.S. President who held office after every U.S. President's first term of office, is false (there is no one yet who has held office after George Bush's first term).

9.a. True. The first conjunct, 'Bb', is true. The second conjunct is also true, since no positive integer that is greater than 2 is equal to 2.

c. True. No positive integer x is equal to any number than which it is greater.

e. True. The antecedent is true, since it is not the case that every positive integer is greater than every positive integer. But 'Mcba' is also true—$3 - 2 = 1$.

g. True. No positive integer z that is even is such that the result of subtracting 1 from z is also even.

i. False. Not every positive integer (in fact, *no* positive integer) is such that it equals itself if and only if there are not two positive integers of which it is the difference. Every positive integer equals itself, but every positive integer is also the difference of two positive integers.

8.2E

1.a. The sentence is false on the following interpretation:

U.D.: set of people
Fx: x is a father
Gx: x is a male

Every father is a male, but not every person is a male.

c. The sentence is false on the following interpretation:

U.D.: set of people
Bxy: x is the child of y

Everyone is someone's child, but no one is the parent of everyone.

e. The sentence is false on the following interpretation:

U.D.: set of people
Fx: x is a woman
Gx: x has blonde hair

The antecedent, '(∀x)Fx ⊃ (∀w)Gw' is true, since *its* antecedent, '(∀x)Fx', is false. But the consequent, '(∀z)(Fz ⊃ Gz)', is false, since some women do not have blonde hair.

g. The sentence is false on the following interpretation:

U.D.: set of positive integers
  Gx: x is negative
  Fxy: x equals y

No positive integer is negative, but not every positive integer is such that if it equals itself (which everyone does) then it is negative.

2.a. The sentence is true on the following interpretation:

U.D.: set of positive integers
  Bxy: x equals y

The sentence to the left of ' ≡ ' is true, since it is not the case that all positive integers equal one another; and the sentence to the right of ' ≡ ' is true, since each positive integer is equal to itself.

c. The sentence is true on the following interpretation:

U.D.: set of people
  Fx: x is twenty years old
  Gx: x weighs ten pounds

At least one person is twenty years old, and at least one person weighs ten pounds, but no twenty-year-old person weighs ten pounds.

e. The sentence is true on the following interpretation:

U.D.: set of people
  Fx: x weighs 1510 pounds
  Gx: x is happy

Trivially, every person who weighs 1510 pounds is happy since no person weighs 1510 pounds; and every person who is happy does not weigh 1510 pounds.

g. The sentence is true on the following interpretation:

U.D.: set of positive integers
  Bx: x is prime
  Hx: x is odd

The antecedent is false—not every positive integer is such that it is prime if and only if it is odd, and the consequent is true—at least one positive integer is both prime and odd.

i. U.D.: set of positive integers
    Bxy: x is greater than y

The greater-than relation is transitive, making the first conjunct true; for every positive integer there is a greater one, making the second conjunct true; and the greater-than relation is irreflexive, making the third conjunct true.

3.a. The sentence is true on the following interpretation:

U.D.: set of people
Fx: x is female
Gx: x is thirteen years old

At least one female person is thirteen years old, and at least one person is neither female nor thirteen years old.
The sentence is false on the following interpretation:

U.D.: set of people
Fx: x has a heart
Gx: x has a lung

At least one person has a heart and a lung, but no person lacks both.

c. The sentence is true on the following interpretation:

U.D.: set of people
Bxy: x is the parent of y
n: Richard Nixon

The antecedent, '(∀x)Bnx', is false on this interpretation.
The sentence is false on the following interpretation:

U.D.: set of U.S. citizens
Bxy: x is a citizen of the same country as y
n: Richard Nixon

Every U.S. citizen is a citizen of the same country as Richard Nixon, so the antecedent is true and the consequent false.

e. The sentence is true on the following interpretation:

U.D.: set of positive integers
Nxy: x equals y

Each positive integer x is such that each positive integer w that is equal to x is equal to itself.
The sentence is false on the following interpretation:

U.D.: set of positive integers
Nxy: x is greater than y

No positive integer x is such that every positive integer w that is greater or smaller than x is greater than itself.

     g. The sentence is true on the following interpretation:

       U.D.: set of positive integers
        Cx: x is greater than 0
        Dx: x is prime

Every positive integer is either greater than 0 or prime (because every positive integer is greater than 0), and at least one positive integer is both greater than 0 and prime. The biconditional is therefore true on this interpretation.
     The sentence is false on the following interpretation:

       U.D.: set of positive integers
        Cx: x is even
        Dx: x is odd

Every positive integer is either even or odd, but no positive integer is both. The biconditional is therefore false on this interpretation.

     4.a. If the antecedent is true on an interpretation, then at least one member x of the U.D., let's assume a, stands in the relation B to every member y of the U.D. But then it follows that for every member y of the U.D., there is at least one member x that stands in the relation B to y—namely, a. So the consequent is also true. If the antecedent is false on an interpretation, then the conditional is trivially true. So the sentence is true on every interpretation.
     c. If 'Fa' is true on an interpretation, then 'Fa ∨ [(∀x)Fx ⊃ Ga]' is true. If 'Fa' is false on an interpretation, then '(∀x)Fx' is false, making '(∀x)Fx ⊃ Ga' true. Either way, the disjunction is true.
     e. If '(∃x)Hx' is true on an interpretation, then the disjunction is true on that interpretation. If '(∃x)Hx' is false on an interpretation, then no member of the U.D. is H. In this case, every member of the U.D. is such that if it is H (which it is not) then it is J, and so the second disjunct is true, making the ̄disjunction true as well. ̄Either way, then, the disjunction is true.

     5.a. No member of any U.D. is such that it is in the extension of 'B' if and only if it isn't in the extension of 'B'. So the existentially quantified sentence is false on every interpretation.
     c. The second conjunct is true on an interpretation if and only if no member of the U.D. is G and no member of the U.D. is not F—that is, every member of the U.D. *is* F. But then the first conjunct must be false, because its antecedent is true but its consequent is false. Thus there is no interpretation on which the entire conjunction is true; it is quantificationally false.

8.3E

1.a. The first sentence is false and the second true on the following interpretation:

> U.D.: set of people
> Fx: x is female
> Gx: x is a university professor
> a: Paul Newman

Some person is female and Paul Newman is not a university professor, so '($\exists$x)Fx $\supset$ Ga' is false. But every nonfemale person is trivially such that if that person is female (which *he* is not) then Paul Newman is a university professor, so '($\exists$x)(Fx $\supset$ Ga)' is true.

c. The first sentence is false and the second true on the following interpretation:

> U.D.: set of integers
> Fx: x is a multiple of 2
> Gx: x is an odd number

It is false that either every integer is a multiple of 2 or every integer is odd, but it is true that every integer is either a multiple of 2 or odd.

e. The first sentence is false and the second true on the following interpretation:

> U.D.: set of people
> Fx: x is female
> Gx: x is a parent

A female who is not a parent is not such that she is female if and only if she is a parent. But '($\exists$x)Fx $\equiv$ ($\exists$x)Gx' is true, since '($\exists$x)Fx' and '($\exists$x)Gx' are both true.

g. The first sentence is true and the second false on the following interpretation:

> U.D.: set of positive integers
> Bx: x is less than 5
> Dxy: x is divisible by y without remainder

The number 1 is less than 5 and divides every positive integer without remainder. But '($\forall$x)(Bx $\supset$ ($\forall$y)Dyx)' is false, for 2 is less than 5 but does not divide any odd number without remainder.

i. The first sentence is false and the second true on the following interpretation:

> U.D.: set of positive integers
> Fx: x is odd
> Kxy: x is smaller than y

The number 1 does not satisfy the condition that if it is odd (which it is) then there is a positive integer that is smaller than it. But at least one positive integer does satisfy the condition—in fact, every other positive integer does.

2.a. Suppose that '(∀x)Fx ⊃ Ga' is true on an interpretation. Then either '(∀x)Fx' is false or 'Ga' is true. If '(∀x)Fx' is false, then some member of the U.D. is not in the extension of 'F'. But then that object is trivially such that if it is F (which it is not) then a is G. So '(∃x)(Fx ⊃ Ga)' is true. If 'Ga' is true, then trivially every member x of the U.D. is such that if x is F then a is G, so '(∃x)(Fx ⊃ Ga)' is true in this case as well.

Now suppose that '(∀x)Fx ⊃ Ga' is false on some interpretation. Then '(∀x)Fx' is true, and 'Ga' is false. Every object in the U.D. is then in the extension of 'F'; hence no member x is such that if it is F (which it is) then a is G (which is false). So '(∃x)(Fx ⊃ Ga)' is false as well.

c. Suppose that '(∃x)(Fx ∨ Gx)' is true on an interpretation. Then at least one member of the U.D. is either in the extension of 'F' or in the extension of 'G'. This individual therefore does not satisfy ' ~Fy & ~Gy', so '(∀y)(~Fy & ~Gy)' is false and its negation true.

Now suppose that '(∃x)(Fx ∨ Gx)' is false on an interpretation. Then no member of the U.D. satisfies 'Fx ∨ Gx'—no member of the U.D. is in the extension of 'F' or in the extension of 'G'. In this case, every member of the U.D. satisfies ' ~Fy & ~Gy', so '(∀y)(~Fy & ~Gy)' is true and its negation false.

3.a. All the set members are true on the following interpretation:

    U.D.: set of people
     Bx: x is a barber
     Cx: x is a child

Some person is a barber, some person is a child, and some person is neither a barber nor a child.

c. All the set members are true on the following interpretation:

    U.D.: set of positive integers
     Fx: x is greater than 10
     Gx: x is greater than 5
     Nx: x is smaller than 3
     Mx: x is smaller than 5

Every positive integer that is greater than 10 is greater than 5, every positive integer that is smaller than 3 is smaller than 5, and no positive integer that is greater than 5 is also smaller than 5.

e. All the set members are true on the following interpretation:

    U.D.: set of people
     Nx: x has three hearts
     Mx: x is 4100 years old
    Cxy: x loves y

The two sentences are trivially true, the first because no person has three hearts and the second because no person is 4100 years old.

g. All the set members are true on the following interpretation:

U.D.: set of positive integers
Nx: x is prime
Mx: x is an even number

The first sentence is true, because 3 is prime but not even. Hence not all primes are even numbers. The second is true because any nonprime integer is such that if it is prime (which it is not) then it is even. Hence it is false that all positive integers fail to satisfy this condition.

i. All the set members are true on the following interpretation:

U.D.: set of positive integers
Fxy: x evenly divides y
Gxy: x is greater than y
a: 1

At least one positive integer is evenly divisible by 1, at least one positive integer is such that 1 is not greater than that integer, and every positive integer is either evenly divisible by 1 or such that 1 is greater than it.

4.a. If the set is quantificationally consistent, then there is an interpretation on which both set members are true. But, if '(∃x)(Bx & Cx)' is true on an interpretation, then at least one member x of the U.D. is in the extensions of both 'B' and 'C'. That member is *not* neither B nor C, so, if '(∃x)(Bx & Cx)' is true, then '(∀x) ~(Bx ∨ Cx)' is false. There is no interpretation on which both set members are true.

c. If the first set member is true on an interpretation, then every pair x and y of members of the U.D. is such that either x stands in the relation B to y or y stands in the relation B to x. In particular, each pair consisting of a member of the U.D. and itself must satisfy the condition and so must stand in the relation B to itself. This being so, the second set member is false on such an interpretation. Thus there can be no interpretation on which both set members are true.

5. Suppose that $\mathscr{P}$ and $\mathscr{Q}$ are quantificationally equivalent. Then on every interpretation $\mathscr{P}$ and $\mathscr{Q}$ have the same truth-value. Thus the biconditional $\mathscr{P} \equiv \mathscr{Q}$ is true on every interpretation (since a biconditional is true when its immediate components have the same truth-value); hence it is quantificationally true.

Suppose that $\mathscr{P} \equiv \mathscr{Q}$ is quantificationally true. Therefore it is true on every interpretation. Then $\mathscr{P}$ and $\mathscr{Q}$ have the same truth-value on every interpretation (since a biconditional is true only if its immediate components have the same truth-value) and are quantificationally equivalent.

8.4E

1.a. The set members are true and '(∃x)(Hx & Fx)' false on the following interpretation:

> U.D.: set of people
> Fx: x is a teenager
> Hx: x is middle-aged
> Gx: x has a heart

Every teenager has a heart, and every middle-aged person has a heart, but no teenager is middle-aged.

c. The set member is true and 'Fa' is false on the following interpretation:

> U.D.: set of mammals
> Fx: x is a gorilla
> a: Pablo Picasso

Some mammal is a gorilla, but Pablo Picasso is not a gorilla.

e. The set members are true and '(∃x)Bx' is false on the following interpretation:

> U.D.: set of mammals
> Bx: x is a planet
> Cx: x has four legs

Every mammal is trivially such that if it is a planet then it has four legs, for no mammal is a planet. There is at least one mammal that has four legs, but there is no mammal that is a planet.

g. The set member is true and '(∀x) ~ Lxx' is false on the following interpretation:

> U.D.: set of positive integers
> Lxy: x is greater than or equal to y

Every positive integer x is such that for some positive integer y, x is not greater than or equal to y. But it is false that every positive integer is not greater than or equal to itself.

2.a. The premises are true and the conclusion false on the following interpretation:

> U.D.: set of people
> Fx: x has a heart
> Gx: x has four legs
> Nx: x has antennae

The first premise is true, since its antecedent is false. The second premise is trivially true because no person has antennae. The conclusion is false, for no person either lacks a heart or has four legs.

c. The premises are true and the conclusion false on the following interpretation:

U.D.: set of people
Fx: x is fat
Gx: x is a child
Hx: x is old

Some child is fat, and some old person is fat, but no child is an old person.

e. The premises are true and the conclusion false on the following interpretation:

U.D.: set of people
Fx: x is a tree
Gx: x is a child

The first premise is trivially true, for no person is a tree. For the same reason, the second premise is true. But some person is a child, so the conclusion is false.

g. The premises are true and the conclusion false on the following interpretation:

U.D.: set of positive integers
Gx: x is prime
Dxy: x equals y

Some positive integer is prime, and every prime number equals itself, but there is no prime number that is equal to every positive integer.

i. The premises are true and the conclusion false on the following interpretation:

U.D.: set of positive integers
Fx: x is odd
Gx: x is positive
Hx: x is prime

Every odd positive integer is positive, and every prime positive integer is positive, but not every positive integer is odd or prime.

3.a. A symbolization of the first argument is

$(\forall x)Bx$
_____
$(\exists x)Bx$

To see that this argument is quantificationally valid, assume that '$(\forall x)Bx$' is true on some interpretation. Then every member of the U.D. is B. Since every U.D. is nonempty, it follows that there is at least one member that is B. So '$(\exists x)Bx$' is true as well.

A symbolization of the second argument is

$(\forall x)(Px \supset Bx)$

$(\exists x)(Px \ \& \ Bx)$

The premise is true and the conclusion false on the following interpretation:

U.D.: set of positive integers
Px: x is purple
Bx: x is beautiful

c. One symbolization of the first argument is

$(\exists x)(\forall y)Lxy$

$(\forall y)(\exists x)Lxy$

To see that the argument is quantificationally valid, assume that the premise is true on some interpretation. Then some member x of the U.D.—let's call it a—stands in the relation L to every member of the U.D. Thus, for each member y of the U.D., there is some member—namely, a—who stands in the relation L to y. So the conclusion is true as well.

A symbolization of the second argument is

$(\forall x)(\exists y)Lyx$

$(\exists y)(\forall x)Lyx$

The following interpretation makes the premise true and the conclusion false:

U.D.: set of positive integers
Lxy: x is larger than y

For each positive integer, there is a larger one, but no positive integer is the largest.

e. A symbolization of the first argument is

$(\exists x)(Tx \ \& \ Sx) \ \& \ (\exists x)(Tx \ \& \ \sim Hx)$

$(\exists x)(Tx \ \& \ (Sx \ \lor \ \sim Hx))$

To see that this argument is quantificationally valid, assume that the premise is true on some interpretation. Then at least one member of the U.D.—let's call it a —is both a student and smart and at least one member of the U.D. is both a student and not happy. a satisfies the condition of being both a student and either smart or happy, so the conclusion is true as well.

A symbolization of the second argument is

$$(\forall x)(Tx \supset Sx) \ \& \ \sim(\exists x)(Tx \ \& \ Hx)$$
$$(\exists x)(Tx \ \& \ (Sx \lor \sim Hx))$$

The following interpretation makes the premise true and the conclusion false:

> U.D.: set of positive integers
> Tx: x is negative
> Sx: x is odd
> Hx: x is prime

Every negative positive integer (there are none) is odd, and there is no positive integer that is negative and prime. But it is false that some positive integer is both negative and either odd or not prime.

g. A symbolization of the first argument is

$$(\forall x)(Ax \supset Cx) \ \& \ (\forall x)(Cx \supset Sx)$$
$$(\forall x)(Ax \supset Sx)$$

To see that the argument is quantificationally valid, assume that the premise is true on some interpretation. Then every member of the U.D. that is A is also C, and every member of the U.D. that is C is also S. So if a member of the U.D. is A, it is C and therefore S as well, which is what the conclusion says.

A symbolization of the second argument is

$$(\forall x)(Sx \supset Cx) \ \& \ (\forall x)(Cx \supset Ax)$$
$$(\forall x)(Ax \supset Sx)$$

The premise is true and the conclusion false on the following interpretation:

> U.D.: set of positive integers
> Ax: x is positive
> Cx: x is greater than 1
> Sx: x is even

Every even positive integer is greater than 1, and every positive integer that is greater than 1 is positive. But not every positive integer that is positive is greater than 1, for 1 itself does not satisfy this condition.

8.5E

1.a. Ca $\supset$ Daa
c. Ba $\lor$ Faa
e. Ca $\supset$ (N $\supset$ Ba)
g. Ba $\supset$ Ca
i. Ca $\lor$ (Daa $\lor$ Ca)

2. Remember that, in expanding a sentence containing the individual constant 'g', we must use that constant.

a. Dag & Dgg

c. [Aa & (Daa ∨ Dba)] ∨ [Ab & (Dab ∨ Dbb)]

e. [Ua ⊃ ((Daa ∨ Daa) ∨ (Dab ∨ Dba))] & [Ub ⊃ ((Dba ∨ Dab) ∨ (Dbb ∨ Dbb))]

g. [Dag ⊃ ((~Ua & Daa) ∨ (~Ug & Dag))] & [Dgg ⊃ ((~Ua & Dga) ∨ (~Ug & Dgg))]

i. ~(K ∨ ((Daa & Dab) ∨ (Dba & Dbb)))

3. Remember that if any individual constants occur in a sentence, those constants must be used in the expansion of the sentence.

a. Bb & [(Gab ⊃ ~Eab) & (Gbb ⊃ ~Ebb)]

c. [(Gaa ⊃ ~Eaa) & (Gab ⊃ ~Eab)] & [(Gba ⊃ ~Eba) & (Gbb ⊃ ~Ebb)]

e. Impossible! This sentence contains three individual constants, 'a', 'b', and 'c'; so it can be expanded only for sets of at least three constants.

g. [Ba ⊃ ~((Ba & Maaa) ∨ (Bb & Maab))] & [Bb ⊃ ~((Ba & Mbaa) ∨ (Bb & Mbab))]

i. [Eaa ≡ ~((Maaa ∨ Maba) ∨ (Mbaa ∨ Mbba))] & [Ebb ≡ ~((Maab ∨ Mabb) ∨ (Mbab ∨ Mbbb))]

4.a. [(Ga ⊃ Naa) & (Gb ⊃ Nbb)] & (Gc ⊃ Ncc)

c. ((N ≡ Ba) ∨ (N ≡ Bb)) ∨ (N ≡ Bc)

5. The truth-table for an expansion for the set {'a'} is

Fa	(Fa	&	~Fa)	⊃ (↓)	~Fa
T	T	F	F T	T	F T
F	F	F	T F	T	T F

This truth-table shows that the sentence

((∃x)Fx & (∃y) ~Fy) ⊃ (∀x) ~Fx

is true on every interpretation with a one-member U.D. The truth-table for an expansion for the set {'a', 'b'} is

Fa	Fb	[(Fa	∨	Fb)	&	(~Fa	∨	~Fb)]	⊃ (↓)	(~Fa	&	~Fb)
T	T	T	T	T	F	F T	F	F T	T	F T	F	F T
T	F	T	T	F	T	F T	T	T F	F	F T	F	T F
F	T	F	T	T	T	T F	T	F T	F	T F	F	F T
F	F	F	F	F	F	T F	T	T F	T	T F	T	T F

This truth-table shows that the sentence

$$((\exists x)Fx \ \& \ (\exists y) \sim Fy) \supset (\forall x) \sim Fx$$

is true on at least one interpretation with a two-member U.D. and false on at least one interpretation with a two-member U.D.

6.a. One assignment to its atomic components for which the expansion

$$[Naa \lor (Naa \lor Nan)] \ \& \ [Nnn \lor (Nna \lor Nnn)]$$

is true is

								↓						
Naa	Nan	Nna	Nnn	[Naa	∨	(Naa	∨	Nan)]	&	[Nnn	∨	(Nna	∨	Nnn)]
T	T	T	T	T	T	T	T	T	T	T	T	T	T	T

Using this information, we shall construct an interpretation with a two-member U.D. such that the relation N holds between each two members of the U.D.:

    U.D.: the set consisting of the Sun and Venus
    Nxy: x is in the same galaxy as y

Every member of the U.D. is in the same galaxy as itself and as every other member, so '$(\forall x)(Nxx \lor (\exists y)Nxy)$' is true on this interpretation.

b. There is only one assignment to its atomic components for which the expansion 'Saan & Snnn' is true.

Saan	Snnn	Saan	↓ &	Snnn
T	T	T	T	T

Using this information, we construct an interpretation with a two-member U.D.:

U.D.: set consisting of the number 0 and the number 1
Sxyz: x minus y equals z
n: 0

Because $0 - 0 = 0$ and $1 - 1 = 0$, '$(\forall y)$Syyn' is true on this interpretation.

7.a.

Fa	Ga	(Fa	⊃	Ga)	↓ ⊃	Ga
F	F	F	T	F	F	F

c.

Baa	Bab	Bba	Bbb	[(Baa	∨	Bab)	&	(Bba	∨	Bbb)]
T	F	F	T	T	T	F	T	F	T	T

	↓ ⊃	[(Baa	&	Bba)	∨	(Bab	&	Bbb)]
	F	T	F	F	F	F	F	T

e.

Fa	Ga	Fb	Gb	[(Fa	&	Fb)	⊃	(Ga	&	Gb)]	↓ ⊃	[(Fa	⊃	Ga)	&	(Fb	⊃	Gb)]
T	F	F	T	T	F	F	T	F	F	T	F	T	F	F	F	F	T	T

g.

Faa	Ga	~Ga	↓ ⊃	(Faa	⊃	Ga)
T	F	T F	F	T	F	F

8.a.

Baa	Bab	Bba	Bbb	~[(Baa	&	Bab)	&	(Bba	&	Bbb)]	↓ ≡	(Baa	&	Bbb)
T	F	F	T	T T	F	F	F	F	F	T	T	T	T	T

c.

Fa	Fb	Ga	Gb		[(Fa	∨	Fb)	&	(Ga	∨	Gb)]
T	F	F	T		T	T	F	T	F	T	T

↓
	&	~[(Fa	&	Ga)	∨	(Fb	&	Gb)]
	T	T T	F	F	F	F	F	T

e.

↓ (above &)

Fa	Ga		(Fa	⊃	Ga)	&	(Ga	⊃	~Fa)
F	T		F	T	T	T	T	T	T F

g.

↓ (above ⊃)

Ba	Ha		(Ba	≡	Ha)	⊃	(Ba	&	Ha)
T	T		T	T	T	T	T	T	T

i. Sneaky. This one can't be done because, as pointed out in Section 8.2, the sentence is false on all interpretations with finite U.D.s.

9.a.

Fa	Fb	Ga	Gb		((Fa	&	Ga)	∨	(Fb	&	Gb))
T	T	F	F		T	F	F	F	T	F	F

↓
	⊃	(~(Fa	∨	Ga)	∨	~(Fb	∨	Gb))
	T	F T	T	F	F	F T	T	F

Fa	Fb	Ga	Gb		((Fa	&	Ga)	∨	(Fb	&	Gb))
T	F	T	T		T	T	T	T	F	F	T

↓
	⊃	(~(Fa	∨	Ga)	∨	~(Fb	∨	Gb))
	F	F T	T	T	F	F F	T	T

c.

↓ (above ⊃)

Bnn		Bnn	⊃	~Bnn
F		F	T	T F

	↓		
Bnn	Bnn	⊃	~Bnn
T	T	F	F T

e.

				↓	
Naa	(Naa	∨	Naa)	⊃	Naa
T	T	T	T	T	T

Naa	Nab	Nba	Nbb	[[(Naa	∨	Naa)	⊃	Naa]
T	T	T	F	T	T	T	T	T

		↓					↓						
&	[(Nba	∨	Nab)	⊃	Nbb]]	&	[[(Nab	∨	Nba)	⊃	Naa]
F	T	T	T	F	F	F	T	T	T	T	T

&	[(Nbb	∨	Nbb)	⊃	Nbb]]
T	F	F	F	T	F

g.

						↓			
Ca	Da	(Ca	∨	Da)	≡	(Ca	&	Da)
T	T	T	T	T	T	T	T	T

Ca	Da	(Ca	∨	Da)	≡	(Ca	&	Da)
T	F	T	T	F	F	T	F	F

11. The expanded sentence 'Ga & ~Ga' is a truth-functional compound. It is false on every truth-value assignment, so it is quantificationally false. But the fact that this sentence is quantificationally false only shows that '(∃y)Gy & (∃y) ~Gy' is not true on any interpretation that has a one-member U.D.—for it is an

expansion using only one constant. The sentence is in fact not quantificationally false, for it is true on some interpretations with larger universes of discourse. We may expand the sentence for the set {'a', 'b'} to show this:

```
                          ↓
Ga  Gb │ (Ga  ∨  Gb)  &  (~Ga  ∨  ~Gb)
────────────────────────────────────────
 T   F │  T   T   F   T   F T   T   T F
```

12.a.
```
                        ↓                    ↓
Fa  Fb  Ga │ (Fa  ∨  Fb)  ⊃  Ga  (Fa  ⊃  Ga)  ∨  (Fb  ⊃  Ga)
────────────────────────────────────────────────────────────
 T   F   F │  T   T   F   F   F    T   F   F   T   F   T   F
```

c.
```
                          ↓                      ↓
Fa Fb Ga Gb │ (Fa ∨ Fb)  &  (Ga ∨ Gb) (Fa & Ga)  ∨  (Fb & Gb)
──────────────────────────────────────────────────────────────
 T  F  F  T │  T  T  F   T   F  T  T    T  F  F    F   F  F  T
```

e.
```
                          ↓                      ↓
Fa Fb Ga Gb │ (Fa ≡ Ga)  &  (Fb ≡ Gb) (Fa ∨ Fb)  ≡  (Ga ∨ Gb)
──────────────────────────────────────────────────────────────
 T  F  F  T │  T  F  F    F   F  F  T    T  T  F    T   F  T  T
```

g.
```
                                                ↓
Ba Bb Daa Dab Dba Dbb │ (Ba & (Daa & Dba))  ∨  (Bb & (Dab & Dbb))
──────────────────────────────────────────────────────────────────
 F  F  T   T   T   T  │  F   F   T   T  T    F   F   F   T   T  T
```

```
                              ↓
(Ba  ⊃  (Daa  &  Dba))  &  (Bb  ⊃  (Dab  &  Dbb))
──────────────────────────────────────────────────
 F   T    T   T   T     T   F   T    T   T   T
```

i.
```
                                                  ↓
Fa Fb Kaa Kab Kba Kbb │ ((Fa ⊃ Kaa) ∨ (Fa ⊃ Kba))  &  ((Fb ⊃ Kab) ∨ (Fb ⊃ Kbb))
──────────────────────────────────────────────────────────────────────────────────
 T  T  F   T   F   T  │  T   F  F   F  T  F  F       F   T  T  T   T  T  T  T
```

```
                                        ↓
((Fa  ⊃  Kaa)  ∨  (Fa  ⊃  Kba))  ∨  ((Fb  ⊃  Kab)  ∨  (Fb  ⊃  Kbb))
──────────────────────────────────────────────────────────────────────
  T   F   F    F   F   T   F      F    T   T   T    T   T   T   T
```

13a.

$$Ba\ Bb\ Ca\ Cb\ |\ Ba \lor Bb\ Ca \lor Cb \sim [(Ba \lor Ca)\ \&\ (Bb \lor Cb)]$$

```
Ba Bb Ca Cb | Ba  ∨  Bb  Ca  ∨  Cb  ~ [(Ba ∨ Ca) & (Bb ∨ Cb)]
                 ↓          ↓      ↓
 T  F  T  F | T   T  F   T   T  F   T   T   T  T   F  F   F  F
```

c.

```
Fa  Ga  Ma  Na | Fa  ⊃  Ga  Na  ⊃  Ma  Ga  ⊃  ~Ma
                         ↓           ↓          ↓
 F   F   F   F | F   T  F   F   T  F   F   T  T F
```

e.

```
Caa  Ma  Na | Na  ⊃  (Ma  &  Caa)  Ma  ⊃  ~Caa
                    ↓                   ↓
 T   F   F | F   T  F   F   T   F   T  F T
```

g.

```
Ma  Mb  Na  Nb | ~[(Na  ⊃  Ma)  &  (Nb  ⊃  Mb)]
                   ↓
 F   T   T   T | T   T   F   F   F   T   T   T
```

```
~[~(Na  ⊃  Ma)  &  ~(Nb  ⊃  Mb)]
↓
T T T   F   F   F   F T   T   T
```

i.

```
Faa  Gaa | Faa  ~Gaa  Faa  ∨  Gaa
             ↓    ↓          ↓
 T   F  | T   T F   T   T  F
```

15.a.

```
Fa  Ga  Na | (Fa  ⊃  Ga)  ⊃  Na  Na  ⊃  Ga  ~Fa  ∨  Ga
                          ↓          ↓          ↓
 T   F   F | T   F   F   T   F   F   T   F   F T   F  F
```

c.

```
Fa  Fb  Ga  Gb  Ha  Hb | (Fa  &  Ga)  ∨  (Fb  &  Gb)
                                        ↓
 T   T   T   F   F   T | T   T   T   T   T   F   F
```

```
(Fa  &  Ha)  ∨  (Fb  &  Hb)  (Ga  &  Ha)  ∨  (Gb  &  Hb)
             ↓                            ↓
 T   F   F   T   T   T   T   F   F   F   F   F   F T
```

e.

$$\downarrow \quad \downarrow \quad \downarrow$$

Fa	Ga	Fa	⊃	Ga	~Fa	~Ga
F	T	F	T	T	T F	F T

g.

$$\downarrow \qquad\qquad \downarrow$$

Daa	Dab	Dba	Dbb	Ga	Gb	Ga	∨	Gb	(Ga	⊃	Daa)	&	(Gb	⊃	Dbb)
T	F	F	T	F	T	F	T	T	F	T	T	T	T	T	T

$$\downarrow$$

[(Ga	&	Daa)	&	(Ga	&	Dab)]	∨	[(Gb	&	Dba)	&	(Gb	&	Dbb)]
F	F	T	F	F	F	F	F	T	F	F	F	T	T	T

i.

$$\downarrow \qquad\qquad \downarrow \qquad\qquad \downarrow$$

Fa	Ga	Ha	Fa	⊃	Ga	Ha	⊃	Ga	Fa	∨	Ha
F	F	F	F	T	F	F	T	F	F	F	F

8.6E

1.a. **F**
  c. **T**
  e. **T**
  g. **F**
  i. **F**

2.a. The sentence is false on the following interpretation:

    U.D.: set of positive integers

There is no positive integer that is identical to every positive integer.

  c. The sentence is false on the following interpretation:

    U.D.: set consisting of the numbers 1, 2, and 3

It is not true that for any three members of the U.D., at least two are identical.

  e. The sentence is false on the following interpretation:

    U.D.: set consisting of the number 1
    Gxy: x is greater than y

It is not true that there is a pair of members of the U.D. such that either the members of the pair are not identical or one member is greater than the other. The only pair of members of the U.D. consists of 1 and 1.

3.a. Consider any interpretation and any members x, y, and z of its U.D. If x and y are not the same member or if y and z are not the same member, then these members do not satisfy the condition specified by '$(x = y \mathbin{\&} y = z)$' and so they do satisfy '$[(x = y \mathbin{\&} y = z) \supset x = z]$'. On the other hand, if x and y are the same and y and z are the same, then x and z must be the same, satisfying the consequent '$x = z$'. In this case as well, then, x, y, and z satisfy '$[(x = y \mathbin{\&} y = z) \supset x = z]$'. Therefore the universal claim is true on every interpretation.

c. Consider any interpretation and any members x and y of its U.D. If x and y are not the same, they do not satisfy '$x = y$' and so do satisfy '$[x = y \supset (Gxy = Gyx)]$'. If x and y are the same, and hence satisfy '$x = y$', they must satisfy '$(Gxy = Gyx)$' as well—the pair consisting of the one object and itself is either in the extension or not. Therefore the universal claim must be true on every interpretation.

4.a. The first sentence is true and the second false on the following interpretation:

U.D.: set of positive integers

Every positive integer is identical to at least one positive integer (itself), but not even one positive integer is identical to every positive integer.

c. The first sentence is false and the second is true on the following interpretation:

U.D.: set of positive integers
a: 1
b: 1
c: 2
d: 3

5.a. The sentences are all true on the following interpretation:

U.D.: set of positive integers
a: 1
b: 1
c: 1
d: 2

c. The sentences are all true on the following interpretation:

U.D.: set of positive integers

The first sentence is true because there are at least two positive integers. The second sentence is true because for any positive integer x, we can find a pair of positive integers z and w such that either x is identical to z or x is identical to w—just let one of the pair be x itself.

6.a. The following interpretation shows that the entailment does not hold:

U.D.: set consisting of the numbers 1 and 2

It is true that for any x, y, and z in the U.D., at least two of x, y, and z must be identical. But it is not true that for any x and y in the U.D., x and y must be identical.

c. The following interpretation shows that the entailment does not hold:

U.D.: set consisting of the numbers 1 and 2
Gxy: x is greater than or equal to y

At least one member of the U.D. (the number 2) is greater than or equal to every member of the U.D., and at least one member of the U.D. (the number 1) is not greater than or equal to any member of the U.D. other than itself. But no member of the U.D. is not greater than or equal to itself.

7.a. The argument can be symbolized as

$$(\forall x)[Mx \supset (\exists y)(\sim y = x \& Lxy)] \& (\forall x)[Mx \supset (\forall y)(Pxy \supset Lxy)]$$
$$(\forall x)(Mx \supset \sim Pxx)$$

The argument is quantificationally invalid, as the following interpretation shows:

U.D.: set of U.S. states
Mx: x is on the East Coast
Lxy: x and y are in the same country
Pxy: x and y are on the same coast

For every U.S. state on the East Coast, there is at least one nonidentical state on the same coast (there are at least two East Coast states), and every East Coast state is such that every U.S. state on the same coast is in the same country. However, the conclusion, which says that no East Coast state is on the same coast as itself, is false.

c. The argument can be symbolized as

$$(\forall x)[(Fx \& (\exists y)(Pxy \& Lxy)) \supset Lxx]$$
$$(\forall x)[Fx \supset (\exists y)(\exists z)((Lxy \& Lxz) \& \sim y = z)]$$

The argument is quantificationally invalid, as the following interpretation shows:

U.D.: set of positive integers
Fx: x is odd
Lxy: x is greater than y
Pxy: x is less than y

Trivially, every odd positive integer that is both less than and greater than some positive integer (there are none) is less than itself. But not all odd positive integers are greater than at least two positive integers—the number 1 is not.

e. The argument may be symbolized as

$(\forall x) \sim (\exists y)(\exists z)(\exists w)([[(Pyx \ \& \ Pzx) \ \& \ Pwx]$
$\quad \& \ [(\sim y = z \ \& \ \sim z = w) \ \& \ \sim w = y]]$
$\quad \& \ (\forall x_1)[Px_1 x \supset ((x_1 = y \lor x_1 = z) \lor x_1 = w)])$
$(\forall x)(\exists y)(\exists z)[(Pyx \ \& \ Pzx) \ \& \ \sim y = z)]$

$\overline{}$

$(\forall x)(\exists y)(\exists z)[((Pyx \ \& \ Pzx) \ \& \ \sim y = z) \ \& \ (\forall w)(Pwx \supset (w = y \lor w = z))]$

The argument is quantificationally invalid, as the following interpretation shows:

      U.D.: set of positive integers
      Pxy: x is greater than y

No positive integer is less than exactly three positive integers (for any positive integer, there are infinitely many positive integers that are greater). Every positive integer is less than at least two positive integers. But no positive integer is less than exactly two positive integers.

8.a.

	↓
a = a	~a = a
T	F T

a = a	a = b	b = a	b = b	(~a = a	∨	~b = a)	↓∨	(~a = b	∨	~b = b)
T	F	F	T	F T	T	T F	T	T F	T	F T

c.

a = a	Gaa	(Gaa	∨	Gaa)	↓∨	a = a	↓ Gaa
T	F	F	F	F	T	T	F

e.

a = a	a = b	b = a	b = b	a = a	↓&	b = b	(~a = a	∨	~a = b)	↓∨	(~b = a	∨	~b = b)
T	F	F	T	T	T	T	F T	T	T F	T	T F	T	F T

(~a = a	&	~a = b)	↓∨	(~b = a	&	~b = b)
F T	F	T F	F	T F	F	F T

8.7E

1.a. Let **d** be a variable assignment for this interpretation. **d** satisfies the antecedent ' ~(∀x)Ex' just in case it fails to satisfy '(∀x)Ex'. **d** will fail to satisfy '(∀x)Ex' just in case there is at least one member **u** of the U.D. such that **d**[**u**/x] fails to satisfy 'Ex'. The number 1 is such a member: **d**[1/x] fails to satisfy 'Ex' because ⟨**d**[1/x](x)⟩, which is ⟨1⟩, is a not member of I(E), the set of 1-tuples of even positive integers. So **d** does satisfy ' ~(∀x)Ex'.

d satisfies the consequent '(∃y)Lyo' just in case there is at least one member **u** of the U.D. such that **d**[**u**/y] satisfies 'Lyo', that is, just in case there is at least one member **u** such that ⟨**d**[**u**/y](y), I(o)⟩, which is ⟨**u**, 1⟩, is in I(L). There is no such member, for there is no positive integer that is less than 1. Therefore **d** does not satisfy '(∃y)Lyo' and consequently **d** does not satisfy the conditional '(∀x)Ex ⊃ (∃y)Lyo'. The sentence is false on this interpretation.

c. Let **d** be a variable assignment for this interpretation. **d** satisfies '(∃x)(K ∨ Ex)' just in case there is some member **u** of the U.D. such that **d**[**u**/x] satisfies 'K ∨ Ex'. There is such a member—take 2 as an example. **d**[2/x] satisfies 'K ∨ Ex' because **d**[2/x] satisfies the second disjunct. **d**[2/x] satisfies 'Ex' because ⟨**d**[2/x](x)⟩, which is ⟨2⟩, is a member of I(E)—2 is even. Therefore **d** satisfies '(∃x)(K ∨ Ex)'. The sentence is true on this interpretation.

e. Let **d** be a variable assignment for this interpretation. **d** satisfies '(K ≡ (∀x)Ex) ⊃ (∃y)(∃z)Lyz' if and only if either **d** fails to satisfy the antecedent or **d** does satisfy the consequent. **d** satisfies the antecedent because it fails to satisfy either 'K' (which is interpreted to be false) or '(∀x)Ex'. **d** does not satisfy the latter because not every member **u** of the U.D. is such that **d**[**u**/x] satisfies 'Ex'—no odd number is in the extension of 'E'.

d also satisfies the consequent '(∃y)(∃z)Lyz' because, for example, **d**[1/y] satisfies '(∃z)Lyz'. The latter is the case because, for example, **d**[1/y, 2/z] satisfies 'Lyz'; ⟨1, 2⟩ is in the extension of 'L'. The sentence is true on this interpretation.

2.a. Let **d** be a variable assignment for this interpretation. **d** satisfies '(∃x)(Ex ⊃ (∀y)Ey)' just in case there is at least one member **u** of the U.D. such that **d**[**u**/x] satisfies 'Ex ⊃ (∀y)Ey'. There is such a member; take 1 as an example. **d**[1/x] satisfies 'Ex ⊃ (∀y)Ey' because it fails to satisfy 'Ex'. **d**[1/x] fails to satisfy 'Ex' because ⟨**d**[1/x](x)⟩, which is ⟨1⟩, is not a member of I(E)—1 is not even. So **d** satisfies '(∃x)(Ex ⊃ (∀y)Ey)'. The sentence is true on this interpretation.

c. Let **d** be a variable assignment for this interpretation. **d** satisfies '(∀x)(Tx ⊃ (∃y)Gyx)' just in case every member **u** of the U.D. is such that **d**[**u**/x] satisfies 'Tx ⊃ (∃y)Gyx', that is, just in case both **d**[1/x] and **d**[3/x] satisfy 'Tx ⊃ (∃y)Gyx'. **d**[1/x] satisfies 'Tx ⊃ (∃y)Gyx' because it satisfies '(∃y)Gyx'. **d**[1/x] satisfies '(∃y)Gyx' because there is at least one member **u** of the U.D. such that **d**[1/x, **u**/y] satisfies 'Gyx'—3 is such a member. **d**[1/x, 3/y] satisfies 'Gyx' because ⟨**d**[1/x, 3/y](y), **d**[1/x, 3/y](x)⟩, which is ⟨3, 1⟩, is a member of I(G)— 3 is greater than 1.

$\mathbf{d}[3/x]$ satisfies 'Tx $\supset$ ($\exists$y)Gyx' because $\mathbf{d}[3/x]$ does not satisfy 'Tx'. $\mathbf{d}[3/x]$ does not satisfy 'Tx' because $\langle \mathbf{d}[3/x](x) \rangle$, which is $\langle 3 \rangle$, is not a member of $\mathbf{I}(T)$—3 is not less than 2. So both $\mathbf{d}[1/x]$ and $\mathbf{d}[3/x]$ satisfy 'Tx $\supset$ ($\exists$y)Gyx' and therefore $\mathbf{d}$ satisfies '($\forall$x)(Tx $\supset$ ($\exists$y)Gyx)'. The sentence is true on this interpretation.

e. Let $\mathbf{d}$ be a variable assignment for this interpretation. $\mathbf{d}$ satisfies this sentence just in case for every member $\mathbf{u}$ of the U.D., $\mathbf{d}[\mathbf{u}/x]$ satisfies '($\forall$y)Gxy $\lor$ ($\exists$y)Gxy'. However, the number 1 is *not* such that $\mathbf{d}[1/x]$ satisfies the formula. $\mathbf{d}[1/x]$ does not satisfy '($\forall$y)Gxy', because there is not even one member $\mathbf{u}$ of the U.D. such that $\mathbf{d}[1/x, \mathbf{u}/y]$ satisfies 'Gxy'—no 2-tuple $\langle 1, \mathbf{u} \rangle$ is in the extension of 'G'. $\mathbf{d}[1/x]$ also does not satisfy '($\exists$y)Gxy', for the same reason. Because $\mathbf{d}[1/x]$ does not satisfy '($\forall$y)Gxy $\lor$ ($\exists$y)Gxy', $\mathbf{d}$ does not satisfy the universally quantified sentence. The sentence is false on this interpretation.

3.a. Let $\mathbf{d}$ be a variable assignment for this interpretation. $\mathbf{d}$ satisfies 'Mooo $\equiv$ Pooo' just in case either $\mathbf{d}$ satisfies both 'Mooo' and 'Pooo' or $\mathbf{d}$ satisfies neither of 'Mooo' and 'Pooo'. $\mathbf{d}$ does not satisfy 'Mooo' because $\langle \mathbf{I}(o), \mathbf{I}(o), \mathbf{I}(o) \rangle$, which is $\langle 1, 1, 1 \rangle$, is not a member of $\mathbf{I}(M)$—$1 - 1 \neq 1$. $\mathbf{d}$ does not satisfy 'Pooo' because $\langle \mathbf{I}(o), \mathbf{I}(o), \mathbf{I}(o) \rangle$, which again is $\langle 1, 1, 1 \rangle$, is not a member of $\mathbf{I}(P)$—$1 + 1 \neq 1$. So $\mathbf{d}$ satisfies neither immediate component and therefore does satisfy 'Mooo $\equiv$ Pooo'. The sentence is true on this interpretation.

c. Let $\mathbf{d}$ be a variable assignment for this interpretation. $\mathbf{d}$ satisfies '($\forall$x)($\forall$y)($\forall$z)(Mxyz $\equiv$ Pxyz)' just in case every member $\mathbf{u}$ of the U.D. is such that $\mathbf{d}[\mathbf{u}/x]$ satisfies '($\forall$y)($\forall$z)(Mxyz $\equiv$ Pxyz)'. $\mathbf{d}[\mathbf{u}/x]$ satisfies '($\forall$y)($\forall$z)(Mxyz $\equiv$ Pxyz)' just in case every member $\mathbf{u}_1$ of the U.D. is such that $\mathbf{d}[\mathbf{u}/x, \mathbf{u}_1/y]$ satisfies '($\forall$z)(Mxyz $\equiv$ Pxyz)'. $\mathbf{d}[\mathbf{u}/x, \mathbf{u}_1/y]$ satisfies '($\forall$z)(Mxyz $\equiv$ Pxyz)' just in case every member $\mathbf{u}_2$ of the U.D. is such that $\mathbf{d}[\mathbf{u}/x, \mathbf{u}_1/y, \mathbf{u}_2/z]$ satisfies 'Mxyz $\equiv$ Pxyz'. So $\mathbf{d}$ satisfies '($\forall$x)($\forall$y)($\forall$z)(Mxyz $\equiv$ Pxyz)' just in case for any members $\mathbf{u}, \mathbf{u}_1$, and $\mathbf{u}_2$ of the U.D., $\mathbf{d}[\mathbf{u}/x, \mathbf{u}_1/y, \mathbf{u}_2/z]$ satisfies 'Mxyz $\equiv$ Pxyz'. But this is not the case. For example, $\mathbf{d}[1/x, 2/y, 3/z]$ does not satisfy 'Mxyz', because $\langle \mathbf{d}[1/x, 2/y, 3/z](x), \mathbf{d}[1/x, 2/y, 3/z](y), \mathbf{d}[1/x, 2/y, 3/z](z) \rangle$, which is $\langle 1, 2, 3 \rangle$, is not a member of $\mathbf{I}(M)$—$1 - 2 \neq 3$. On the other hand, $\mathbf{d}[1/x, 2/y, 3/z]$ does satisfy 'Pxyz', because $\langle \mathbf{d}[1/x, 2/y, 3/z](x), \mathbf{d}[1/x, 2/y, 3/z](y), \mathbf{d}[1/x, 2/y, 3/z](z) \rangle$, which again is $\langle 1, 2, 3 \rangle$, is a member of $\mathbf{I}(P)$—$1 + 2 = 3$. The assignment $\mathbf{d}[1/x, 2/y, 3/z]$ therefore does not satisfy 'Mxyz $\equiv$ Pxyz', and so $\mathbf{d}$ does not satisfy '($\forall$x)($\forall$y)($\forall$z)(Mxyz $\equiv$ Pxyz)'. The sentence is false on this interpretation.

e. Let $\mathbf{d}$ be a variable assignment for this interpretation. $\mathbf{d}$ satisfies this sentence if and only if for every member $\mathbf{u}$ of the U.D., $\mathbf{d}[\mathbf{u}/y]$ satisfies '($\exists$z)(Pyoz $\supset$ Pooo)'. The latter is the case for a member $\mathbf{u}$ of the U.D. if and only if there is a member $\mathbf{u}_1$ of the U.D. such that $\mathbf{d}[\mathbf{u}/y, \mathbf{u}_1/z]$ satisfies 'Pyoz $\supset$ Pooo'. No variable assignment can satisfy 'Pooo', for $\langle 1, 1, 1 \rangle$ is not in the extension of 'P'. But for any member $\mathbf{u}$ of the U.D. we can find a member $\mathbf{u}_1$ such that $\langle \mathbf{u}, 1, \mathbf{u}_1 \rangle$ is not in the extension of 'P'; pick any number other than the number that is the successor of $\mathbf{u}$. The sentence is true on this interpretation.

5. We shall show that the sentence is true on every interpretation. Let **I** be any interpretation. '(∀x)((∀y)Fy ⊃ Fx)' is true on **I** if and only if every variable assignment satisfies the sentence. A variable assignment **d** satisfies '(∀x)((∀y)Fy ⊃ Fx)' if and only if every member **u** of the U.D. is such that **d**[**u**/x] satisfies '(∀y)Fy ⊃ Fx'. Consider any member **u** of the U.D. If ⟨**u**⟩ is a member of **I**(F), then **d**[**u**/x] satisfies 'Fx' and hence also satisfies '(∀y)Fy ⊃ Fx'. If ⟨**u**⟩ is not a member of **I**(F), then **d**[**u**/x] does not satisfy '(∀y)Fy'. This is because **u** is such that **d**[**u**/x, **u**/y] does not satisfy 'Fy'—⟨**d**[**u**/x, **u**/y](y)⟩, which is ⟨**u**⟩, is not a member of **I**(F). So if ⟨**u**⟩ is not a member of **I**(F), then **d**[**u**/x] satisfies '(∀y)Fy ⊃ Fx' because it fails to satisfy the antecedent. Each member **u** of the U.D. is such that either ⟨**u**⟩ is a member of **I**(F) or it isn't, so each member **u** of the U.D. is such that **d**[**u**/x] satisfies '(∀y)Fy ⊃ Fx'. Therefore **d** must satisfy '(∀x)((∀y)Fy ⊃ Fx)'. The sentence is true on every interpretation.

7. Assume that 'Fa' is true on an interpretation. Then every variable assignment for this interpretation satisfies 'Fa'. So we know that ⟨**I**(a)⟩ is in the extension of 'F'. We shall now show that every variable assignment also satisfies '(∃x)Fx'. Let **d** be any such assignment. **d** satisfies '(∃x)Fx' if and only if there is some member **u** of the U.D. such that **d**[**u**/x] satisfies 'Fx'. We know that there is such a member, namely, **I**(a). **d**[**I**(a)/x] satisfies 'Fx' because ⟨**I**(a)⟩ is in the extension of 'F'. Therefore '(∃x)Fx' is true on the interpretation as well.

9.a. Let **d** be a variable assignment for this interpretation. Then **d** satisfies '(∀x)(∀y)[~x = y ⊃ (Ex ⊃ Gxy)]' if and only if for every positive integer **u**, **d**[**u**/x] satisfies '(∀y)[~x = y ⊃ (Ex ⊃ Gxy)]'. This will be the case if and only if for every pair of positive integers **u** and **u**₁, **d**[**u**/x, **u**₁/y] satisfies ' ~x = y ⊃ (Ex ⊃ Gxy)'. But **d**[2/x, 3/y], for example, does not satisfy the open sentence. **d**[2/x, 3/y] does satisfy ' ~x = y', for 2 and 3 are distinct members of the U.D. **d**[2/x, 3/y] does not satisfy 'Ex ⊃ Gxy', for it satisfies its antecedent and fails to satisfy its consequent. **d**[2/x, 3/y] satisfies 'Ex' because ⟨**d**[2/x, 3/y](x)⟩, which is ⟨2⟩, is a member of **I**(E). **d**[2/x, 3/y] fails to satisfy 'Gxy' because ⟨**d**[2/x, 3/y](x), **d**[2/x, 3/y](y)⟩, which is ⟨2, 3⟩, is not a member of **I**(G)—2 is not greater than 3. We conclude that '(∀x)(∀y)[~x = y ⊃ (Ex ⊃ Gxy)]' is false on this interpretation.

    c. Let **d** be a variable assignment for this interpretation. Then **d** satisfies the sentence if and only if for every member **u** of the U.D., **d**[**u**/x] satisfies 'Ex ⊃ (∃y)(~x = y & ~Gxy)]. Every odd positive integer **u** is such that **d**[**u**/x] satisfies the formula, because every odd positive integer **u** is such that **d**[**u**/x] fails to satisfy 'Ex'. Every even positive integer **u** is such that **d**[**u**/x] satisfies the formula, because every positive integer (odd or even) satisfies the consequent, '(∃y)(~x = y & ~Gxy)'. For every positive integer **u** there is a positive integer **u**₁ such that **d**[**u**/x, **u**₁/y] satisfies ' ~x = y & ~Gxy': Let **u**₁ be any integer that is greater than **u**. In this case, **d**[**u**/x, **u**₁/y] will satisfy ' ~x = y' because **u** and **u**₁ are not identical, and the variant will also satisfy ' ~Gxy' because ⟨**u**, **u**₁⟩ is not in the extension of 'G'. The sentence is therefore true on this interpretation.

10.a. A sentence of the form $(\forall x)x = x$ is true on an interpretation **I** if and only if every variable assignment satisfies the sentence on **I**. A variable assignment **d** satisfies $(\forall x)x = x$ if and only if for every member **u** of the U.D., $\mathbf{d}[\mathbf{u}/x]$ satisfies $x = x$—and this is the case if and only for every member **u** of the U.D., $\mathbf{d}[\mathbf{u}/x](x)$ is identical to $\mathbf{d}[\mathbf{u}/x](x)$. Trivially, this is so. Therefore $(\forall x)x = x$ is satisfied by every variable assignment on every interpretation; it is quantification-ally true.

CHAPTER NINE

9.1E

a. 1. $(\exists x)Fx$✔   SM
   2. $(\exists x) \sim Fx$✔   SM

   3.   Fa   1 $\exists$D
   4. $\sim$Fb   2 $\exists$D

The tree is open.

c. 1. $(\exists x)(Fx \ \& \ \sim Gx)$✔   SM
   2. $(\forall x)(Fx \supset Gx)$ SM

   3.   Fa & $\sim$Ga✔   1 $\exists$D
   4.   Fa   3 & D
   5. $\sim$Ga   3 & D
   6.   Fa $\supset$ Ga✔   2 $\forall$D

   7. $\sim$Fa   Ga   6 $\supset$ D
         $\times$ $\times$

The tree is closed.

e. 1. $\sim(\forall x)(Fx \supset Gx)$✔   SM
   2. $\sim(\exists x)Fx$✔   SM
   3. $\sim(\exists x)Gx$✔   SM

   4. $(\exists x) \sim(Fx \supset Gx)$✔   1 $\sim\forall$D
   5. $(\forall x) \sim Fx$ 2 $\sim\exists$D
   6. $(\forall x) \sim Gx$ 3 $\sim\exists$D
   7. $\sim(Fa \supset Ga)$✔   4 $\exists$D
   8.   Fa   7 $\sim\supset$ D
   9. $\sim$Ga   7 $\sim\supset$ D
  10. $\sim$Fa   5 $\forall$D
          $\times$

The tree is closed.

g. 1.   (∃x)Fx✔   SM
    2.   (∃y)Gy✔   SM
    3.   (∃z)(Fz & Gz)✔   SM

    4.   Fa   1 ∃D
    5.   Gb   2 ∃D
    6.   Fc & Gc✔   3 ∃D
    7.   Fc   6 & D
    8.   Gc   6 & D

The tree is open.

i. 1.   (∀x)(∀y)(Fxy ⊃ Fyx)   SM
    2.   (∃x)(∃y)(Fxy & ~Fyx)✔   SM

    3.   (∃y)(Fay & ~Fya)✔   2 ∃D
    4.   Fab & ~Fba✔   3 ∃D
    5.   Fab   4 & D
    6.   ~Fba   4 & D
    7.   (∀y)(Fay ⊃ Fya)   1 ∀D
    8.   Fab ⊃ Fba✔   7 ∀D

    9.   ~Fab   Fba   8 ⊃ D
                 ×   ×

The tree is closed.

k. 1.   (∃x)Fx ⊃ (∀x)Fx✔   SM
    2.   ~(∀x)(Fx ⊃ (∀y)Fy)✔   SM

    3.   (∃x) ~(Fx ⊃ (∀y)Fy)✔   2 ~∀D
    4.   ~(Fa ⊃ (∀y)Fy)✔   3 ∃D
    5.   Fa   4 ~⊃ D
    6.   ~(∀y)Fy✔   4 ~⊃ D
    7.   (∃y) ~Fy✔   6 ~∀D
    8.   ~Fb   7 ∃D

    9.   ~(∃x)Fx✔   (∀x)Fx   1 ⊃ D
   10.   (∀x) ~Fx | 9 ~∃D
   11.   ~Fa | 10 ∀D
   12.   ×   Fb   9 ∀D
                              ×

The tree is closed.

m. 1.   (∀x)(Fx ⊃ (∃y)Gyx)   SM
    2.   ~(∀x) ~Fx✔   SM
    3.   (∀x)(∀y) ~Gxy   SM

    4.   (∃x) ~~Fx✔   2 ~∀D
    5.   ~~Fa✔   4 ∃D
    6.   Fa   5 ~~D
    7.   Fa ⊃ (∃y)Gya✔   1 ∀D

    8.   ~Fa   (∃y)Gya✔   7 ⊃ D
    9.   ×   Gba   8 ∃D
   10.   (∀y) ~Gby   3 ∀D
   11.   ~Gba   10 ∀D
                      ×

The tree is closed.

o. 1.   (∃x)Lxx✔   SM
    2.   ~(∃x)(∃y)(Lxy & Lyx)✔   SM

    3.   (∀x) ~(∃y)(Lxy & Lyx)   2 ~∃D
    4.   Laa   1 ∃D
    5.   ~(∃y)(Lay & Lya)✔   3 ∀D
    6.   (∀y) ~(Lay & Lya)   5 ~∃D
    7.   ~(Laa & Laa)✔   6 ∀D

    8.   ~Laa   ~Laa   7 ~ & D
          ×   ×

The tree is closed.

q. 1. $(\exists x)(Fx \lor Gx)$✔   SM
    2. $(\forall x)(Fx \supset \sim Gx)$ SM
    3. $(\forall x)(Gx \supset \sim Fx)$ SM
    4. $\sim(\exists x)(\sim Fx \lor \sim Gx)$✔   SM

    5. $(\forall x) \sim(\sim Fx \lor \sim Gx)$ 4 $\sim\exists$D
    6. $Fa \lor Ga$ 1 $\exists$D
    7. $Fa \supset \sim Ga$✔   2 $\forall$D
    8. $Ga \supset \sim Fa$ 3 $\forall$D
    9. $\sim(\sim Fa \lor \sim Ga)$✔   5 $\forall$D
    10. $\sim\sim Fa$✔   9 $\sim\lor$D
    11. $\sim\sim Ga$✔   9 $\sim\lor$D
    12. Ga 11 $\sim\sim$D
    13. Fa 10 $\sim\sim$D

    14. $\sim Fa$ $\sim Ga$ 7 $\supset$D
          $\times$ $\times$

The tree is closed.

9.2E

Note: In these answers, whenever a tree is open we give a complete tree. This is because the strategems we have suggested do not uniquely determine the order of decomposition, so the first open branch to be completed on your tree may not be the first such branch completed on our tree. In accordance with strategem 5, you should stop when your tree has one completed open branch.

a. 1. $(\forall x)Fx \lor (\exists y)Gy$✔   SM
    2. $(\exists x)(Fx \mathbin{\&} Gb)$✔   SM

    3. $Fa \mathbin{\&} Gb$✔   2 $\exists$D
    4. Fa 3 $\&$D
    5. Gb 3 $\&$D

    6. $(\forall x)Fx$ $(\exists y)Gy$✔   1 $\lor$D
    7. Fa 6 $\forall$D
    8. Fb 6 $\forall$D
    9. Gc 6 $\exists$D

The tree is open (both branches are completed open branches). The set is quantificationally consistent.

c. 1. $(\forall x)(Fx \supset Gxa)$ SM


```
c.  1.            (∀x)(Fx ⊃ Gxa)        SM
    2.            (∃x)Fx✔               SM
    3.            (∀y) ~Gya             SM

    4.                Fb                2 ∃D
    5.            Fb ⊃ Gba✔             1 ∀D
                    /\
    6.      ~Fb          Gba           5 ⊃ D
    7.       ×          ~Gba           3 ∀D
                          ×
```

The tree is closed. The set is quantificationally inconsistent.

```
e.  1.            (∀x)(Fx ⊃ Gxa)        SM
    2.            (∃x)Fx✔               SM
    3.            (∀y)Gya               SM

    4.                Fb                2 ∃D
    5.            Fb ⊃ Gba✔             1 ∀D
                    /\
    6.      ~Fb          Gba           5 ⊃ D
    7.       ×          Gba            3 ∀D
    8.                  Gaa            3 ∀D
    9.              Fa ⊃ Gaa✔          1 ∀D
                       /\
    10.            ~Fa    Gaa          9 ⊃ D
```

The tree is open (the two right-hand branches are completed open branches). The set is quantificationally consistent.

```
g.  1.          (∀x)(Fx ∨ Gx)       SM
    2.        ~(∃y)(Fy ∨ Gy)✔       SM

    3.        (∀y) ~(Fy ∨ Gy)       2 ~∃D
    4.          ~(Fa ∨ Ga)✔         3 ∀D
    5.              ~Fa             4 ~∨D
    6.              ~Ga             4 ~∨D
    7.            Fa ∨ Ga✔          1 ∀D
                    /\
    8.         Fa     Ga           7 ∨D
                ×     ×
```

The tree is closed. The set is quantificationally inconsistent.

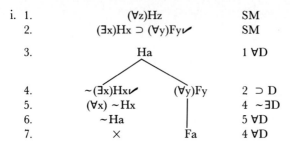

i. 1.   (∀z)Hz   SM
   2.   (∃x)Hx ⊃ (∀y)Fy✔   SM

   3.   Ha   1 ∀D

   4.   ~(∃x)Hx✔   (∀y)Fy   2 ⊃ D
   5.   (∀x) ~Hx   4 ~∃D
   6.   ~Ha   5 ∀D
   7.   ×   Fa   4 ∀D

The tree is open (the right-hand branch is a completed open branch). The set is quantificationally consistent.

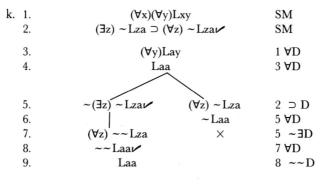

k. 1.   (∀x)(∀y)Lxy   SM
   2.   (∃z) ~Lza ⊃ (∀z) ~Lza✔   SM

   3.   (∀y)Lay   1 ∀D
   4.   Laa   3 ∀D

   5.   ~(∃z) ~Lza✔   (∀z) ~Lza   2 ⊃ D
   6.   ~Laa   5 ∀D
   7.   (∀z) ~~Lza   ×   5 ~∃D
   8.   ~~Laa✔   7 ∀D
   9.   Laa   8 ~~D

The tree is open (the left-hand branch is a completed open branch). The set is quantificationally consistent.

m.

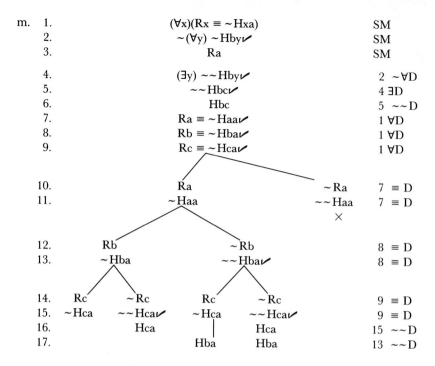

1.	(∀x)(Rx ≡ ~Hxa)	SM
2.	~(∀y) ~Hby✔	SM
3.	Ra	SM
4.	(∃y) ~~Hby✔	2 ~∀D
5.	~~Hbc✔	4 ∃D
6.	Hbc	5 ~~D
7.	Ra ≡ ~Haa✔	1 ∀D
8.	Rb ≡ ~Hba✔	1 ∀D
9.	Rc ≡ ~Hca✔	1 ∀D
10.	Ra ~Ra	7 ≡ D
11.	~Haa ~~Haa	7 ≡ D
	×	
12.	Rb ~Rb	8 ≡ D
13.	~Hba ~~Hba✔	8 ≡ D
14.	Rc ~Rc Rc ~Rc	9 ≡ D
15.	~Hca ~~Hca✔ ~Hca ~~Hca✔	9 ≡ D
16.	Hca Hca	15 ~~D
17.	Hba Hba	13 ~~D

The tree is open (all but the right-most branch are completed open branches). The set is quantificationally consistent.

9.3E

1.a.

1.	~((∃x)Fx ∨ ~(∃x)Fx)✔	SM
2.	~(∃x)Fx✔	1 ~∨D
3.	~~(∃x)Fx✔	1 ~∨D
4.	(∀x) ~Fx	2 ~∃D
5.	(∃x)Fx✔	3 ~~D
6.	Fa	5 ∃D
7.	~Fa	4 ∀D
	×	

The tree is closed. The sentence '(∃x)Fx ∨ ~(∃x)Fx' is quantificationally true.

c. 1. $\sim((\forall x)Fx \lor (\forall x)\sim Fx)\checkmark$ SM

    2. $\sim(\forall x)Fx\checkmark$ 1 $\sim\lor D$

    3. $\sim(\forall x)\sim Fx\checkmark$ 1 $\sim\lor D$

    4. $(\exists x)\sim Fx\checkmark$ 2 $\sim\forall D$

    5. $(\exists x)\sim\sim Fx\checkmark$ 3 $\sim\forall D$

    6. $\sim Fa$ 4 $\exists D$

    7. $\sim\sim Fb\checkmark$ 5 $\exists D$

    8. Fb 7 $\sim\sim D$

The tree is open. The sentence '$(\forall x)Fx \lor (\forall x)\sim Fx$' is not quantificationally true.

e. 1. $\sim((\forall x)Fx \lor (\exists x)\sim Fx)\checkmark$ SM

    2. $\sim(\forall x)Fx\checkmark$ 1 $\sim\lor D$

    3. $\sim(\exists x)\sim Fx\checkmark$ 1 $\sim\lor D$

    4. $(\exists x)\sim Fx\checkmark$ 2 $\sim\forall D$

    5. $(\forall x)\sim\sim Fx$ 3 $\sim\exists D$

    6. $\sim Fa$ 4 $\exists D$

    7. $\sim\sim Fa\checkmark$ 5 $\forall D$

    8. Fa 7 $\sim\sim D$

        $\times$

The tree is closed. The sentence '$(\forall x)Fx \lor (\exists x)\sim Fx$' is quantificationally true.

g. 1 $\sim((\forall x)(Fx \lor Gx) \supset ((\exists x)\sim Fx \supset (\exists x)Gx))\checkmark$ SM

    2. $(\forall x)(Fx \lor Gx)$ 1 $\sim\supset D$

    3. $\sim((\exists x)\sim Fx \supset (\exists x)Gx)\checkmark$ 1 $\sim\supset D$

    4. $(\exists x)\sim Fx\checkmark$ 3 $\sim\supset D$

    5. $\sim(\exists x)Gx\checkmark$ 3 $\sim\supset D$

    6. $(\forall x)\sim Gx$ 5 $\sim\exists D$

    7. $\sim Fa$ 4 $\exists D$

    8. $Fa \lor Ga\checkmark$ 2 $\forall D$

    9. Fa Ga 8 $\lor D$

    10. $\times$ $\sim Ga$ 6 $\forall D$

                $\times$

The tree is closed. The sentence '$(\forall x)(Fx \lor Gx) \supset [(\exists x)\sim Fx \supset (\exists x)Gx]$' is quantificationally true.

i. 1. $\sim(((\forall x)Fx \lor (\forall x)Gx) \supset (\forall x)(Fx \lor Gx))\checkmark$ SM

2. $(\forall x)Fx \lor (\forall x)Gx\checkmark$ 1 $\sim\supset$ D
3. $\sim(\forall x)(Fx \lor Gx)\checkmark$ 1 $\sim\supset$ D
4. $(\exists x)\sim(Fx \lor Gx)\checkmark$ 3 $\sim\forall$D
5. $\sim(Fa \lor Ga)\checkmark$ 4 $\exists$D
6. $\sim Fa$ 5 $\sim\lor$D
7. $\sim Ga$ 5 $\sim\lor$D

8. $(\forall x)Fx$ $(\forall x)Gx$ 2 $\lor$D
9. Fa Ga 8 $\forall$D
    $\times$ $\times$

The tree is closed. The sentence '$((\forall x)Fx \lor (\forall x)Gx) \supset (\forall x)(Fx \lor Gx)$' is quantificationally true.

k. 1. $\sim((\exists x)(Fx \ \& \ Gx) \supset ((\exists x)Fx \ \& \ (\exists x)Gx))\checkmark$ SM

2. $(\exists x)(Fx \ \& \ Gx)\checkmark$ 1 $\sim\supset$ D
3. $\sim((\exists x)Fx \ \& \ (\exists x)Gx)\checkmark$ 1 $\sim\supset$ D
4. $Fa \ \& \ Ga\checkmark$ 2 $\exists$D
5. Fa 4 $\&$ D
6. Ga 4 $\&$ D

7. $\sim(\exists x)Fx\checkmark$ $\sim(\exists x)Gx\checkmark$ 3 $\sim \&$ D
8. $(\forall x)\sim Fx$ $(\forall x)\sim Gx$ 7 $\sim\exists$D
9. $\sim Fa$ $\sim Ga$ 8 $\forall$D
   $\times$ $\times$

The tree is closed. The sentence '$(\exists x)(Fx \ \& \ Gx) \supset ((\exists x)Fx \ \& \ (\exists x)Gx)$' is quantificationally true.

m. 1. $\sim(\sim(\exists x)Fx \lor (\forall x)\sim Fx)\checkmark$ SM

2. $\sim\sim(\exists x)Fx\checkmark$ 1 $\sim\lor$D
3. $\sim(\forall x)\sim Fx\checkmark$ 1 $\sim\lor$D
4. $(\exists x)Fx\checkmark$ 2 $\sim\sim$D
5. $(\exists x)\sim\sim Fx\checkmark$ 3 $\sim\forall$D
6. Fa 4 $\exists$D
7. $\sim\sim Fb\checkmark$ 5 $\exists$D
8. Fb 7 $\sim\sim$D

The tree is open. The sentence ' $\sim(\exists x)Fx \lor (\forall x)\sim Fx$' is not quantificationally true.

o. 1.   ~((∀x)((Fx & Gx) ⊃ Hx) ⊃ (∀x)(Fx ⊃ (Gx & Hx)))✔   SM

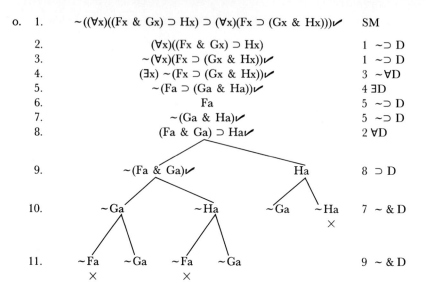

2.   (∀x)((Fx & Gx) ⊃ Hx)   1 ~⊃ D
3.   ~(∀x)(Fx ⊃ (Gx & Hx))✔   1 ~⊃ D
4.   (∃x) ~(Fx ⊃ (Gx & Hx))✔   3 ~∀D
5.   ~(Fa ⊃ (Ga & Ha))✔   4 ∃D
6.   Fa   5 ~⊃ D
7.   ~(Ga & Ha)✔   5 ~⊃ D
8.   (Fa & Ga) ⊃ Ha✔   2 ∀D

9.   ~(Fa & Ga)✔   Ha   8 ⊃ D

10.   ~Ga   ~Ha   ~Ga   ~Ha   7 ~ & D
                                             ×

11. ~Fa   ~Ga   ~Fa   ~Ga   9 ~ & D
     ×   ×

The tree is open. The sentence '(∀x)[(Fx & Gx) ⊃ Hx] ⊃ (∀x)[Fx ⊃ (Gx & Hx)]' is not quantificationally true.

q. 1.   ~((∀x)(Fx ⊃ Gx) ⊃ (∀x)(Fx ⊃ (∀y)Gy))✔   SM

2.   (∀x)(Fx ⊃ Gx)   1 ~⊃ D
3.   ~(∀x)(Fx ⊃ (∀y)Gy)✔   1 ~⊃ D
4.   (∃x) ~(Fx ⊃ (∀y)Gy)✔   3 ~∀D
5.   ~(Fa ⊃ (∀y)Gy)✔   4 ∃D
6.   Fa   5 ~⊃ D
7.   ~(∀y)Gy✔   5 ~⊃ D
8.   (∃y) ~Gy✔   7 ~∀D
9.   ~Gb   8 ∃D
10.   Fa ⊃ Ga✔   2 ∀D

11.   ~Fa   Ga   10 ⊃ D
12.   ×   Fb ⊃ Gb✔   2 ∀D

13.   ~Fb   Gb   12 ⊃ D
                                    ×

The tree is open. The sentence '(∀x)(Fx ⊃ Gx) ⊃ (∀x)[Fx ⊃ (∀y)Gy]' is not quantificationally true.

s. 1. $\sim((\forall x)Gxx \supset (\forall x)(\forall y)Gxy)\checkmark$ SM

2. $(\forall x)Gxx$ 1 $\sim\supset$ D
3. $\sim(\forall x)(\forall y)Gxy\checkmark$ 1 $\sim\supset$ D
4. $(\exists x)\sim(\forall y)Gxy\checkmark$ 3 $\sim\forall$D
5. $\sim(\forall y)Gay\checkmark$ 4 $\exists$D
6. $(\exists y)\sim Gay\checkmark$ 5 $\sim\forall$D
7. $\sim Gab$ 6 $\exists$D
8. Gaa 2 $\forall$D
9. Gbb 2 $\forall$D

The tree is open. The sentence '$(\forall x)Gxx \supset (\forall x)(\forall y)Gxy$' is not quantificationally true.

u. 1. $\sim((\exists x)(\forall y)Gxy \supset (\forall x)(\exists y)Gyx)\checkmark$ SM

2. $(\exists x)(\forall y)Gxy\checkmark$ 1 $\sim\supset$ D
3. $\sim(\forall x)(\exists y)Gyx\checkmark$ 1 $\sim\supset$ D
4. $(\exists x)\sim(\exists y)Gyx\checkmark$ 3 $\sim\forall$D
5. $(\forall y)Gay$ 2 $\exists$D
6. $\sim(\exists y)Gyb\checkmark$ 4 $\exists$D
7. $(\forall y)\sim Gyb$ 6 $\sim\exists$D
8. Gab 5 $\forall$D
9. $\sim Gab$ 7 $\forall$D
          $\times$

The tree is closed. The sentence '$(\exists x)(\forall y)Gxy \supset (\forall x)(\exists y)Gyx$' is quantificationally true.

w. 1. $\sim(((\exists x)Lxx \supset (\forall y)Lyy) \supset (Laa \supset Lgg))\checkmark$ SM

2. $(\exists x)Lxx \supset (\forall y)Lyy\checkmark$ 1 $\sim\supset$ D
3. $\sim(Laa \supset Lgg)\checkmark$ 1 $\sim\supset$ D
4. Laa 3 $\sim\supset$ D
5. $\sim Lgg$ 3 $\sim\supset$ D

6. $\sim(\exists x)Lxx\checkmark$ $(\forall y)Lyy$ 2 $\supset$ D
7. $(\forall x)\sim Lxx$ 6 $\sim\exists$D
8. $\sim Laa$ 7 $\forall$D
9. $\times$ Lgg 6 $\forall$D
          $\times$

The tree is closed. The sentence '$[(\exists x)Lxx \supset (\forall y)Lyy] \supset (Laa \supset Lgg)$' is quantificationally true.

2.a. 1.   (∀x)Fx & (∃x) ~Fx✓   SM

    2.   (∀x)Fx   1 & D
    3.   (∃x) ~Fx✓   1 & D
    4.   ~Fa   3 ∃D
    5.   Fa   2 ∀D
                   ×

The tree is closed. Therefore the sentence is quantificationally false.

c. 1.   (∃x)Fx & (∃x) ~Fx✓   SM

    2.   (∃x)Fx✓   1 & D
    3.   (∃x) ~Fx✓   1 & D
    4.   Fa   2 ∃D
    5.   ~Fb   3 ∃D

The tree is open. Therefore the sentence is not quantificationally false.

e. 1.   (∀x)(Fx ⊃ (∀y) ~Fy)   SM

    2.   Fa ⊃ (∀y) ~Fy✓   1 ∀D

    3.   ~Fa   (∀y) ~Fy   2 ⊃ D
    4.   ~Fa   3 ∀D

The tree is open. Therefore the sentence is not quantificationally false.

g. 1.   (∀x)(Fx ≡ ~Fx)   SM

    2.   Fa ≡ ~Fa✓   1 ∀D

    3.   Fa   ~Fa   2 ≡ D
    4.   ~Fa   ~~Fa✓   2 ≡ D
    5.   ×   Fa   4 ~~D
                  ×

The tree is closed. Therefore the sentence is quantificationally false.

i. 1.   (∃x)(∃y)(Fxy & ~Fyx)✓   SM

    2.   (∃y)(Fay & ~Fya)✓   1 ∃D
    3.   Fab & ~Fba✓   2 ∃D
    4.   Fab   3 & D
    5.   ~Fba   3 & D

The tree is open. Therefore the sentence is not quantificationally false.

k. 1. $(\forall x)(\forall y)(Fxy \supset \sim Fyx)$ SM

  2. $(\forall y)(Fay \supset \sim Fya)$ 1 $\forall$D
  3.   Faa $\supset \sim$ Faa✔ 2 $\forall$D

  4. $\sim$Faa $\sim$Faa 3 $\supset$ D

The tree is open. Therefore the sentence is not quantificationally false.

m. 1. $(\exists x)(\forall y)Gxy$ & $\sim(\forall y)(\exists x)Gxy$✔ SM

  2. $(\exists x)(\forall y)Gxy$✔ 1 & D
  3. $\sim(\forall y)(\exists x)Gxy$✔ 1 & D
  4. $(\exists y) \sim(\exists x)Gxy$✔ 3 $\sim\forall$D
  5. $(\forall y)Gay$ 2 $\exists$D
  6. $\sim(\exists x)Gxb$✔ 4 $\exists$D
  7. $(\forall x) \sim Gxb$ 6 $\sim\exists$D
  8.   Gab 5 $\forall$D
  9. $\sim$Gab 7 $\forall$D
        ×

The tree is closed. Therefore the sentence is quantificationally false.

3.a. 1. $\sim((\exists x)Fxx \supset (\exists x)(\exists y)Fxy)$✔ SM

  2. $(\exists x)Fxx$✔ 1 $\sim\supset$ D
  3. $\sim(\exists x)(\exists y)Fxy$✔ 1 $\sim\supset$ D
  4. $(\forall x) \sim(\exists y)Fxy$ 3 $\sim\exists$D
  5.   Faa 2 $\exists$D
  6. $\sim(\exists y)Fay$✔ 4 $\forall$D
  7. $(\forall y) \sim Fay$ 6 $\sim\exists$D
  8. $\sim$Faa 7 $\forall$D
        ×

The tree for the negation of '$(\exists x)Fxx \supset (\exists x)(\exists y)Fxy$' is closed. Therefore the latter sentence is quantificationally true.

c. 1. $\sim((\exists x)(\forall y)Lxy \supset (\exists x)Lxx)$✔ SM

  2. $(\exists x)(\forall y)Lxy$✔ 1 $\sim\supset$ D
  3. $\sim(\exists x)Lxx$✔ 1 $\sim\supset$ D
  4. $(\forall x) \sim Lxx$ 3 $\sim\exists$D
  5. $(\forall y)Lay$ 2 $\exists$D
  6. $\sim$Laa 4 $\forall$D
  7.   Laa 5 $\forall$D
        ×

The tree for the negation of '$(\exists x)(\forall y)Lxy \supset (\exists x)Lxx$' is closed. Therefore the latter sentence is quantificationally true.

e. 1. $\sim((\forall x)(Fx \supset (\exists y)Gya) \supset (Fb \supset (\exists y)Gya))\checkmark$ SM

2. $\qquad\qquad (\forall x)(Fx \supset (\exists y)Gya)$ 1 $\sim\supset$ D
3. $\qquad\qquad \sim(Fb \supset (\exists y)Gya)\checkmark$ 1 $\sim\supset$ D
4. $\qquad\qquad Fb$ 3 $\sim\supset$ D
5. $\qquad\qquad \sim(\exists y)Gya\checkmark$ 3 $\sim\supset$ D
6. $\qquad\qquad (\forall y)\sim Gya$ 5 $\sim\exists$D
7. $\qquad\qquad Fb \supset (\exists y)Gya\checkmark$ 2 $\forall$D

8. $\qquad\sim Fb \qquad\qquad (\exists y)Gya\checkmark$ 7 $\supset$ D
9. $\qquad\times \qquad\qquad\quad Gca$ 8 $\exists$D
10. $\qquad\qquad\qquad\quad\ \sim Gca$ 6 $\forall$D
$\qquad\qquad\qquad\qquad\quad\ \times$

The tree for the negation of '$(\forall x)(Fx \supset (\exists y)Gya) \supset (Fb \supset (\exists y)Gya)$' is closed. Therefore the latter sentence is quantificationally true.

g. 1. $\sim((\forall x)(Fx \supset (\forall y)Gxy) \supset (\exists x)(Fx \supset \sim(\forall y)Gxy))\checkmark$ SM

2. $\qquad\qquad (\forall x)(Fx \supset (\forall y)Gxy)$ 1 $\sim\supset$ D
3. $\qquad\qquad \sim(\exists x)(Fx \supset \sim(\forall y)Gxy)\checkmark$ 1 $\sim\supset$ D
4. $\qquad\qquad (\forall x)\sim(Fx \supset \sim(\forall y)Gxy)$ 3 $\sim\exists$D
5. $\qquad\qquad \sim(Fa \supset \sim(\forall y)Gay)\checkmark$ 4 $\forall$D
6. $\qquad\qquad Fa$ 5 $\sim\supset$ D
7. $\qquad\qquad \sim\sim(\forall y)Gay\checkmark$ 5 $\sim\supset$ D
8. $\qquad\qquad (\forall y)Gay$ 7 $\sim\sim$D
9. $\qquad\qquad Fa \supset (\forall y)Gay\checkmark$ 2 $\forall$D

10. $\qquad\sim Fa \qquad\qquad (\forall y)Gay$ 9 $\supset$ D
11. $\qquad\times \qquad\qquad\quad Gaa$ 10 $\forall$D
12. $\qquad\qquad\qquad\qquad Gaa$ 8 $\forall$D

1. $(\forall x)(Fx \supset (\forall y)Gxy) \supset (\exists x)(Fx \supset \sim(\forall y)Gxy)\checkmark$ SM

2. $\sim(\forall x)(Fx \supset (\forall y)Gxy)\checkmark \qquad (\exists x)(Fx \supset \sim(\forall y)Gxy)\checkmark$ 1 $\supset$ D
3. $(\exists x)\sim(Fx \supset (\forall y)Gxy)\checkmark$ 2 $\sim\forall$
4. $\sim(Fa \supset (\forall y)Gay)\checkmark$ 3 $\exists$D
5. Fa 4 $\sim\supset$ D
6. $\sim(\forall y)Gay\checkmark$ 4 $\sim\supset$ D
7. $(\exists y)\sim Gay\checkmark$ 6 $\sim\forall$D
8. $\sim Gab$ 7 $\exists$D
9. $\qquad\qquad\qquad Fa \supset \sim(\forall y)Gay\checkmark$ 2 $\exists$D

10. $\qquad\qquad\quad \sim Fa \qquad \sim(\forall y)Gay\checkmark$ 9 $\supset$ D
11. $\qquad\qquad\qquad\qquad\quad (\exists y)\sim Gay\checkmark$ 10 $\sim\forall$D
12. $\qquad\qquad\qquad\qquad\quad\ \sim Gab$ 11 $\exists$D

Both the tree for the given sentence and the tree for its negations are open. Therefore the given sentence is quantificationally indeterminate.

4.a. 1.

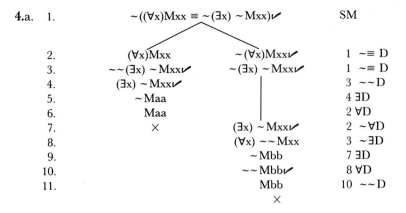

1.	~((∀x)Mxx ≡ ~(∃x) ~Mxx)✔		SM
2.	(∀x)Mxx	~(∀x)Mxx✔	1 ~≡ D
3.	~~(∃x) ~Mxx✔	~(∃x) ~Mxx✔	1 ~≡ D
4.	(∃x) ~Mxx✔		3 ~~D
5.	~Maa		4 ∃D
6.	Maa		2 ∀D
7.	×	(∃x) ~Mxx✔	2 ~∀D
8.		(∀x) ~~Mxx	3 ~∃D
9.		~Mbb	7 ∃D
10.		~~Mbb✔	8 ∀D
11.		Mbb	10 ~~D
		×	

The tree is closed. Therefore the sentences '(∀x)Mxx' and ' ~(∃x) ~Mxx' are quantificationally equivalent.

c. 1.

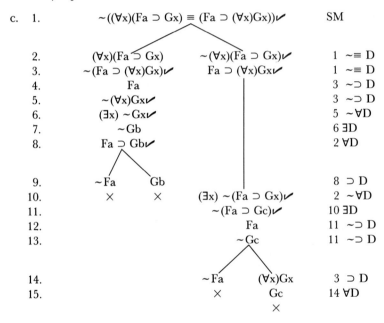

1.	~((∀x)(Fa ⊃ Gx) ≡ (Fa ⊃ (∀x)Gx))✔		SM
2.	(∀x)(Fa ⊃ Gx)	~(∀x)(Fa ⊃ Gx)✔	1 ~≡ D
3.	~(Fa ⊃ (∀x)Gx)✔	Fa ⊃ (∀x)Gx✔	1 ~≡ D
4.	Fa		3 ~⊃ D
5.	~(∀x)Gx✔		3 ~⊃ D
6.	(∃x) ~Gx✔		5 ~∀D
7.	~Gb		6 ∃D
8.	Fa ⊃ Gb✔		2 ∀D
9.	~Fa Gb		8 ⊃ D
10.	× ×	(∃x) ~(Fa ⊃ Gx)✔	2 ~∀D
11.		~(Fa ⊃ Gc)✔	10 ∃D
12.		Fa	11 ~⊃ D
13.		~Gc	11 ~⊃ D
14.	~Fa (∀x)Gx		3 ⊃ D
15.	× Gc		14 ∀D
	×		

The tree is closed. Therefore the sentences '(∀x)(Fa ⊃ Gx)' and 'Fa ⊃ (∀x)Gx' are quantificationally equivalent.

e. 1.   ~(((∃x)Fx ⊃ Ga) ≡ (∃x)(Fx ⊃ Ga))✔   SM

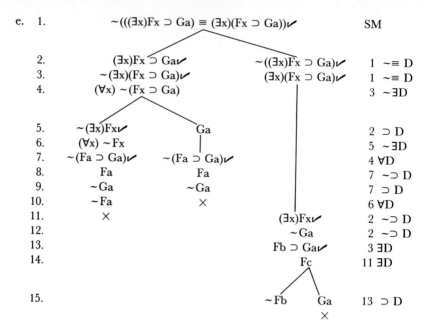

2.	(∃x)Fx ⊃ Ga✔		~((∃x)Fx ⊃ Ga)✔	1 ~≡ D
3.	~(∃x)(Fx ⊃ Ga)✔		(∃x)(Fx ⊃ Ga)✔	1 ~≡ D
4.	(∀x) ~(Fx ⊃ Ga)			3 ~∃D
5.	~(∃x)Fx✔	Ga		2 ⊃ D
6.	(∀x) ~Fx			5 ~∃D
7.	~(Fa ⊃ Ga)✔	~(Fa ⊃ Ga)✔		4 ∀D
8.	Fa	Fa		7 ~⊃ D
9.	~Ga	~Ga		7 ⊃ D
10.	~Fa	×		6 ∀D
11.	×		(∃x)Fx✔	2 ~⊃ D
12.			~Ga	2 ~⊃ D
13.			Fb ⊃ Ga✔	3 ∃D
14.			Fc	11 ∃D
15.			~Fb Ga	13 ⊃ D
			×	

The tree is open. Therefore the sentences '(∃x)Fx ⊃ Ga' and '(∃x)(Fx ⊃ Ga)' are not quantificationally equivalent.

g. 1.   ~(((∀x)Fx ⊃ Ga) ≡ (∃x)(Fx ⊃ Ga))✔   SM

2.	(∀x)Fx ⊃ Ga✔		~((∀x)Fx ⊃ Ga)✔	1 ~≡ D
3.	~(∃x)(Fx ⊃ Ga)✔		(∃x)(Fx ⊃ Ga)✔	1 ~≡ D
4.	(∀x) ~(Fx ⊃ Ga)			3 ~∃D
5.	~(∀x)Fx✔	Ga		2 ⊃ D
6.	(∃x) ~Fx✔			5 ~∀D
7.	~Fb			6 ∃D
8.	~(Fb ⊃ Ga)✔	~(Fb ⊃ Ga)✔		4 ∀D
9.	Fb	Fa		8 ~⊃ D
10.	~Ga	~Ga		8 ~⊃ D
11.	×	×	(∀x)Fx	2 ~⊃ D
12.			~Ga	2 ~⊃ D
13.			Fc ⊃ Ga✔	3 ∃D
14.		~Fc	Ga	13 ⊃ D
15.		Fc	×	11 ∀D
		×		

The tree is closed. Therefore the sentences '(∀x)Fx ⊃ Ga' and '(∃x)(Fx ⊃ Ga)' are quantificationally equivalent.

i. 1. $\sim((\forall x)(\forall y)(Fx \supset Gy) \equiv (\forall x)(Fx \supset (\forall y)Gy))\checkmark$ SM

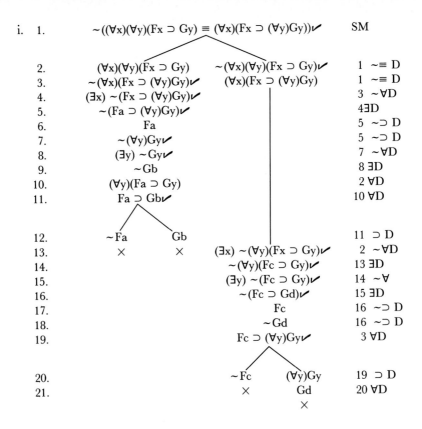

2.	$(\forall x)(\forall y)(Fx \supset Gy)$	$\sim(\forall x)(\forall y)(Fx \supset Gy)\checkmark$	1 $\sim\equiv$ D
3.	$\sim(\forall x)(Fx \supset (\forall y)Gy)\checkmark$	$(\forall x)(Fx \supset (\forall y)Gy)$	1 $\sim\equiv$ D
4.	$(\exists x)\sim(Fx \supset (\forall y)Gy)\checkmark$		3 $\sim\forall$D
5.	$\sim(Fa \supset (\forall y)Gy)\checkmark$		4$\exists$D
6.	Fa		5 $\sim\supset$ D
7.	$\sim(\forall y)Gy\checkmark$		5 $\sim\supset$ D
8.	$(\exists y)\sim Gy\checkmark$		7 $\sim\forall$D
9.	$\sim Gb$		8 $\exists$D
10.	$(\forall y)(Fa \supset Gy)$		2 $\forall$D
11.	$Fa \supset Gb\checkmark$		10 $\forall$D

12.	$\sim Fa$	Gb		11 $\supset$ D
13.	$\times$	$\times$	$(\exists x)\sim(\forall y)(Fx \supset Gy)\checkmark$	2 $\sim\forall$D
14.			$\sim(\forall y)(Fc \supset Gy)\checkmark$	13 $\exists$D
15.			$(\exists y)\sim(Fc \supset Gy)\checkmark$	14 $\sim\forall$
16.			$\sim(Fc \supset Gd)\checkmark$	15 $\exists$D
17.			Fc	16 $\sim\supset$ D
18.			$\sim Gd$	16 $\sim\supset$ D
19.			$Fc \supset (\forall y)Gy\checkmark$	3 $\forall$D

20.	$\sim Fc$	$(\forall y)Gy$	19 $\supset$ D
21.	$\times$	Gd	20 $\forall$D
		$\times$	

The tree is closed. Therefore the sentences '$(\forall x)(\forall y)(Fx \supset Gy)$' and '$(\forall x)(Fx \supset (\forall y)Gy)$' are quantificationally equivalent.

k.   1. $\sim((\forall x)(Fa \equiv Gx) \equiv (Fa \equiv (\forall x)Gx))\checkmark$ SM

2. $(\forall x)(Fa \equiv Gx)$ $\sim(\forall x)(Fa \equiv Gx)\checkmark$ 1 $\sim\equiv$ D
3. $\sim(Fa \equiv (\forall x)Gx)\checkmark$ $Fa \equiv (\forall x)Gx\checkmark$ 1 $\sim\equiv$ D

4.   Fa $\sim$Fa   3 $\sim\equiv$ D
5. $\sim(\forall x)Gx\checkmark$ $(\forall x)Gx$ 3 $\sim\equiv$ D
6. $(\exists x)\sim Gx\checkmark$ 5 $\sim\forall$ D
7. $\sim$Gb   6 $\exists$D
8. $Fa \equiv Gb\checkmark$ $Fa \equiv Gb\checkmark$ 2 $\forall$D

9.   Fa $\sim$Fa   Fa $\sim$Fa   8 $\equiv$ D
10.   Gb $\sim$Gb   Gb $\sim$Gb   8 $\equiv$ D
11.   ×   ×   ×   Gb   5 $\forall$D
12.   × $(\exists x)\sim(Fa \equiv Gx)\checkmark$ 2 $\sim\forall$D
13. $\sim(Fa \equiv Gc)\checkmark$ 12 $\exists$D
                                                   5 $\forall$D

14.   Fa $\sim$Fa   3 $\equiv$ D
15. $(\forall x)Gx$ $\sim(\forall x)Gx\checkmark$ 3 $\equiv$ D

16.   Fa $\sim$Fa   Fa $\sim$Fa   13 $\sim\equiv$ D
17. $\sim$Gc   Gc $\sim$Gc   Gc   13 $\sim\equiv$ D
18.   Gc   ×   ×   15 $\forall$D
19.   × $(\exists x)\sim Gx\checkmark$ 15 $\sim\forall$D
20. $\sim$Gd   19 $\exists$D

The tree is open. Therefore the sentences '$(\forall x)(Fa \equiv Gx)$' and '$(Fa \equiv (\forall x)Gx)$' are not quantificationally equivalent.

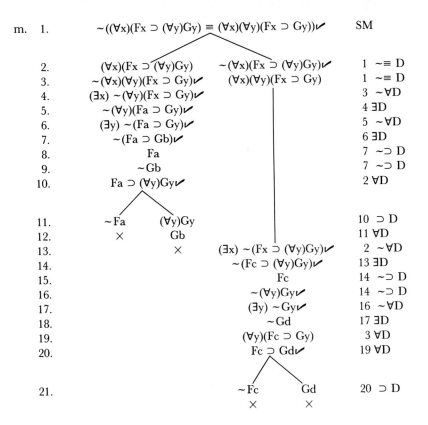

m. 1.   ~((∀x)(Fx ⊃ (∀y)Gy) ≡ (∀x)(∀y)(Fx ⊃ Gy))✔   SM

2.	(∀x)(Fx ⊃ (∀y)Gy)	~(∀x)(Fx ⊃ (∀y)Gy)✔	1 ~≡ D
3.	~(∀x)(∀y)(Fx ⊃ Gy)✔	(∀x)(∀y)(Fx ⊃ Gy)	1 ~≡ D
4.	(∃x) ~(∀y)(Fx ⊃ Gy)✔		3 ~∀D
5.	~(∀y)(Fa ⊃ Gy)✔		4 ∃D
6.	(∃y) ~(Fa ⊃ Gy)✔		5 ~∀D
7.	~(Fa ⊃ Gb)✔		6 ∃D
8.	Fa		7 ~⊃ D
9.	~Gb		7 ~⊃ D
10.	Fa ⊃ (∀y)Gy✔		2 ∀D

11.	~Fa	(∀y)Gy		10 ⊃ D
12.	×	Gb		11 ∀D
13.		×	(∃x) ~(Fx ⊃ (∀y)Gy)✔	2 ~∀D
14.			~(Fc ⊃ (∀y)Gy)✔	13 ∃D
15.			Fc	14 ~⊃ D
16.			~(∀y)Gy✔	14 ~⊃ D
17.			(∃y) ~Gy✔	16 ~∀D
18.			~Gd	17 ∃D
19.			(∀y)(Fc ⊃ Gy)	3 ∀D
20.			Fc ⊃ Gd✔	19 ∀D

21.		~Fc Gd	20 ⊃ D
		× ×	

The tree is closed. Therefore the sentences '(∀x)(Fx ⊃ (∀y)Gy)' and '(∀x)(∀y)(Fx ⊃ Gy)' are quantificationally equivalent.

5.a.
1.	(∀x)(Fx ⊃ Gx)	SM
2.	Ga	SM
3.	~Fa	SM
4.	Fa ⊃ Ga✔	1 ∀D
5.	~Fa Ga	4 ⊃ D

The tree is open. Therefore the argument is quantificationally invalid.

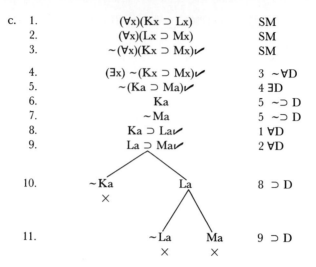

c. 1. $(\forall x)(Kx \supset Lx)$ SM
    2. $(\forall x)(Lx \supset Mx)$ SM
    3. $\sim(\forall x)(Kx \supset Mx)\checkmark$ SM

    4. $(\exists x)\sim(Kx \supset Mx)\checkmark$ 3 $\sim\forall$D
    5. $\sim(Ka \supset Ma)\checkmark$ 4 $\exists$D
    6. Ka 5 $\sim\supset$ D
    7. $\sim Ma$ 5 $\sim\supset$ D
    8. $Ka \supset La\checkmark$ 1 $\forall$D
    9. $La \supset Ma\checkmark$ 2 $\forall$D

    10. $\sim Ka$ La 8 $\supset$ D
            $\times$

    11. $\sim La$ Ma 9 $\supset$ D
                        $\times$ $\times$

The tree is closed. Therefore the argument is quantificationally valid.

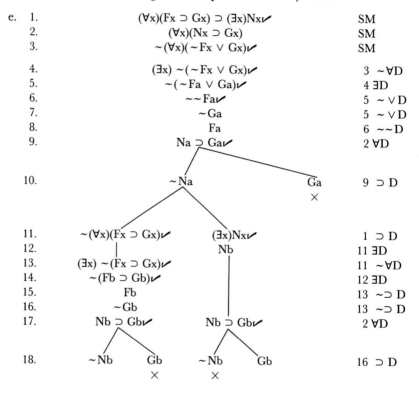

e. 1. $(\forall x)(Fx \supset Gx) \supset (\exists x)Nx\checkmark$ SM
    2. $(\forall x)(Nx \supset Gx)$ SM
    3. $\sim(\forall x)(\sim Fx \vee Gx)\checkmark$ SM

    4. $(\exists x)\sim(\sim Fx \vee Gx)\checkmark$ 3 $\sim\forall$D
    5. $\sim(\sim Fa \vee Ga)\checkmark$ 4 $\exists$D
    6. $\sim\sim Fa\checkmark$ 5 $\sim\vee$ D
    7. $\sim Ga$ 5 $\sim\vee$ D
    8. Fa 6 $\sim\sim$D
    9. $Na \supset Ga\checkmark$ 2 $\forall$D

    10. $\sim Na$ Ga 9 $\supset$ D
                                    $\times$

    11. $\sim(\forall x)(Fx \supset Gx)\checkmark$ $(\exists x)Nx\checkmark$ 1 $\supset$ D
    12. Nb 11 $\exists$D
    13. $(\exists x)\sim(Fx \supset Gx)\checkmark$ 11 $\sim\forall$D
    14. $\sim(Fb \supset Gb)\checkmark$ 12 $\exists$D
    15. Fb 13 $\sim\supset$ D
    16. $\sim Gb$ 13 $\sim\supset$ D
    17. $Nb \supset Gb\checkmark$ $Nb \supset Gb\checkmark$ 2 $\forall$D

    18. $\sim Nb$ Gb $\sim Nb$ Gb 16 $\supset$ D
            $\times$ $\times$

The tree is open. Therefore the argument is quantificationally invalid.

g.
1. $(\forall x)(\sim Ax \supset Kx)$ SM
2. $(\exists y) \sim Ky$✔   SM
3. $\sim(\exists w)(Aw \vee \sim Lwf)$✔   SM

4. $(\forall w) \sim (Aw \vee \sim Lwf)$ 3 $\sim\exists$D
5. $\sim Ka$ 2 $\exists$D
6. $\sim Aa \supset Ka$✔   1 $\forall$D
7. $\sim(Aa \vee \sim Laf)$✔   4 $\forall$D
8. $\sim Aa$ 7 $\sim\vee$D
9. $\sim\sim Laf$✔   7 $\sim\vee$D
10. Laf 9 $\sim\sim$D

11. $\sim\sim Aa$✔ Ka 6 $\supset$D
12. Aa ×   11 $\sim\sim$D
     ×

The tree is closed. Therefore the argument is quantificationally valid.

i.
1. $(\forall x)(\forall y)Cxy$ SM
2. $\sim((Caa \& Cab) \& (Cba \& Cbb))$✔   SM

3. $(\forall y)Cay$ 1 $\forall$D
4. $(\forall y)Cby$ 1 $\forall$D
5. Caa 3 $\forall$D
6. Cab 3 $\forall$D
7. Cba 4 $\forall$D
8. Cbb 4 $\forall$D

9. $\sim(Caa \& Cab)$✔ $\sim(Cba \& Cbb)$✔   2 $\sim \& $D

10. $\sim Caa$ $\sim Cab$ $\sim Cba$ $\sim Cbb$ 9 $\sim \& $D
   ×   ×   ×   ×

The tree is closed. Therefore the argument is quantificationally valid.

k.
1. $(\forall x)(Fx \supset Gx)$ SM
2. $\sim(\exists x)Fx$✔   SM
3. $\sim\sim(\exists x)Gx$✔   SM

4. $(\exists x)Gx$✔   3 $\sim\sim$D
5. Ga 4 $\exists$D
6. $(\forall x) \sim Fx$ 2 $\sim\exists$D
7. $Fa \supset Ga$✔   1 $\forall$D
8. $\sim Fa$ 6 $\forall$D

9. $\sim Fa$ Ga 7 $\supset$D

The tree is open. Therefore the argument is quantificationally invalid.

m. 1.   (∃x)Cx ⊃ Ch✔   SM
    2.   ~((∃x)Cx ≡ Ch)✔   SM

    3.   (∃x)Cx✔   ~(∃x)Cx✔   2 ~≡ D
    4.   ~Ch   Ch   2 ~≡ D
    5.   (∀x) ~Cx   3 ~∃
    6.   ~Ch   5 ∀D
    7.   Ca   ×   3 ∃D

    8.   ~(∃x)Cx✔   Ch   1 ⊃ D
    9.   (∀x) ~Cx   ×   8 ~∃D
    10.   ~Ca   9 ∀D
              ×

The tree is closed. Therefore the argument is quantificationally valid.

6.a. 1.   (∀x) ~Jx   SM
      2.   (∃y)(Hby ∨ Ryy) ⊃ (∃x)Jx✔   SM
      3.   ~(∀y) ~(Hby ∨ Ryy)✔   SM

      4.   (∃y) ~~(Hby ∨ Ryy)✔   3 ~∀D
      5.   ~~(Hba ∨ Raa)✔   4 ∃D
      6.   Hba ∨ Raa✔   5 ~~D
      7.   ~Ja   1 ∀D
      8.   ~Jb   1 ∀D

      9.   ~(∃y)(Hby ∨ Ryy)✔   (∃x)Jx✔   2 ⊃ D
      10.   Jc   9 ∃D
      11.   ~Jc   1 ∀D
      12. (∀y) ~(Hby ∨ Ryy)   ×   9 ~∃
      13.   ~(Hba ∨ Raa)✔   12 ∀D
      14.   ~Hba   13 ~∨D
      15.   ~Raa   13 ~∨D

      16.   Hba   Raa   6 ∨D
              ×   ×

The tree is closed. Therefore the entailment does hold.

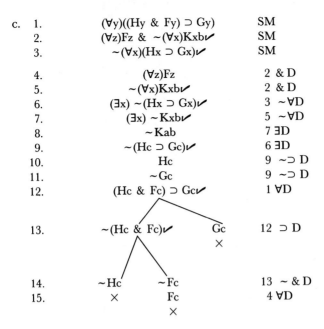

c.	1.	$(\forall y)((Hy \ \& \ Fy) \supset Gy)$	SM
	2.	$(\forall z)Fz \ \& \ \sim(\forall x)Kxb$✔	SM
	3.	$\sim(\forall x)(Hx \supset Gx)$✔	SM
	4.	$(\forall z)Fz$	2 & D
	5.	$\sim(\forall x)Kxb$✔	2 & D
	6.	$(\exists x) \sim(Hx \supset Gx)$✔	3 $\sim\forall$D
	7.	$(\exists x) \sim Kxb$✔	5 $\sim\forall$D
	8.	$\sim Kab$	7 $\exists$D
	9.	$\sim(Hc \supset Gc)$✔	6 $\exists$D
	10.	Hc	9 $\sim\supset$ D
	11.	$\sim Gc$	9 $\sim\supset$ D
	12.	$(Hc \ \& \ Fc) \supset Gc$✔	1 $\forall$D

13. $\sim(Hc \ \& \ Fc)$✔ Gc 12 $\supset$ D
                        $\times$

14. $\sim Hc$ $\sim Fc$ 13 $\sim$ & D
15. $\times$ Fc 4 $\forall$D
              $\times$

The tree is closed. Therefore the entailment does hold.

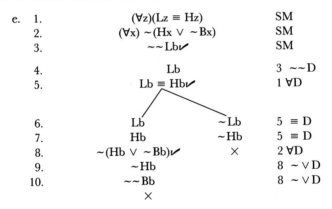

e.	1.	$(\forall z)(Lz \equiv Hz)$	SM
	2.	$(\forall x) \sim(Hx \vee \sim Bx)$	SM
	3.	$\sim\sim Lb$✔	SM
	4.	Lb	3 $\sim\sim$D
	5.	$Lb \equiv Hb$✔	1 $\forall$D

6. Lb $\sim Lb$ 5 $\equiv$ D
7. Hb $\sim Hb$ 5 $\equiv$ D
8. $\sim(Hb \vee \sim Bb)$✔ $\times$ 2 $\forall$D
9. $\sim Hb$ 8 $\sim \vee$ D
10. $\sim\sim Bb$ 8 $\sim \vee$ D
       $\times$

The tree is closed. Therefore the entailment does hold.

9.4E

1.a.
	1.	(∀x)Fxx	SM
	2.	(∃x)(∃y) ~Fxy✓	SM
	3.	(∀x)x = a	SM
	4.	(∃y) ~Fby✓	2 ∃D
	5.	~Fbc	4 ∃D
	6.	Faa	1 ∀D
	7.	c = a	3 ∀D
	8.	Fac	6, 7 = D
	9.	b = a	3 ∀D
	10.	Fbc	8, 9 = D
		×	

The tree is closed. Therefore the set is quantificationally inconsistent.

c.
	1.	(∀x)(x = a ⊃ Gxb)	SM
	2.	~(∃x)Gxx✓	SM
	3.	a = b	SM
	4.	(∀x) ~Gxx	2 ~∃D
	5.	a = a ⊃ Gab✓	1 ∀D

	6.	~a = a	Gab	5 ⊃ D
	7.	×	~Gaa	4 ∀D
	8.		Gaa	3, 6 = D
			×	

The tree is closed. Therefore the set is quantificationally inconsistent.

e.
	1.	(∀x)((Fx & ~Gx) ⊃ ~x = a)	SM
	2.	Fa & ~Ga✓	SM
	3.	Fa	2 & D
	4.	~Ga	2 & D
	5.	(Fa & ~Ga) ⊃ ~a = a✓	1 ∀D

	6.	~(Fa & ~Ga)✓	~a = a	5 ⊃ D
			×	

	7.	~Fa	~~Ga✓	6 ~ & D
	8.	×	Ga	7 ~~D
			×	

The tree is closed. Therefore the set is quantificationally inconsistent.

2.a. 1. $\sim(a = b \equiv b = a)$✔   SM

2. $a = b$ $\sim a = b$ 1 $\sim\equiv$ D
3. $\sim b = a$ $b = a$ 1 $\sim\equiv$ D
4. $\sim a = a$ $\sim b = b$ 2, 3 $=$ D
          ×   ×

The tree is closed. Therefore 'a = b ≡ b = a' is quantificationally false.

c. 1. $\sim((Gab \ \& \ \sim Gba) \supset \sim a = b)$✔   SM
2. $Gab \ \& \ \sim Gba$✔   1 $\sim\supset$ D
3. $\sim\sim a = b$✔   1 $\sim\supset$ D
4. Gab 2 & D
5. $\sim Gba$ 2 & D
6. $a = b$ 3 $\sim\sim$ D
7. Gaa 4, 6 $=$ D
8. $\sim Gaa$ 5, 6 $=$ D
               ×

The tree is closed. Therefore the sentence '(Gab & ~Gba) ⊃ ~a = b' is quantificationally true.

e. 1. $\sim(Fa \equiv (\exists x)(Fx \ \& \ x = a))$✔   SM

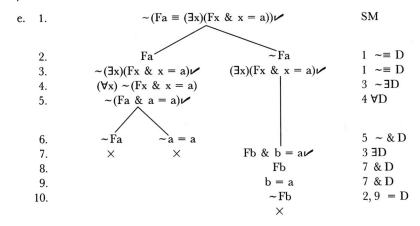

2. Fa $\sim Fa$ 1 $\sim\equiv$ D
3. $\sim(\exists x)(Fx \ \& \ x = a)$✔ $(\exists x)(Fx \ \& \ x = a)$✔   1 $\sim\equiv$ D
4. $(\forall x) \sim (Fx \ \& \ x = a)$ 3 $\sim\exists$ D
5. $\sim(Fa \ \& \ a = a)$✔   4 $\forall$ D

6. $\sim Fa$ $\sim a = a$ 5 $\sim$ & D
7.   ×   × $Fb \ \& \ b = a$✔   3 $\exists$ D
8. Fb 7 & D
9. $b = a$ 7 & D
10. $\sim Fb$ 2, 9 $=$ D
                          ×

The tree is closed. Therefore the sentence 'Fa ≡ (∃x)(Fx & x = a)' is quantificationally true.

g. 1. $\sim((\forall x)x = a \supset ((\exists x)Fx \supset (\forall x)Fx))\checkmark$ SM

    2. $(\forall x)x = a$ 1 $\sim\supset$ D

    3. $\sim((\exists x)Fx \supset (\forall x)Fx)\checkmark$ 1 $\sim\supset$ D

    4. $(\exists x)Fx\checkmark$ 3 $\sim\supset$ D

    5. $\sim(\forall x)Fx\checkmark$ 3 $\sim\supset$ D

    6. $(\exists x) \sim Fx\checkmark$ 5 $\sim\forall$D

    7.   Fb   4 $\exists$D

    8. $\sim$Fc   6 $\exists$D

    9.   c = a   2 $\forall$D

  10.   b = a   2 $\forall$D

  11.   c = b   9, 10 = D

  12.   Fc   7, 11 = D

                               $\times$

The tree is closed. Therefore the sentence '$(\forall x)x = a \supset ((\exists x)Fx \supset (\forall x)Fx)$' is quantificationally true.

i. 1. $(\forall x)(\forall y) \sim x = y$ SM

    2. $(\forall y) \sim a = y$ 1 $\forall$D

    3. $\sim a = a$ 2 $\forall$D

                   $\times$

The tree is closed. Therefore the sentence '$(\forall x)(\forall y) \sim x = y$' is quantificationally false.

k. 1. $(\exists x)(\exists y) \sim x = y\checkmark$ SM

    2. $(\exists y) \sim a = y\checkmark$ 1 $\exists$D

    3. $\sim a = b$ 2 $\exists$D

    1. $\sim(\exists x)(\exists y) \sim x = y\checkmark$ SM

    2. $(\forall x) \sim(\exists y) \sim x = y$ 1 $\sim\exists$D

    3. $\sim(\exists y) \sim a = y\checkmark$ 2 $\forall$D

    4. $(\forall y) \sim\sim a = y$ 3 $\sim\exists$D

    5. $\sim\sim a = a\checkmark$ 4 $\forall$D

    6.   a = a   5 $\sim\sim$D

Both trees are open. Therefore the sentence '$(\exists x)(\exists y) \sim x = y$' is quantificationally indeterminate.

m. 1. $\sim(\forall x)(\forall y)((Fx \equiv Fy) \supset x = y)$✔   SM

    2. $(\exists x) \sim(\forall y)((Fx \equiv Fy) \supset x = y)$✔   1 $\sim\forall$D
    3. $\sim(\forall y)((Fa \equiv Fy) \supset a = y)$✔   2 $\exists$D
    4. $(\exists y) \sim((Fa \equiv Fy) \supset a = y)$✔   3 $\sim\forall$D
    5. $\sim((Fa \equiv Fb) \supset a = b)$✔   4 $\exists$D
    6. $Fa \equiv Fb$✔   5 $\sim\supset$ D
    7. $\sim a = b$ 5 $\sim\supset$ D

    8.   Fa $\sim$Fa   6 $\equiv$ D
    9.   Fb $\sim$Fb   6 $\equiv$ D

    1. $(\forall x)(\forall y)((Fx \equiv Fy) \supset x = y)$ SM
    2. $(\forall y)((Fa \equiv Fy) \supset a = y)$ 1 $\forall$D
    3. $(Fa \equiv Fa) \supset a = a$✔   2 $\forall$D

    4. $\sim(Fa \equiv Fa)$✔ $a = a$ 3 $\supset$ D

    5.   Fa $\sim$Fa   4 $\sim\equiv$ D
    6. $\sim$Fa   Fa   4 $\sim\equiv$ D
            ✗   ✗

Both trees are open. Therefore the sentence '$(\forall x)(\forall y)(Fx \equiv Fy) \supset x = y)$' is quantificationally indeterminate.

    o. 1. $\sim(((\exists x)Gax \& \sim(\exists x)Gxa) \supset (\forall x)(Gxa \supset \sim x = a))$✔   SM

        2. $(\exists x)Gax \& \sim(\exists x)Gxa$✔   1 $\sim\supset$ D
        3. $\sim(\forall x)(Gxa \supset \sim x = a)$✔   1 $\sim\supset$ D
        4. $(\exists x)Gax$✔   2 & D
        5. $\sim(\exists x)Gxa$✔   2 & D
        6. $(\forall x) \sim Gxa$ 5 $\sim\exists$D
        7. $(\exists x) \sim(Gxa \supset \sim x = a)$✔   3 $\sim\forall$D
        8. $\sim(Gba \supset \sim b = a)$✔   7 $\exists$D
        9.   Gac   4 $\exists$D
        10.   Gba   8 $\sim\supset$ D
        11. $\sim\sim b = a$ 8 $\sim\supset$ D
        12. $\sim$Gba   6 $\forall$D
                ✗

The tree is closed. Therefore the sentence '$[(\exists x)Gax \& \sim(\exists x)Gxa] \supset (\forall x)(Gxa \supset x = a)$' is quantificationally true.

3.a. 1. $\sim(\sim a = b \equiv \sim b = a)\checkmark$ SM

2.	$\sim a = b$	$\sim\sim a = b\checkmark$	1 $\sim\equiv$ D
3.	$\sim\sim b = a\checkmark$	$\sim b = a$	1 $\sim\equiv$ D
4.	$b = a$		3 $\sim\sim$ D
5.	$\sim b = b$		2, 4 = D
6.	$\times$	$a = b$	2 $\sim\sim$ D
7.		$\sim a = a$	6, 3 = D
		$\times$	

The tree is closed. Therefore the sentences ' $\sim a = b$' and ' $\sim b = a$' are quantificationally equivalent.

     c.   1. $\sim((\forall x)x = a \equiv (\forall x)x = b)\checkmark$ SM

2.	$(\forall x)x = a$	$\sim(\forall x)x = a\checkmark$	1 $\sim\equiv$ D
3.	$\sim(\forall x)x = b\checkmark$	$(\forall x)x = b$	1 $\sim\equiv$ D
4.	$(\exists x) \sim x = b\checkmark$		3 $\sim\forall$D
5.	$\sim c = b$		4 $\exists$D
6.	$b = a$		2 $\forall$D
7.	$c = a$		2 $\forall$D
8.	$c = b$		6, 7 = D
9.	$\times$	$(\exists x) \sim x = a\checkmark$	2 $\sim\forall$D
10.		$\sim c = a$	9 $\exists$D
11.		$c = b$	3 $\forall$D
12.		$a = b$	3 $\forall$D
13.		$c = a$	11, 12 = D
		$\times$	

The tree is closed. Therefore the sentences '$(\forall x)x = a$' and '$(\forall x)x = b$' are quantificationally equivalent.

e.　1.　　　　　　　$\sim((\forall x)(\forall y)x = y \equiv (\forall x)x = a)$✓　　　　SM

　　2.　　　$(\forall x)(\forall y)x = y$　　　$\sim(\forall x)(\forall y)x = y$✓　　　1　$\sim\equiv$ D
　　3.　　　$\sim(\forall x)x = a$✓　　　　　$(\forall x)x = a$　　　　　　1　$\sim\equiv$ D
　　4.　　　$(\exists x)\sim x = a$✓　　　　　　　　　　　　　　　　　　3　$\sim\forall$D
　　5.　　　$\sim b = a$　　　　　　　　　　　　　　　　　　　　　　　4　$\exists$D
　　6.　　　$(\forall y)b = y$　　　　　　　　　　　　　　　　　　　　　2　$\forall$D
　　7.　　　$b = a$　　　　　　　　　　　　　　　　　　　　　　　　　6　$\forall$D
　　8.　　　×　　　　　　　$(\exists x)\sim(\forall y)x = y$✓　　　2　$\sim\forall$D
　　9.　　　　　　　　　　　$\sim(\forall y)b = y$✓　　　　　　8　$\exists$D
　　10.　　　　　　　　　　$(\exists y)\sim b = y$✓　　　　　　9　$\sim\forall$D
　　11.　　　　　　　　　　$\sim b = c$　　　　　　　　　10　$\exists$D
　　12.　　　　　　　　　　$b = a$　　　　　　　　　　3　$\forall$D
　　13.　　　　　　　　　　$c = a$　　　　　　　　　　3　$\forall$D
　　14.　　　　　　　　　　$b = c$　　　　　　　　　12, 13　= D
　　　　　　　　　　　　　　　　×

The tree is closed. Therefore the sentences '$(\forall x)(\forall y)x = y$' and '$(\forall x)x = a$' are quantificationally equivalent.

g. 1. $\sim((\forall x)(Fx \supset x = a) \equiv (\forall x)(Fa \supset x = a))\checkmark$ SM

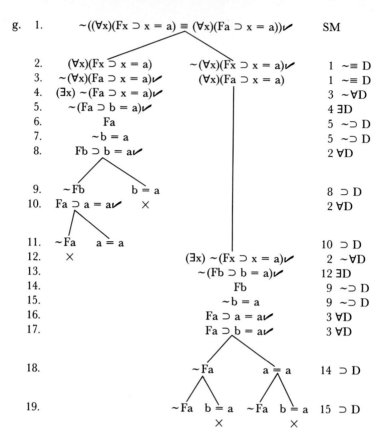

2. $(\forall x)(Fx \supset x = a)$ $\sim(\forall x)(Fx \supset x = a)\checkmark$ 1 $\sim\equiv$ D
3. $\sim(\forall x)(Fa \supset x = a)\checkmark$ $(\forall x)(Fa \supset x = a)$ 1 $\sim\equiv$ D
4. $(\exists x) \sim(Fa \supset x = a)\checkmark$ 3 $\sim\forall$D
5. $\sim(Fa \supset b = a)\checkmark$ 4 $\exists$D
6. Fa 5 $\sim\supset$ D
7. $\sim b = a$ 5 $\sim\supset$ D
8. $Fb \supset b = a\checkmark$ 2 $\forall$D

9. $\sim Fb$ $b = a$ 8 $\supset$ D
10. $Fa \supset a = a\checkmark$ $\times$ 2 $\forall$D

11. $\sim Fa$ $a = a$ 10 $\supset$ D
12. $\times$ $(\exists x) \sim(Fx \supset x = a)\checkmark$ 2 $\sim\forall$D
13. $\sim(Fb \supset b = a)\checkmark$ 12 $\exists$D
14. Fb 9 $\sim\supset$ D
15. $\sim b = a$ 9 $\sim\supset$ D
16. $Fa \supset a = a\checkmark$ 3 $\forall$D
17. $Fa \supset b = a\checkmark$ 3 $\forall$D

18. $\sim Fa$ $a = a$ 14 $\supset$ D

19. $\sim Fa$ $b = a$ $\sim Fa$ $b = a$ 15 $\supset$ D
         $\times$ $\times$

The tree is open. Therefore the sentences '$(\forall x)(Fx \supset x = a)$' and '$(\forall x)(Fa \supset x = a)$' are not quantificationally equivalent.

i. 1.   ~(((∀x)Fx ∨ (∀x) ~Fx) ≡ (∀y)(Fy ⊃ y = b))✔   SM

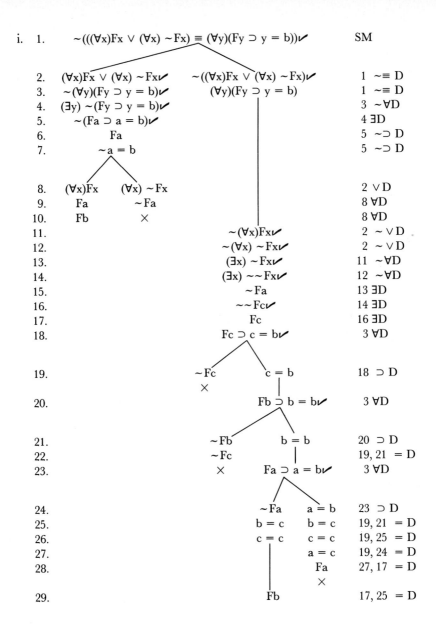

2.	(∀x)Fx ∨ (∀x) ~Fx✔ ~((∀x)Fx ∨ (∀x) ~Fx)✔	1 ~≡ D
3.	~(∀y)(Fy ⊃ y = b)✔ (∀y)(Fy ⊃ y = b)	1 ~≡ D
4.	(∃y) ~(Fy ⊃ y = b)✔	3 ~∀D
5.	~(Fa ⊃ a = b)✔	4 ∃D
6.	Fa	5 ~⊃ D
7.	~a = b	5 ~⊃ D
8.	(∀x)Fx (∀x) ~Fx	2 ∨D
9.	Fa ~Fa	8 ∀D
10.	Fb ×	8 ∀D
11.	~(∀x)Fx✔	2 ~∨D
12.	~(∀x) ~Fx✔	2 ~∨D
13.	(∃x) ~Fx✔	11 ~∀D
14.	(∃x) ~~Fx✔	12 ~∀D
15.	~Fa	13 ∃D
16.	~~Fc✔	14 ∃D
17.	Fc	16 ∃D
18.	Fc ⊃ c = b✔	3 ∀D
19.	~Fc c = b	18 ⊃ D
	×	
20.	Fb ⊃ b = b✔	3 ∀D
21.	~Fb b = b	20 ⊃ D
22.	~Fc	19, 21 = D
23.	× Fa ⊃ a = b✔	3 ∀D
24.	~Fa a = b	23 ⊃ D
25.	b = c b = c	19, 21 = D
26.	c = c c = c	19, 25 = D
27.	a = c	19, 24 = D
28.	Fa	27, 17 = D
	×	
29.	Fb	17, 25 = D

The tree is open. Therefore the sentences '(∀x)Fx ∨ (∀x) ~Fx' and '(∀y)(Fy ⊃ y = b)' are not quantificationally equivalent.

k.   1.   ~$((\exists x)(x = a \ \& \ x = b) \equiv a = b)$✔   SM

2. $(\exists x)(x = a \ \& \ x = b)$✔   ~$(\exists x)(x = a \ \& \ x = b)$✔   1 ~$\equiv$ D
3.   ~$a = b$ $a = b$ 1 ~$\equiv$ D
4. $(\forall x)$ ~$(x = a \ \& \ x = b)$ 2 ~$\exists$D
5.   ~$(a = a \ \& \ a = b)$✔   4 $\forall$D
6.   ~$(b = a \ \& \ b = b)$ 4 $\forall$D

7.   ~$a = a$ ~$a = b$ 5 ~ $\&$ D
8. $c = a \ \& \ c = b$✔   ✕   ✕   2 $\exists$D
9. $c = a$ 8 $\&$ D
10. $c = b$ 8 $\&$ D
11.   ~$c = b$ 3, 9 = D
                   ✕

The tree is closed. Therefore the sentences '$(\exists x)(x = a \ \& \ x = b)$' and '$a = b$' are quantificationally equivalent.

4.a. 1. $a = b \ \& \ $~$Bab$✔   SM
           2.   ~~$(\forall x)Bxx$✔   SM

           3. $(\forall x)Bxx$ 2 ~~D
           4. $a = b$ 1 $\&$ D
           5.   ~Bab 1 $\&$ D
           6. Bbb 3 $\forall$D
           7. Bab 4, 6 = D
                           ✕

The tree is closed. Therefore the argument is quantificationally valid.

c.   1. $(\forall z)(Gz \supset (\forall y)(Ky \supset Hzy))$ SM
     2. $(Ki \ \& \ Gj) \ \& \ i = j$✔   SM
     3.   ~Hii SM

     4. $Ki \ \& \ Gj$✔   2 $\&$ D
     5. $i = j$ 2 $\&$ D
     6. Ki 4 $\&$ D
     7. Gj 4 $\&$ D
     8. $Gj \supset (\forall y)(Ky \supset Hjy)$✔   1 $\forall$D

     9.   ~Gj $(\forall y)(Ky \supset Hjy)$ 8 $\supset$ D
     10.   ✕ $Ki \supset Hji$✔   9 $\forall$D

     11.   ~Ki Hji 10 $\supset$ D
     12.   ✕ Hii 5, 11 = D
                                  ✕

The tree is closed. Therefore the argument is quantificationally valid.

e.	1.	$a = b$		SM
	2.	$\sim(Ka \vee \sim Kb)$✓		SM
	3.	$\sim Ka$		2 $\sim\forall$D
	4.	$\sim\sim Kb$✓		2 $\sim\forall$D
	5.	Kb		4 $\sim\sim$D
	6.	Ka		1, 5 $=$D
		×		

The tree is closed. Therefore the argument is quantificationally valid.

g.	1.	$(\forall x)(x = a \vee x = b)$		SM
	2.	$(\exists x)(Fxa \ \& \ Fbx)$✓		SM
	3.	$\sim(\exists x)Fxx$		SM
	4.	$(\forall x) \sim Fxx$		3 $\sim\exists$D
	5.	$Fca \ \& \ Fbc$✓		2 $\exists$D
	6.	Fca		5 &D
	7.	Fbc		5 &D
	8.	$c = a \vee c = b$✓		1 $\forall$D
	9.			
	10.	$c = a$	$c = b$	8 $\cup$D
	11.	Faa		6, 10 $=$D
	12.		Fcc	7, 10 $=$D
	13.	$\sim Faa$	$\sim Fcc$	4 $\forall$D
		×	×	

The tree is closed. Therefore the argument is quantificationally valid.

i.	1.	$(\forall x)(\forall y)(Fxy \vee Fyx)$		SM
	2.	$a = b$		SM
	3.	$\sim(\forall x)(Fxa \vee Fbx)$✓		SM
	4.	$(\exists x) \sim(Fxa \vee Fbx)$✓		3 $\sim\forall$D
	5.	$\sim(Fca \vee Fbc)$✓		4 $\exists$D
	6.	$\sim Fca$		5 $\sim\forall$D
	7.	$\sim Fbc$		5 $\sim\forall$D
	8.	$(\forall y)(Fay \vee Fya)$		1 $\forall$D
	9.	$Fac \vee Fca$✓		8 $\forall$D
	10.	Fac	Fca	9 $\forall$D
	11.	$\sim Fac$	×	2, 7 $=$D
		×		

The tree is closed. Therefore the argument is quantificationally valid.

k. 1. $(\forall x)(Fx \equiv {\sim}Gx)$ SM

2.   Fa   SM

3.   Gb   SM

4. ${\sim}{\sim}a = b$✔   SM

5. $a = b$ 4 ${\sim}{\sim}$D

6.   Fa $\equiv$ ${\sim}$Ga✔   1 $\forall$D

7.   Fa ${\sim}$Fa   6 $\equiv$ D

8. ${\sim}$Ga ${\sim}{\sim}$Ga   6 $\equiv$ D

9.   Ga   ✕   3, 5 $=$ D

       ✕

The tree is closed. Therefore the argument is quantificationally valid.

m. 1. $(\forall x)(\forall y)x = y$ SM

2. ${\sim}{\sim}(\exists x)(\exists y)(Fx \;\&\; {\sim}Fy)$✔   SM

3. $(\exists x)(\exists y)(Fx \;\&\; {\sim}Fy)$✔   2 ${\sim}{\sim}$D

4. $(\exists y)(Fa \;\&\; {\sim}Fy)$✔   3 $\exists$D

5.   Fa $\&$ ${\sim}$Fb✔   4 $\exists$D

6.   Fa   5 $\&$ D

7. ${\sim}$Fb   5 $\&$ D

8. $(\forall y)a = y$ 1 $\forall$D

9. $a = b$ 8 $\forall$D

10. ${\sim}$Fa   7, 9 $=$ D

       ✕

The tree is closed. Therefore the argument is quantificationally valid.

5.a.
1.		$(\forall x)(Fx \supset (\exists y)(Gyx \ \& \ {\sim}y = x))$	SM
2.		$(\exists x)Fx\checkmark$	SM
3.		${\sim}(\exists x)(\exists y) \ {\sim}x = y\checkmark$	SM
4.		$(\forall x) \ {\sim}(\exists y) \ {\sim}x = y$	3 ${\sim}\exists$D
5.		Fa	2 $\exists$D
6.		$Fa \supset (\exists y)(Gya \ \& \ {\sim}y = a)\checkmark$	1 $\forall$D

7.	${\sim}Fa$	$(\exists y)(Gya \ \& \ {\sim}y = a)\checkmark$	6 $\supset$D
8.	$\times$	$Gba \ \& \ {\sim}b = a\checkmark$	7 $\exists$D
9.		Gba	8 & D
10.		${\sim}b = a$	8 & D
11.		${\sim}(\exists y) \ {\sim}a = y\checkmark$	4 $\forall$D
12.		${\sim}(\exists y) \ {\sim}b = y\checkmark$	4 $\forall$D
13.		$(\forall y) \ {\sim}{\sim}a = y$	11 ${\sim}\exists$D
14.		$(\forall y) \ {\sim}{\sim}b = y$	12 ${\sim}\exists$D
15.		${\sim}{\sim}a = a\checkmark$	13 $\forall$D
16.		${\sim}{\sim}a = b\checkmark$	13 $\forall$D
17.		${\sim}{\sim}b = a\checkmark$	14 $\forall$D
18.		${\sim}{\sim}b = b\checkmark$	14 $\forall$D
19.		$a = a$	18 ${\sim}{\sim}$D
20.		$a = b$	16 ${\sim}{\sim}$D
21.		$b = a$	17 ${\sim}{\sim}$D
22.		$b = b$	18 ${\sim}{\sim}$D
23.		${\sim}b = b$	10, 21 $=$ D
		$\times$	

The tree is closed. Therefore the alleged entailment does hold.

c.
1.		$(\forall x)(Fx \supset {\sim}x = a)$	SM
2.		$(\exists x)Fx\checkmark$	SM
3.		${\sim}(\exists x)(\exists y) \ {\sim}x = y\checkmark$	SM
4.		Fb	2 $\exists$D
5.		$(\forall x) \ {\sim}(\exists y) \ {\sim}x = y$	3 ${\sim}\exists$D
6.		$Fb \supset {\sim}b = a\checkmark$	1 $\forall$D

7.	${\sim}Fb$	${\sim}b = a$	6 $\supset$D
8.	$\times$	${\sim}(\exists y) \ {\sim}a = y\checkmark$	5 $\forall$D
9.		$(\forall y) \ {\sim}{\sim}a = y$	8 ${\sim}\exists$D
10.		${\sim}{\sim}a = b\checkmark$	9 $\forall$D
11.		$a = b$	10 ${\sim}{\sim}$D
12.		${\sim}a = a$	7, 11 $\equiv$ D
		$\times$	

The tree is closed. Therefore the alleged entailment does hold.

e. 1. $(\exists w)(\exists z) \sim w = z$✓   SM
   2. $(\exists w)Hw$✓   SM
   3. $\sim(\exists w) \sim Hw$✓   SM

   4. $(\forall w) \sim\sim Hw$ 3 $\sim\exists$D
   5. $(\exists z) \sim a = z$✓   1 $\exists$D
   6. Hb 2 $\exists$D
   7. $\sim a = c$ 5 $\exists$D
   8. $\sim\sim Ha$✓   4 $\forall$D
   9. $\sim\sim Hb$✓   4 $\forall$D
  10. $\sim\sim Hc$✓   4 $\forall$D
  11. Ha 8 $\sim\sim$D
  12. Hb 9 $\sim\sim$D
  13. Hc 10 $\sim\sim$D

The tree is open. Therefore the alleged entailment does not hold.

g. 1. $(\forall x)(\forall y)((Fx \equiv Fy) \equiv x = y)$ SM
   2. $(\exists z)Fz$✓   SM
   3. $\sim(\exists x)(\exists y)(\sim x = y \,\&\, (Fx \,\&\, \sim Fy))$✓   SM

   4. $(\forall x) \sim(\exists y)(\sim x = y \,\&\, (Fx \,\&\, \sim Fy))$ 3 $\sim\exists$D
   5. Fa 2 $\exists$D
   6. $\sim(\exists y)(\sim a = y \,\&\, (Fa \,\&\, \sim Fy))$✓   4 $\forall$D
   7. $(\forall y) \sim(\sim a = y \,\&\, (Fa \,\&\, \sim Fy))$ 6 $\sim\exists$D
   8. $\sim(\sim a = a \,\&\, (Fa \,\&\, \sim Fa))$✓   7 $\forall$D
   9. $(\forall y)((Fa \equiv Fy) \equiv a = y)$ 1 $\forall$D
  10. $(Fa \equiv Fa) \equiv a = a$✓   9 $\forall$D

  11. $\sim\sim a = a$✓ $\sim(Fa \,\&\, \sim Fa)$✓   8 $\sim\,\&\,$D
  12. $a = a$ 11 $\sim\sim$D
  13. $\sim Fa$ $\sim\sim Fa$✓   11 $\sim\,\&\,$D
  14.   × Fa 13 $\sim\sim$D

  15. $Fa \equiv Fa$✓ $\sim(Fa \equiv Fa)$✓ $Fa \equiv Fa$✓ $\sim(Fa \equiv Fa)$✓   10 $\equiv$D
  16. $a = a$ $\sim a = a$ $a = a$ $\sim a = a$ 10 $\equiv$D
  17.   ×   ×

  18. Fa $\sim Fa$ Fa $\sim Fa$ 15 $\equiv$D
  19. Fa $\sim Fa$ Fa $\sim Fa$ 15 $\equiv$D
  20.   ×   ×

The tree is open. Therefore the alleged entailment does not hold.

9.5E

Note: Branches which are open but not completed are so indicated by a series of dots below the branch.

1.a.

1.	$(\forall x)Jx$	SM
2.	$(\forall x)(Jx \equiv (\exists y)(Gyx \lor Ky))$	SM
3.	Ja	1 $\forall$D
4.	Ja $\equiv (\exists y)(Gya \lor Ky)\checkmark$	2 $\forall$D

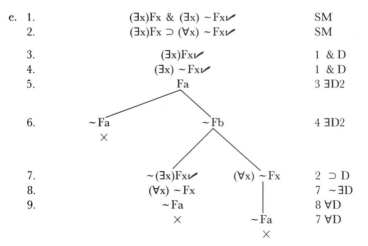

5.	Ja		$\sim$Ja	4 $\equiv$ D
6.	$(\exists y)(Gya \lor Ky)\checkmark$		$\sim\exists y)(Gya \lor Ky)$	4 $\equiv$ D
			$\times$	
7.	Gaa $\lor$ Ka$\checkmark$	Gba $\lor$ Kb$\checkmark$		6 $\exists$D2
8.	Gaa Ka	Gba Kb		7 $\lor$ D
	$\vdots$ $\vdots$	$\vdots$ $\vdots$		

The tree has at least one completed open branch. Therefore the set is quantificationally consistent.

c.

1.	$(\exists x)Fx\checkmark$	SM
2.	$(\exists x) \sim Fx\checkmark$	SM
3.	Fa	1 $\exists$D2
4.	$\sim$Fa $\sim$Fb	2 $\exists$D2
	$\times$	

The tree has a completed open branch. Therefore, the set is quantificationally consistent.

e.

1.	$(\exists x)Fx$ & $(\exists x) \sim Fx\checkmark$	SM
2.	$(\exists x)Fx \supset (\forall x) \sim Fx\checkmark$	SM
3.	$(\exists x)Fx\checkmark$	1 & D
4.	$(\exists x) \sim Fx\checkmark$	1 & D
5.	Fa	3 $\exists$D2
6.	$\sim$Fa $\sim$Fb	4 $\exists$D2
	$\times$	
7.	$\sim(\exists x)Fx\checkmark$ $(\forall x) \sim Fx$	2 $\supset$ D
8.	$(\forall x) \sim Fx$	7 $\sim\exists$D
9.	$\sim$Fa	8 $\forall$D
	$\times$ $\sim$Fa	7 $\forall$D
	$\times$	

The tree is closed. Therefore the set is quantificationally inconsistent.

g. 1.   (∀x)(∃y)Fxy   SM
   2.   (∃y)(∀x) ~Fyx✔   SM

   3.   (∀x) ~Fax   2 ∃D2
   4.   (∃y)Fay✔   1 ∀D
   5.   ~Faa   3 ∀D

   6.   Faa   Fab   4 ∃D2
   7.   ×   (∃y)Fby   1 ∀D
   8.   ~Fab   3 ∀D
                  ×

The tree is closed. Therefore the set is quantificationally inconsistent.

i. 1.   (∃x)Hx✔   SM
   2.   ~(∀x)Hx✔   SM
   3.   (∀x)(Hx ⊃ Kx)   SM
   4.   (∃x)(Kx & Hx)✔   SM

   5.   (∃x) ~Hx✔   2 ~∀D
   6.   Ka & Ha✔   4 ∃D2
   7.   Ka   6 & D
   8.   Ha   6 & D

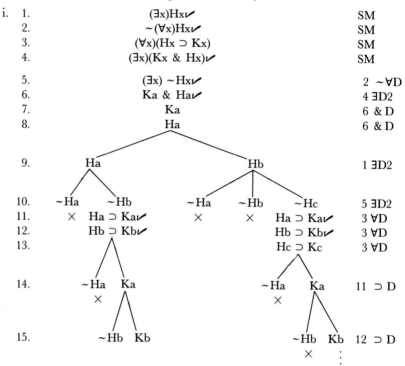

9.   Ha   Hb   1 ∃D2

10. ~Ha   ~Hb   ~Ha   ~Hb   ~Hc   5 ∃D2
11.   ×   Ha ⊃ Ka✔   ×   ×   Ha ⊃ Ka✔   3 ∀D
12.   Hb ⊃ Kb✔   Hb ⊃ Kb✔   3 ∀D
13.   Hc ⊃ Kc   3 ∀D

14.   ~Ha   Ka   ~Ha   Ka   11 ⊃ D
          ×   ×

15.   ~Hb Kb   ~Hb Kb   12 ⊃ D
                              ×

The tree has at least one completed open branch. The set is quantificationally consistent.

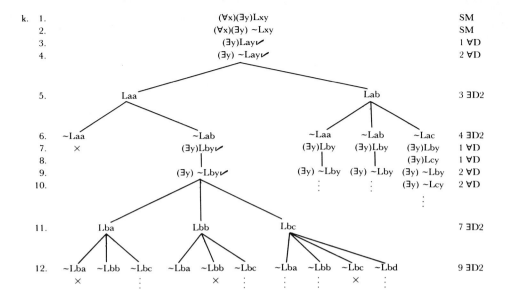

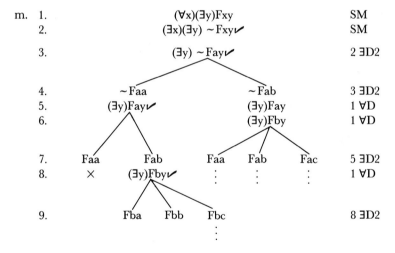

k.

1.	$(\forall x)(\exists y)Lxy$		SM
2.	$(\forall x)(\exists y) \sim Lxy$		SM
3.	$(\exists y)Lay$ ✔		1 $\forall$D
4.	$(\exists y) \sim Lay$ ✔		2 $\forall$D
5.	Laa Lab		3 ∃D2
6.	$\sim$Laa $\sim$Lab $\sim$Laa $\sim$Lab $\sim$Lac		4 ∃D2
7.	× $(\exists y)Lby$✔ $(\exists y)Lby$ $(\exists y)Lby$ $(\exists y)Lby$		1 $\forall$D
8.	$(\exists y)Lcy$		1 $\forall$D
9.	$(\exists y) \sim Lby$✔ $(\exists y) \sim Lby$ $(\exists y) \sim Lby$ $(\exists y) \sim Lby$		2 $\forall$D
10.	$(\exists y) \sim Lcy$		2 $\forall$D
11.	Lba Lbb Lbc		7 ∃D2
12.	$\sim$Lba $\sim$Lbb $\sim$Lbc $\sim$Lba $\sim$Lbb $\sim$Lbc $\sim$Lba $\sim$Lbb $\sim$Lbc $\sim$Lbd		9 ∃D2

The tree has at least one completed open branch. Therefore the set is quantificationally consistent.

m.

1.	$(\forall x)(\exists y)Fxy$		SM
2.	$(\exists x)(\exists y) \sim Fxy$✔		SM
3.	$(\exists y) \sim Fay$✔		2 ∃D2
4.	$\sim Faa$ $\sim Fab$		3 ∃D2
5.	$(\exists y)Fay$✔ $(\exists y)Fay$		1 $\forall$D
6.	$(\exists y)Fby$		1 $\forall$D
7.	Faa Fab Faa Fab Fac		5 ∃D2
8.	× $(\exists y)Fby$✔		1 $\forall$D
9.	Fba Fbb Fbc		8 ∃D2

The tree has at least one completed open branch. Therefore the set is quantificationally consistent.

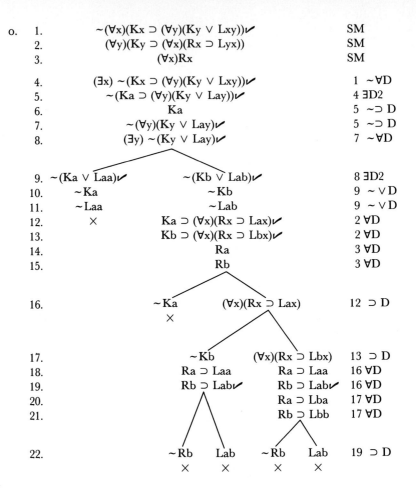

o.
1.	~(∀x)(Kx ⊃ (∀y)(Ky ∨ Lxy))✓		SM
2.	(∀y)(Ky ⊃ (∀x)(Rx ⊃ Lyx))		SM
3.	(∀x)Rx		SM
4.	(∃x) ~(Kx ⊃ (∀y)(Ky ∨ Lxy))✓		1 ~∀D
5.	~(Ka ⊃ (∀y)(Ky ∨ Lay))✓		4 ∃D2
6.	Ka		5 ~⊃ D
7.	~(∀y)(Ky ∨ Lay)✓		5 ~⊃ D
8.	(∃y) ~(Ky ∨ Lay)✓		7 ~∀D

9. ~(Ka ∨ Laa)✓   ~(Kb ∨ Lab)✓   8 ∃D2
10.   ~Ka   ~Kb   9 ~∨D
11.   ~Laa   ~Lab   9 ~∨D
12.   ×   Ka ⊃ (∀x)(Rx ⊃ Lax)✓   2 ∀D
13.   Kb ⊃ (∀x)(Rx ⊃ Lbx)✓   2 ∀D
14.   Ra   3 ∀D
15.   Rb   3 ∀D

16.   ~Ka   (∀x)(Rx ⊃ Lax)   12 ⊃ D
            ×

17.   ~Kb   (∀x)(Rx ⊃ Lbx)   13 ⊃ D
18.   Ra ⊃ Laa   Ra ⊃ Laa   16 ∀D
19.   Rb ⊃ Lab✓   Rb ⊃ Lab✓   16 ∀D
20.   Ra ⊃ Lba   17 ∀D
21.   Rb ⊃ Lbb   17 ∀D

22.   ~Rb   Lab   ~Rb   Lab   19 ⊃ D
         ×   ×   ×   ×

The tree is closed. Therefore the set is quantificationally inconsistent.

2.a. 1.   (∀x)(Fax ⊃ (∃y)Fya)   SM

     2.   Faa ⊃ (∃y)Fya✔   1 ∀D

     3.   ~Faa   (∃y)Fya   2 ⊃ D
                      ⋮

     1.   ~(∀x)(Fax ⊃ (∃y)Fya)✔   SM

     2.   (∃x) ~(Fax ⊃ (∃y)Fya)✔   1 ~∀D

     3.   ~(Faa ⊃ (∃y)Fya)✔   ~(Fab ⊃ (∃y)Fya)✔   2 ∃D2
     4.   Faa   Fab   3 ~⊃ D
     5.   ~(∃y)Fya✔   ~(∃y)Fya✔   3 ~⊃ D
     6.   (∀y) ~Fya   (∀y) ~Fya   5 ~∃D
     7.   ~Faa   ~Faa   6 ∀D
     8.   ×   ~Fba   6 ∀D

Both the tree for the sentence and the tree for its negation have at least one completed open branch. Therefore the sentence is quantificationally indeterminate.

  c. 1.   ~(∀x)(Fx ⊃ (∀y)(Hy ⊃ Fy))✔   SM

     2.   (∃x) ~(Fx ⊃ (∀y)(Hy ⊃ Fy))✔   1 ~∀D
     3.   ~(Fa ⊃ (∀y)(Hy ⊃ Fy))✔   2 ∃D2
     4.   Fa   3 ~⊃ D
     5.   ~(∀y)(Hy ⊃ Fy)✔   3 ~⊃ D
     6.   (∃y) ~(Hy ⊃ Fy)✔   5 ~∀D

     7.   ~(Ha ⊃ Fa)   ~(Hb ⊃ Fb)✔   6 ∃D2
     8.   Ha   Hb   7 ~⊃ D
     9.   ~Fa   ~Fb   7 ~⊃ D
             ×

     1.   (∀x)(Fx ⊃ (∀y)(Hy ⊃ Fy))   SM
     2.   ✔Fa ⊃ (∀y)(Hy ⊃ Fy)   1 ∀D

     3.   ~Fa   (∀y)(Hy ⊃ Fy)   2 ⊃ D
                       ⋮

Both the tree for the sentence and the tree for its negation have at least one completed open branch. Therefore the sentence is quantificationally indeterminate.

e. 1.   ~((∃x)(Fx ∨ ~Fx) ≡ ((∃x)Fx ∨ (∃x) ~Fx))✓   SM

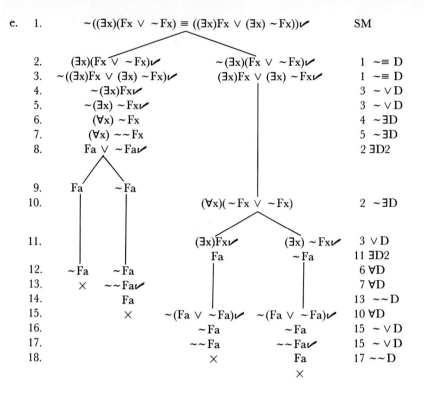

2.   (∃x)(Fx ∨ ~Fx)✓   ~(∃x)(Fx ∨ ~Fx)✓   1 ~≡ D
3.   ~((∃x)Fx ∨ (∃x) ~Fx)✓   (∃x)Fx ∨ (∃x) ~Fx✓   1 ~≡ D
4.   ~(∃x)Fx✓   3 ~∨ D
5.   ~(∃x) ~Fx✓   3 ~∨ D
6.   (∀x) ~Fx   4 ~∃D
7.   (∀x) ~~Fx   5 ~∃D
8.   Fa ∨ ~Fa✓   2 ∃D2

9.   Fa   ~Fa
10.   (∀x)(~Fx ∨ ~Fx)   2 ~∃D

11.   (∃x)Fx✓   (∃x) ~Fx✓   3 ∨D
                             Fa   ~Fa   11 ∃D2
12. ~Fa   ~Fa   6 ∀D
13.   ×   ~~Fa✓   7 ∀D
14.   Fa   13 ~~D
15.   ×   ~(Fa ∨ ~Fa)✓   ~(Fa ∨ ~Fa)✓   10 ∀D
16.   ~Fa   ~Fa   15 ~∨ D
17.   ~~Fa   ~~Fa✓   15 ~∨ D
18.   ×   Fa   17 ~~D
                                     ×

The tree for the negation of the sentence is closed. Therefore the sentence is quantificationally true.

g. 1. ~((∀x)(Fx ⊃ ((∃y)Gyx ⊃ H)) ⊃ (∀x)(Fx ⊃ (∃y)(Gyx ⊃ H)))✓   SM

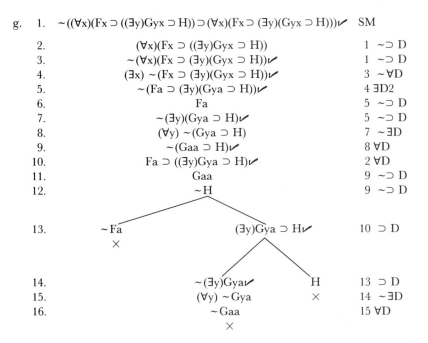

2.   (∀x)(Fx ⊃ ((∃y)Gyx ⊃ H))   1 ~⊃ D
3.   ~(∀x)(Fx ⊃ (∃y)(Gyx ⊃ H))✓   1 ~⊃ D
4.   (∃x) ~(Fx ⊃ (∃y)(Gyx ⊃ H))✓   3 ~∀D
5.   ~(Fa ⊃ (∃y)(Gya ⊃ H))✓   4 ∃D2
6.   Fa   5 ~⊃ D
7.   ~(∃y)(Gya ⊃ H)✓   5 ~⊃ D
8.   (∀y) ~(Gya ⊃ H)   7 ~∃D
9.   ~(Gaa ⊃ H)✓   8 ∀D
10.   Fa ⊃ ((∃y)Gya ⊃ H)✓   2 ∀D
11.   Gaa   9 ~⊃ D
12.   ~H   9 ~⊃ D

13.   ~Fa   (∃y)Gya ⊃ H✓   10 ⊃ D
        ×

14.   ~(∃y)Gya✓   H   13 ⊃ D
15.   (∀y) ~Gya   ×   14 ~∃D
16.   ~Gaa   15 ∀D
                   ×

The tree for the negation of the sentence is closed. Therefore the sentence is quantificationally true.

3.a. 1.   Fa   SM
2.   (∀x)(Fx ⊃ Cx)   SM
3.   ~(∀x)(Fx & Cx)✓   SM

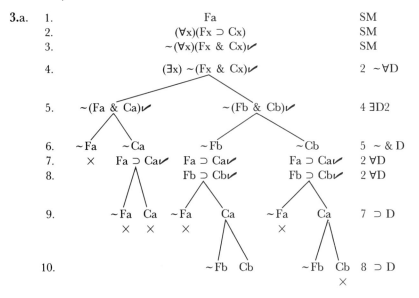

4.   (∃x) ~(Fx & Cx)✓   2 ~∀D

5.   ~(Fa & Ca)✓   ~(Fb & Cb)✓   4 ∃D2

6. ~Fa   ~Ca   ~Fb   ~Cb   5 ~ & D
7.   ×   Fa ⊃ Ca✓   Fa ⊃ Ca✓   Fa ⊃ Ca✓   2 ∀D
8.   Fb ⊃ Cb✓   Fb ⊃ Cb✓   2 ∀D

9.   ~Fa   Ca   ~Fa   Ca   ~Fa   Ca   7 ⊃ D
         ×   ×   ×   ×

10.   ~Fb   Cb   ~Fb   Cb   8 ⊃ D
                                             ×

The tree for the premises and the negation of the conclusion has at least one completed open branch. Therefore the argument is quantificationally invalid.

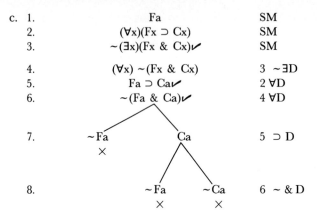

c. 1.   Fa   SM

2.   (∀x)(Fx ⊃ Cx)   SM

3.   ~(∃x)(Fx & Cx)✔   SM

4.   (∀x) ~(Fx & Cx)   3 ~∃D

5.   Fa ⊃ Ca✔   2 ∀D

6.   ~(Fa & Ca)✔   4 ∀D

7.   ~Fa   Ca   5 ⊃ D
      ×

8.   ~Fa   ~Ca   6 ~ & D
           ×   ×

The tree for the premises and the negation of the conclusion is closed. Therefore the argument is quantificationally valid.

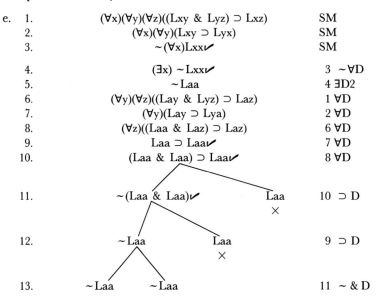

e. 1.   (∀x)(∀y)(∀z)((Lxy & Lyz) ⊃ Lxz)   SM

2.   (∀x)(∀y)(Lxy ⊃ Lyx)   SM

3.   ~(∀x)Lxx✔   SM

4.   (∃x) ~Lxx✔   3 ~∀D

5.   ~Laa   4 ∃D2

6.   (∀y)(∀z)((Lay & Lyz) ⊃ Laz)   1 ∀D

7.   (∀y)(Lay ⊃ Lya)   2 ∀D

8.   (∀z)((Laa & Laz) ⊃ Laz)   6 ∀D

9.   Laa ⊃ Laa✔   7 ∀D

10.   (Laa & Laa) ⊃ Laa✔   8 ∀D

11. ~(Laa & Laa)✔   Laa   10 ⊃ D
                  ×

12.   ~Laa   Laa   9 ⊃ D
                 ×

13. ~Laa   ~Laa   11 ~ & D

The tree for the premises and the negation of the conclusion has at least one completed open branch. Therefore the argument is quantificationally invalid.

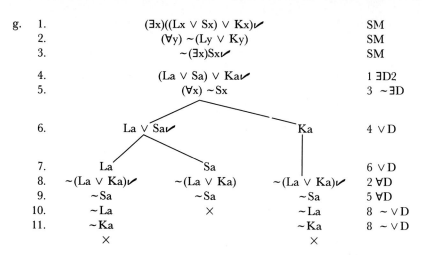

g.
1.	(∃x)((Lx ∨ Sx) ∨ Kx)✓	SM
2.	(∀y) ~(Ly ∨ Ky)	SM
3.	~(∃x)Sx✓	SM
4.	(La ∨ Sa) ∨ Ka✓	1 ∃D2
5.	(∀x) ~Sx	3 ~∃D

6.	La ∨ Sa✓		Ka	4 ∨D
7.	La	Sa		6 ∨D
8.	~(La ∨ Ka)✓	~(La ∨ Ka)	~(La ∨ Ka)✓	2 ∀D
9.	~Sa	~Sa	~Sa	5 ∀D
10.	~La	×	~La	8 ~∨D
11.	~Ka		~Ka	8 ~∨D
	×		×	

The tree for the premises and the negation of the conclusion is closed. Therefore the argument is quantificationally valid.

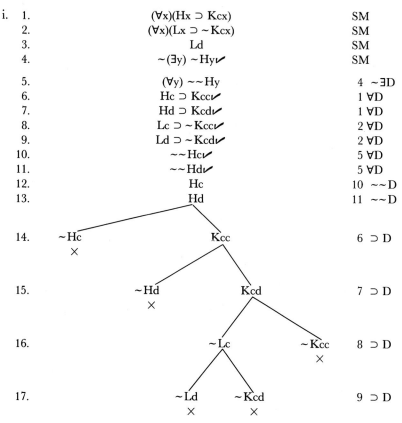

i.
1.	(∀x)(Hx ⊃ Kcx)	SM
2.	(∀x)(Lx ⊃ ~Kcx)	SM
3.	Ld	SM
4.	~(∃y) ~Hy✓	SM
5.	(∀y) ~~Hy	4 ~∃D
6.	Hc ⊃ Kcc✓	1 ∀D
7.	Hd ⊃ Kcd✓	1 ∀D
8.	Lc ⊃ ~Kcc✓	2 ∀D
9.	Ld ⊃ ~Kcd✓	2 ∀D
10.	~~Hc✓	5 ∀D
11.	~~Hd✓	5 ∀D
12.	Hc	10 ~~D
13.	Hd	11 ~~D

14.	~Hc	Kcc		6 ⊃ D
	×			
15.		~Hd	Kcd	7 ⊃ D
		×		
16.			~Lc ⋯ ~Kcc	8 ⊃ D
			×	
17.			~Ld ⋯ ~Kcd	9 ⊃ D
			× ×	

The tree for the premises and the negation of the conclusion is closed. Therefore the argument is quantificationally valid.

4.a.   1. $\sim((\forall x)(\forall y) \sim Sxy \equiv \sim(\exists x)(\exists y)Sxy)\checkmark$ SM

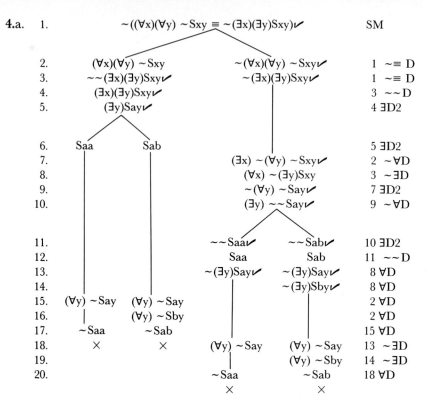

2.	$(\forall x)(\forall y) \sim Sxy$		$\sim(\forall x)(\forall y) \sim Sxy\checkmark$	1 $\sim\equiv$ D
3.	$\sim\sim(\exists x)(\exists y)Sxy\checkmark$		$\sim(\exists x)(\exists y)Sxy\checkmark$	1 $\sim\equiv$ D
4.	$(\exists x)(\exists y)Sxy\checkmark$			3 $\sim\sim$ D
5.	$(\exists y)Say\checkmark$			4 $\exists$D2

6.	Saa	Sab		5 $\exists$D2
7.			$(\exists x) \sim(\forall y) \sim Sxy\checkmark$	2 $\sim\forall$D
8.			$(\forall x) \sim(\exists y)Sxy$	3 $\sim\exists$D
9.			$\sim(\forall y) \sim Say\checkmark$	7 $\exists$D2
10.			$(\exists y) \sim\sim Say\checkmark$	9 $\sim\forall$D

11.			$\sim\sim Saa\checkmark$ $\sim\sim Sab\checkmark$	10 $\exists$D2
12.			Saa Sab	11 $\sim\sim$ D
13.			$\sim(\exists y)Say\checkmark$ $\sim(\exists y)Say\checkmark$	8 $\forall$D
14.			$\sim(\exists y)Sby\checkmark$	8 $\forall$D
15.	$(\forall y) \sim Say$	$(\forall y) \sim Say$		2 $\forall$D
16.		$(\forall y) \sim Sby$		2 $\forall$D
17.	$\sim Saa$	$\sim Sab$		15 $\forall$D
18.	$\times$	$\times$	$(\forall y) \sim Say$ $(\forall y) \sim Say$	13 $\sim\exists$D
19.			$(\forall y) \sim Sby$	14 $\sim\exists$D
20.			$\sim Saa$ $\sim Sab$	18 $\forall$D
			$\times$ $\times$	

The tree for the negation of the corresponding biconditional is closed. Therefore the sentences are equivalent.

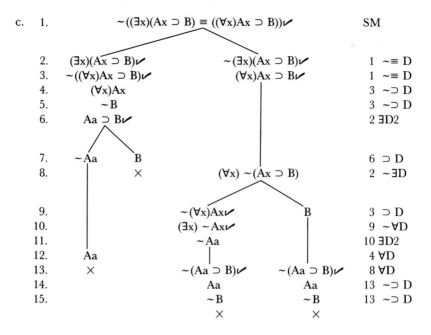

c. 1.   ~((∃x)(Ax ⊃ B) ≡ ((∀x)Ax ⊃ B))✔   SM

2.	(∃x)(Ax ⊃ B)✔	~(∃x)(Ax ⊃ B)✔	1 ~≡ D
3.	~((∀x)Ax ⊃ B)✔	(∀x)Ax ⊃ B✔	1 ~≡ D
4.	(∀x)Ax		3 ~⊃ D
5.	~B		3 ~⊃ D
6.	Aa ⊃ B✔		2 ∃D2
7.	~Aa B		6 ⊃ D
8.	×	(∀x) ~(Ax ⊃ B)	2 ~∃D
9.		~(∀x)Ax✔ B	3 ⊃ D
10.		(∃x) ~Ax✔	9 ~∀D
11.		~Aa	10 ∃D2
12.	Aa		4 ∀D
13.	×	~(Aa ⊃ B)✔ ~(Aa ⊃ B)✔	8 ∀D
14.		Aa Aa	13 ~⊃ D
15.		~B ~B	13 ~⊃ D
		× ×	

The tree for the negation of the corresponding biconditional is closed. Therefore the sentences are equivalent.

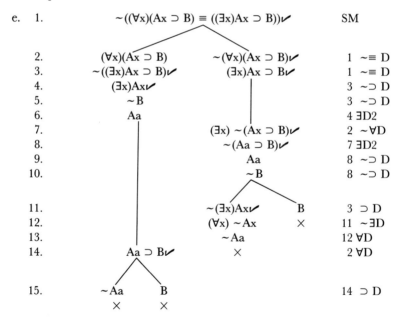

e. 1.   ~((∀x)(Ax ⊃ B) ≡ (∃x)Ax ⊃ B))✔   SM

2.	(∀x)(Ax ⊃ B)	~(∀x)(Ax ⊃ B)✔	1 ~≡ D
3.	~((∃x)Ax ⊃ B)✔	(∃x)Ax ⊃ B✔	1 ~≡ D
4.	(∃x)Ax✔		3 ~⊃ D
5.	~B		3 ~⊃ D
6.	Aa		4 ∃D2
7.		(∃x) ~(Ax ⊃ B)✔	2 ~∀D
8.		~(Aa ⊃ B)✔	7 ∃D2
9.		Aa	8 ~⊃ D
10.		~B	8 ~⊃ D
11.		~(∃x)Ax✔ B	3 ⊃ D
12.		(∀x) ~Ax ×	11 ~∃D
13.		~Aa	12 ∀D
14.	Aa ⊃ B✔	×	2 ∀D
15.	~Aa B		14 ⊃ D
	× ×		

The tree for the negation of the corresponding biconditional is closed. Therefore the sentences are equivalent.

g. 1.   (~((∃x)(∃y)Hxy ≡ (∃y)(∃x)Hxy)✓   SM

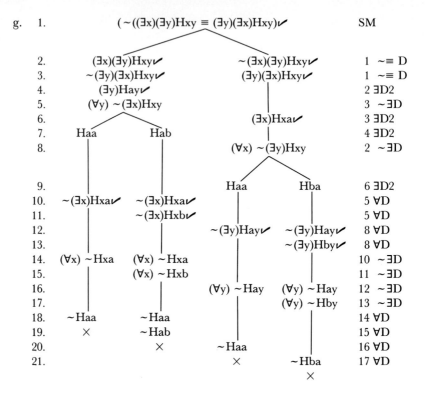

2.	1 ~≡ D
3.	1 ~≡ D
4.	2 ∃D2
5.	3 ~∃D
6.	3 ∃D2
7.	4 ∃D2
8.	2 ~∃D
9.	6 ∃D2
10.	5 ∀D
11.	5 ∀D
12.	8 ∀D
13.	8 ∀D
14.	10 ~∃D
15.	11 ~∃D
16.	12 ~∃D
17.	13 ~∃D
18.	14 ∀D
19.	15 ∀D
20.	16 ∀D
21.	17 ∀D

The tree for the negation of the corresponding biconditional is closed. Therefore the sentences are equivalent.

5.a. 1.   (∀x)(Fax ⊃ Fxa)   SM
     2.   ~(Fab ∨ Fba)✓   SM

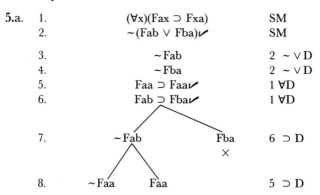

3.	2 ~∨ D
4.	2 ~∨ D
5.	1 ∀D
6.	1 ∀D
7.	6 ⊃ D
8.	5 ⊃ D

The tree has at least one completed open branch. Therefore the given set does not quantificationally entail the given sentence.

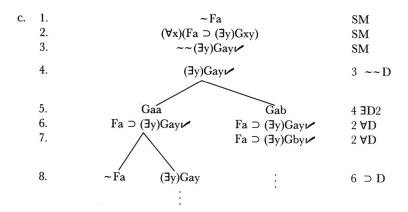

c.
1.	~Fa		SM
2.	(∀x)(Fa ⊃ (∃y)Gxy)		SM
3.	~~(∃y)Gay✔		SM
4.	(∃y)Gay✔		3 ~~D

5.	Gaa	Gab	4 ∃D2
6.	Fa ⊃ (∃y)Gay✔	Fa ⊃ (∃y)Gay✔	2 ∀D
7.		Fa ⊃ (∃y)Gby✔	2 ∀D

8.	~Fa	(∃y)Gay	:	6 ⊃ D

The tree has at least one completed open branch. Therefore the given set does not quantificationally entail the given sentence.

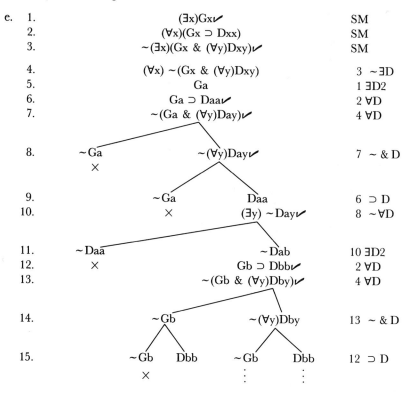

e.
1.	(∃x)Gx✔		SM
2.	(∀x)(Gx ⊃ Dxx)		SM
3.	~(∃x)(Gx & (∀y)Dxy)✔		SM
4.	(∀x) ~(Gx & (∀y)Dxy)		3 ~∃D
5.	Ga		1 ∃D2
6.	Ga ⊃ Daa✔		2 ∀D
7.	~(Ga & (∀y)Day)✔		4 ∀D

8.	~Ga	~(∀y)Day✔		7 ~ & D
	×			

9.	~Ga	Daa		6 ⊃ D
10.	×	(∃y) ~Day✔		8 ~∀D

11.	~Daa	~Dab		10 ∃D2
12.	×	Gb ⊃ Dbb✔		2 ∀D
13.		~(Gb & (∀y)Dby)✔		4 ∀D

14.	~Gb	~(∀y)Dby	13 ~ & D

15.	~Gb	Dbb	~Gb	Dbb	12 ⊃ D
	×		:	:	

The tree is not closed. Therefore the given set does not quantificationally entail the given sentence.

7. If a tree is closed, then on each branch of that tree there is some atomic sentence 𝒫 and its negation, ~𝒫. One of these sentences occurs subsequent to the other on the branch in question. Let $\mathcal{2}$ be the latter of the two sentences, and let n be the number of the line on which $\mathcal{2}$ occurs. Then n is either the last line of the branch or the second to the last line of the branch. The reason is that once both an atomic sentence and its negation have been added to a branch, that branch is closed and no further sentences can be added to the branch after the current decomposition has been completed. (Some decomposition rules do add two sentences to each branch passing through the sentence being decomposed.) Hence such a branch is finite—for no infinite branch can have a last member.

9. No. For example, consider the sentence '$(\exists x)(Fx \ \& \ \sim Fb)$' and its substitution instance 'Fb $\& \ \sim$ Fb'. Clearly, every tree for the unit set of the latter sentence will close, but the systematic tree for the unit set of '$(\exists x)(Fx \ \& \ \sim Fb)$' does not close. Rather it has at least one completed open branch:

1.		$(\exists x)(Fx \ \& \ \sim Fb)$✔	SM
2.	Fb $\& \sim$ Fb	Fa $\& \sim$ Fb	1 $\exists$D2
3.	Fb	Fa	2 & D
4.	$\sim$ Fb	$\sim$ Fa	2 & D
	$\times$		

11. Since it has already been specified that stage 1 is done before stage 2 and stage 2 before stage 3, we would have to specify the order in which work within each stage is to be done, and what constants are to be used in what order.

CHAPTER TEN

10.1.1E

a. Derive: Fa & Fb

1	$(\forall x)Fx$	Assumption
2	Fa	1 $\forall$E
3	Fb	1 $\forall$E
4	Fa & Fb	2, 3 & I

c. Derive: $\sim$ Qe

1	$(\forall z)Mz$	Assumption
2	$(\forall z) \sim Mz$	Assumption
3	Qe	Assumption
4	Ma	1 $\forall$E
5	$\sim$ Ma	2 $\forall$E
6	$\sim$ Qe	3-5 $\sim$ I

10.1.2E

a. Derive: (∃x)(Ax & Jx)

1	Jc	Assumption
2	Ac	Assumption
3	Ac & Jc	1, 2 & I
4	(∃x)(Ax & Jx)	3 ∃I

c. Derive: (∃y)(∃z)Cyz

1	(∀w)(∀z)Cwz	Assumption
2	(∀z)Ckz	1 ∀E
3	Ckr	2 ∀E
4	(∃z)Ckz	3 ∃I
5	(∃y)(∃z)Cyz	4 ∃I

10.1.3E

a. Derive: (∀y)Hy

1	(∀x)Hx	Assumption
2	Ha	1 ∀E
3	(∀y)Hy	2 ∀I

c. Derive: (∀x)(Ex ⊃ Kx)

1	(∀x)(Ex ⊃ Sx)	Assumption
2	(∀x)(Sx ⊃ Kx)	Assumption
3	Es	Assumption
4	Es ⊃ Ss	1 ∀E
5	Ss	3, 4 ⊃ E
6	Ss ⊃ Ks	2 ∀E
7	Ks	5, 6 ⊃ E
8	Es ⊃ Ks	3-7 ⊃ I
9	(∀x)(Ex ⊃ Kx)	8 ∀I

10.1.4E

1.a. Derive: $(\exists y)(Zy \lor Hy)$

1	$(\exists x)Zx$	Assumption
2	$\quad$ Za	Assumption
3	$\quad$ Za $\lor$ Ha	2 $\lor$I
4	$\quad$ $(\exists y)(Zy \lor Hy)$	3 $\exists$I
5	$(\exists y)(Zy \lor Hy)$	1, 2-4 $\exists$E

c. Derive: $(\forall x)(\exists y)Bxy$

1	$(\exists y)(\forall x)Bxy$	Assumption
2	$\quad$ $(\forall x)Bxf$	Assumption
3	$\quad$ Bhf	2 $\forall$E
4	$\quad$ $(\exists y)Bhy$	3 $\exists$I
5	$\quad$ $(\forall x)(\exists y)Bxy$	4 $\forall$I
6	$(\forall x)(\exists y)Bxy$	1, 2-5 $\exists$E

2.a. This sentence can be derived by $\forall$E applied to the sentence on line 1.

  c. This sentence cannot be derived. Note that 'Saaab' is not a substitution instance of '$(\forall x)Saaxx$'. Either 'a' can replace the free variable in the open sentence 'Saaxx', or 'b' can replace it, but they cannot both replace it in forming a substitution instance.

  e. This sentence can be derived by $\exists$I applied to the sentence on line 2.

  g. This sentence can be derived by $\exists$I applied to the sentence on line 2. Note that 'Saabb' is a substitution instance of '$(\exists w)Swwbb$'.

  i. This sentence cannot be derived. Note that $\forall$I cannot be used to derive this sentence, for 'a' occurs in an undischarged assumption on line 1, which violates the first restriction on using $\forall$I.

  k. This sentence cannot be derived. Note that 'Saabb' is *not* a substitution instance of '$(\forall x)Saxxb$'.

3.a. Derive: (Mk & Gh) & Md

1	$(\forall x)(Mx \,\&\, Gx)$	Assumption
2	Mk & Gk	1 $\forall$E
3	Mk	2 & E
4	Mh & Gh	1 $\forall$E
5	Gh	4 & E
6	Mk & Gh	3, 5 & I
7	Md & Gd	1 $\forall$E
8	Md	7 & E
9	(Mk & Gh) & Md	6, 8 & I

c. Derive: $(\exists x)(\sim Bxx \supset (\forall z)Msz)$

1	Bnn ∨ (Kn & Lj)	Assumption
2	~(∀z)Msz ⊃ ~Kn	Assumption
3	~Bnn	Assumption
4	Bnn	Assumption
5	~Kn	Assumption
6	Bnn	4 R
7	~Bnn	3 R
8	Kn	5-7 ~E
9	Kn & Lj	Assumption
10	Kn	9 & E
11	Kn	1, 4-8, 9-10 ∨ E
12	~(∀z)Msz	Assumption
13	~Kn	2, 12 ⊃ E
14	Kn	11 R
15	(∀z)Msz	12-14 ~E
16	~Bnn ⊃ (∀z)Msz	3-15 ⊃ I
17	(∃x)(~Bxx ⊃ (∀z)Msz)	16 ∃I

e. Derive: $((\forall x)Hxg \lor Rg) \lor Lg$

1	(∀z)[(Rz ∨ (∀x)Hxz) ≡ Kzzz]	Assumption
2	Kggg	Assumption
3	(Rg ∨ (∀x)Hxg) ≡ Kggg	1 ∀E
4	Rg ∨ (∀x)Hxg	2, 3 ≡ E
5	Rg	Assumption
6	(∀x)Hxg ∨ Rg	5 ∨I
7	(∀x)Hxg	Assumption
8	(∀x)Hxg ∨ Rg	7 ∨I
9	(∀x)Hxg ∨ Rg	4, 5-6, 7-8 ∨ E
10	((∀x)Hxg ∨ Rg) ∨ Lg	9 ∨I

g. Derive: $(\forall w)(\exists z) \sim (Hz \ \& \ Rzw)$

1	$(\forall z)[Hz \supset (Rzz \supset Gz)]$	Assumption
2	$(\forall z)(Gz \supset Bz) \ \& \ (\forall z) \sim Bz$	Assumption
3	$Ha \supset (Raa \supset Ga)$	1 $\forall$E
4	$(\forall z)(Gz \supset Bz)$	2 & E
5	$Ga \supset Ba$	4 $\forall$E
6	$(\forall z) \sim Bz$	2 & E
7	$Ha \ \& \ Raa$	Assumption
8	Ha	7 & E
9	$Raa \supset Ga$	8, 3 $\supset$ E
10	Raa	7 & E
11	Ga	9, 10 $\supset$ E
12	Ba	5, 11 $\supset$ E
13	$\sim Ba$	6 $\forall$E
14	$\sim(Ha \ \& \ Raa)$	7-13 $\sim$I
15	$(\exists z) \sim (Hz \ \& \ Rza)$	14 $\exists$I
16	$(\forall w)(\exists z) \sim (Hz \ \& \ Rzw)$	15 $\forall$I

i. Derive: Sc

1	$(\exists x)Px \supset Sc$	Assumption
2	$(\exists x)[Txx \ \& \ (\exists y)(Py \ \& \ \sim Jy)]$	Assumption
3	$Taa \ \& \ (\exists y)(Py \ \& \ \sim Jy)$	Assumption
4	$(\exists y)(Py \ \& \ \sim Jy)$	3 & E
5	$Pb \ \& \ \sim Jb$	Assumption
6	Pb	5 & E
7	$(\exists x)Px$	6 $\exists$I
8	Sc	1, 7 $\supset$ E
9	Sc	4, 5-8 $\exists$E
10	Sc	2, 3-9 $\exists$E

10.4E

1. Derivability

a. Derive: $(\forall z)Kzz$

1	$(\forall x)Kxx$	Assumption
2	Kcc	1 $\forall$E
3	$(\forall z)Kzz$	2 $\forall$I

c. Derive: $(\exists y)Hy$

1	$(\forall z)(Gz \supset Hz)$	Assumption
2	Gi	Assumption
3	$Gi \supset Hi$	1 $\forall$E
4	Hi	2, 3 $\supset$ E
5	$(\exists y)Hy$	4 $\exists$I

e. Derive: $(\exists x)(\exists y)(\exists z)Bxyz$

1	$(\exists y)Byyy$	Assumption
2	$Bjjj$	Assumption
3	$(\exists z)Bjjz$	2 $\exists$I
4	$(\exists y)(\exists z)Bjyz$	3 $\exists$I
5	$(\exists x)(\exists y)(\exists z)Bxyz$	4 $\exists$I
6	$(\exists x)(\exists y)(\exists z)Bxyz$	1, 2-5 $\exists$E

2. Validity

a. Derive: $(Caa\ \&\ Cab)\ \&\ (Cba\ \&\ Cbb)$

1	$(\forall x)(\forall y)Cxy$	Assumption
2	$(\forall y)Cay$	1 $\forall$E
3	Caa	2 $\forall$E
4	Cab	2 $\forall$E
5	$Caa\ \&\ Cab$	3, 4 & I
6	$(\forall y)Cby$	1 $\forall$E
7	Cba	6 $\forall$E
8	Cbb	6 $\forall$E
9	$Cba\ \&\ Cbb$	7, 8 & I
10	$(Caa\ \&\ Cab)\ \&\ (Cba\ \&\ Cbb)$	5, 9 & I

c. Derive: $(\forall x)(Hx \supset Gx)$

1	$(\forall y)[(Hy\ \&\ Fy) \supset Gy]$	Assumption
2	$(\forall z)Fz\ \&\ \sim(\forall x)Kxb$	Assumption
3	Hm	Assumption
4	$(Hm\ \&\ Fm) \supset Gm$	1 $\forall$E
5	$(\forall z)Fz$	2 & E
6	Fm	5 $\forall$E
7	$Hm\ \&\ Fm$	3, 6 & I
8	Gm	4, 7 $\supset$ E
9	$Hm \supset Gm$	3-8 $\supset$ I
10	$(\forall x)(Hx \supset Gx)$	9 $\forall$I

e. Derive: (∃w)(Aw ∨ ~Lwf)

1	(∀x)(~Ax ⊃ Kx)	Assumption
2	(∃y) ~Ky	Assumption
3	~Ka	Assumption
4	~Aa ⊃ Ka	1 ∀E
5	~Aa	Assumption
6	Ka	4, 5 ⊃ E
7	~Ka	3 R
8	Aa	5-7 ~E
9	Aa ∨ ~Laf	8 ∨I
10	(∃w)(Aw ∨ ~Lwf)	9 ∃I
11	(∃w)(Aw ∨ ~Lwf)	2, 3-10 ∃E

3. Theorems

a. Derive: (∀x)(∃y)(Ay ⊃ Ax)

1	Ac	Assumption
2	Ac	1 R
3	Ac ⊃ Ac	1-2 ⊃ I
4	(∃y)(Ay ⊃ Ac)	3 ∃I
5	(∀x)(∃y)(Ay ⊃ Ax)	4 ∀I

c. Derive: (∀x)(Ax ⊃ Bx) ⊃ ((∀x)Ax ⊃ (∀x)Bx)

1	(∀x)(Ax ⊃ Bx)	Assumption
2	(∀x)Ax	Assumption
3	Ac ⊃ Bc	1 ∀E
4	Ac	2 ∀E
5	Bc	3, 4 ⊃ E
6	(∀x)Bx	5 ∀I
7	(∀x)Ax ⊃ (∀x)Bx	2-6 ⊃ I
8	(∀x)(Ax ⊃ Bx) ⊃ ((∀x)Ax ⊃ (∀x)Bx)	1-7 ⊃ I

e. Derive: $(\forall x)(B \supset Ax) \equiv (B \supset (\forall x)Ax)$

1	$(\forall x)(B \supset Ax)$	Assumption
2	B	Assumption
3	$B \supset Ac$	1 $\forall$E
4	Ac	2, 3 $\supset$ E
5	$(\forall x)Ax$	4 $\forall$I
6	$B \supset (\forall x)Ax$	2-5 $\supset$ I
7	$B \supset (\forall x)Ax$	Assumption
8	B	Assumption
9	$(\forall x)Ax$	7, 8 $\supset$ E
10	Ac	9 $\forall$E
11	$B \supset Ac$	8-10 $\supset$ I
12	$(\forall x)(B \supset Ax)$	11 $\forall$I
13	$(\forall x)(B \supset Ax) \equiv (B \supset (\forall x)Ax)$	1-6, 7-12 $\equiv$ I

4. Equivalence

a. Derive: $(\forall x)(Ax \& Ax)$

1	$(\forall x)Ax$	Assumption
2	Ak	1 $\forall$E
3	Ak & Ak	2, 2 & I
4	$(\forall x)(Ax \& Ax)$	3 $\forall$I

Derive: $(\forall x)Ax$

1	$(\forall x)(Ax \& Ax)$	Assumption
2	Ai & Ai	1 $\forall$E
3	Ai	2 & E
4	$(\forall x)Ax$	3 $\forall$I

c. Derive: $(\exists x)Ax \lor (\exists x)Bx$

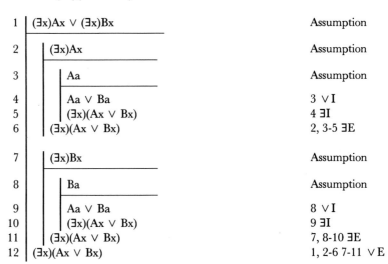

1	$(\exists x)(Ax \lor Bx)$	Assumption
2	$\quad$ Aa $\lor$ Ba	Assumption
3	$\quad\quad$ Aa	Assumption
4	$\quad\quad$ $(\exists x)Ax$	3 $\exists$I
5	$\quad\quad$ $(\exists x)Ax \lor (\exists x)Bx$	4 $\lor$I
6	$\quad\quad$ Ba	Assumption
7	$\quad\quad$ $(\exists x)Bx$	6 $\exists$I
8	$\quad\quad$ $(\exists x)Ax \lor (\exists x)Bx$	7 $\lor$I
9	$\quad$ $(\exists x)Ax \lor (\exists x)Bx$	2, 3-5, 6-8 $\lor$E
10	$(\exists x)Ax \lor (\exists x)Bx$	1, 2-9 $\exists$E

Derive: $(\exists x)(Ax \lor Bx)$

1	$(\exists x)Ax \lor (\exists x)Bx$	Assumption
2	$\quad$ $(\exists x)Ax$	Assumption
3	$\quad\quad$ Aa	Assumption
4	$\quad\quad$ Aa $\lor$ Ba	3 $\lor$I
5	$\quad\quad$ $(\exists x)(Ax \lor Bx)$	4 $\exists$I
6	$\quad$ $(\exists x)(Ax \lor Bx)$	2, 3-5 $\exists$E
7	$\quad$ $(\exists x)Bx$	Assumption
8	$\quad\quad$ Ba	Assumption
9	$\quad\quad$ Aa $\lor$ Ba	8 $\lor$I
10	$\quad\quad$ $(\exists x)(Ax \lor Bx)$	9 $\exists$I
11	$\quad$ $(\exists x)(Ax \lor Bx)$	7, 8-10 $\exists$E
12	$(\exists x)(Ax \lor Bx)$	1, 2-6 7-11 $\lor$E

e. Derive: $(\exists x) \sim Ax$

1	$\sim(\forall x)Ax$	Assumption
2	$\quad$ $\sim(\exists x) \sim Ax$	Assumption
3	$\quad\quad$ $\sim Ac$	Assumption
4	$\quad\quad$ $(\exists x) \sim Ax$	3 $\exists$I
5	$\quad\quad$ $\sim(\exists x) \sim Ax$	2 R
6	$\quad$ Ac	3-5 $\sim$E
7	$\quad$ $(\forall x)Ax$	6 $\forall$I
8	$\quad$ $\sim(\forall x)Ax$	1 R
9	$(\exists x) \sim Ax$	2-8 $\sim$E

Derive: ~(∀x)Ax

```
1 │ (∃x) ~Ax                    Assumption
2 │ │ ~Ac                       Assumption
3 │ │ │ (∀x)Ax                  Assumption
4 │ │ │ Ac                      3 ∀E
5 │ │ │ ~Ac                     2 R
6 │ │ ~(∀x)Ax                   3-5 ~I
7 │ ~(∀x)Ax                     1, 2-6 ∃E
```

5. Inconsistency

a.
```
1 │ (∀x)Hx                      Assumption
2 │ (∀y) ~(Hy ∨ Byy)            Assumption
3 │ Hc                          1 ∀E
4 │ Hc ∨ Bcc                    3 ∨I
5 │ ~(Hc ∨ Bcc)                 2 ∀E
```

c.
```
1 │ (∀x)Rx                      Assumption
2 │ (∃x) ~Rx                    Assumption
3 │ │ ~Ri                       Assumption
4 │ │ │ ~(H & ~H)               Assumption
5 │ │ │ ~Ri                     3 R
6 │ │ │ Ri                      1 ∀E
7 │ │ H & ~H                    4-6 ~E
8 │ H & ~H                      2, 3-7 ∃E
9 │ H                           8 & E
10 │ ~H                         8 & E
```

e.
```
1 │ (∀w)(∀z)(Jwz ≡ ~Jwz)       Assumption
2 │ (∀z)(Jaz ≡ ~Jaz)           1 ∀E
3 │ Jab ≡ ~Jab                 2 ∀E
4 │ │ Jab                       Assumption
5 │ │ ~Jab                      3, 4 ≡ E
6 │ │ Jab                       4 R
7 │ ~Jab                        4-6 ~I
8 │ Jab                         3, 7 ≡ E
```

6. Derivability

a. Derive: (∃x)Bx

1	(∀x)(~Bx ⊃ ~Wx)	Assumption
2	(∃x)Wx	Assumption
3	Wa	Assumption
4	~Ba ⊃ ~Wa	1 ∀E
5	~Ba	Assumption
6	~Wa	4, 5 ⊃ E
7	Wa	3 R
8	Ba	5-7 ~E
9	(∃x)Bx	8 ∃I
10	(∃x)Bx	2, 3-9 ∃E

c. Derive: Ha ⊃ (∃x)Sxcc

1	(∀x)(Hx ⊃ (∀y)Rxyb)	Assumption
2	(∀x)(∀z)(Razx ⊃ Sxzz)	Assumption
3	Ha	Assumption
4	Ha ⊃ (∀y)Rayb	1 ∀E
5	(∀y)Rayb	3, 4 ⊃ E
6	Racb	5 ∀E
7	(∀z)(Razb ⊃ Sbzz)	2 ∀E
8	Racb ⊃ Sbcc	7 ∀E
9	Sbcc	6, 8 ⊃ E
10	(∃x)Sxcc	9 ∃I
11	Ha ⊃ (∃x)Sxcc	3-10 ⊃ I

e. Derive: (∃z)Lz ⊃ (∃y)Ky

1	(∀z)(~Lz ∨ (∃y)Ky)	Assumption
2	(∃z)Lz	Assumption
3	La	Assumption
4	~La ∨ (∃y)Ky	1 ∀E
5	~La	Assumption
6	~(∃y)Ky	Assumption
7	La	3 R
8	~La	5 R
9	(∃y)Ky	6-8 ~E
10	(∃y)Ky	Assumption
11	(∃y)Ky	10 R
12	(∃y)Ky	4, 5-9, 10-11 ∨E
13	(∃y)Ky	2, 3-12 ∃E
14	(∃z)Lz ⊃ (∃y)Ky	2-13 ⊃I

7. Validity

a. Derive: (∀x)(Zx ⊃ (∃y)(Ky ∨ Sy))

1	(∀x)(Zx ⊃ (∃y)Ky)	Assumption
2	Za ⊃ (∃y)Ky	1 ∀E
3	Za	Assumption
4	(∃y)Ky	2, 3 ⊃E
5	Kb	Assumption
6	Kb ∨ Sb	5 ∨I
7	(∃y)(Ky ∨ Sy)	6 ∃I
8	(∃y)(Ky ∨ Sy)	4, 5-7 ∃E
9	Za ⊃ (∃y)(Ky ∨ Sy)	3-8 ⊃I
10	(∀x)(Zx ⊃ (∃y)(Ky ∨ Sy))	9 ∀I

c. Derive: (∃z)[Bz & (∀y)(By ⊃ Hzy)]

1	(∀x)(∀y)[(Hky & Hxk) ⊃ Hxy]		Assumption
2	(∀z)(Bz ⊃ Hkz)		Assumption
3	(∃x)(Bx & Hxk)		Assumption
4		Bi & Hik	Assumption
5			Ba	Assumption
6			Ba ⊃ Hka	2 ∀E
7			Hka	5, 6 ⊃ E
8			Hik	4 & E
9			Hka & Hik	7, 8 & I
10			(∀y)[(Hky & Hik) ⊃ Hiy]	1 ∀E
11			(Hka & Hik) ⊃ Hia	10 ∀E
12			Hia	9, 11 ⊃ E
13		Ba ⊃ Hia	5-12 ⊃ I
14		(∀y)(By ⊃ Hiy)	13 ∀I
15		Bi	4 & E
16		Bi & (∀y)(By ⊃ Hiy)	15, 14 & I
17		(∃z)[Bz & (∀y)(By ⊃ Hzy)]	16 ∃I
18	(∃z)[Bz & (∀y)(By ⊃ Hzy)]		3, 4-17 ∃E

e. Derive: (∀w)([Gw & (∃z)(Gz & Hwz)] ⊃ Hww)

1	(∀x)(∀y)[(Gx & Gy) ⊃ (Hxy ⊃ Hyx)]	Assumption
2	(∀x)(∀y)(∀z)([(Gx & Gy) & Gx] ⊃ [(Hxy & Hyz) ⊃ Hxz])	Assumption
3	Ga & (∃z)(Gz & Haz)	Assumption
4	(∃z)(Gz & Haz)	3 & E
5	Gb & Hab	Assumption
6	(∀y)[(Ga & Gy) ⊃ (Hay ⊃ Hya)]	1 ∀E
7	(Ga & Gb) ⊃ (Hab ⊃ Hba)	6 ∀E
8	Gb	5 & E
9	Ga	3 & E
10	Ga & Gb	9, 8 & I
11	Hab ⊃ Hba	10, 7 ⊃ E
12	Hab	5 & E
13	Hba	11, 12 ⊃ E
14	Hab & Hba	12, 13 & I
15	(∀y)(∀z)([(Ga & Gy) & Gz] ⊃ [(Hay & Hyz) ⊃ Haz])	2 ∀E
16	(∀z)([(Ga & Gb) & Gz] ⊃ [(Hab & Hbz) ⊃ Haz])	15 ∀E
17	[(Ga & Gb) & Ga] ⊃ [(Hab & Hba) ⊃ Haa]	16 ∀E
18	(Ga & Gb) & Ga	10, 9 & I
19	(Hab & Hba) ⊃ Haa	17, 18 ⊃ E
20	Haa	14, 19 ⊃ E
21	Haa	4, 5-20 ∃E
22	[Ga & (∃z)(Gz & Haz)] ⊃ Haa	3-21 ⊃ I
23	(∀w)([Gw & (∃z)(Gz & Hwz)] ⊃ Hww)	22 ∀I

8. Theorems

a. Derive: [(∀x)(∀y)Axy & (∀x)(Axx ⊃ B)] ⊃ B

1	(∀x)(∀y)Axy & (∀x)(Axx ⊃ B)	Assumption
2	(∀x)(Axx ⊃ B)	1 & E
3	Akk ⊃ B	2 ∀E
4	(∀x)(∀y)Axy	1 & E
5	(∀y)Aky	4 ∀E
6	Akk	5 ∀E
7	B	3, 6 ⊃ E
8	[(∀x)(∀y)Axy & (∀x)(Axx ⊃ B)] ⊃ B	1-7 ⊃ I

c. Derive: $(\forall x)Ax \equiv \sim(\exists x) \sim Ax$

1	$(\forall x)Ax$	Assumption
2	$(\exists x) \sim Ax$	Assumption
3	$\sim Ac$	Assumption
4	$(\exists x) \sim Ax$	Assumption
5	Ac	1 $\forall$E
6	$\sim Ac$	3 R
7	$\sim(\exists x) \sim Ax$	4-6 $\sim$I
8	$\sim(\exists x) \sim Ax$	2, 3-7 $\exists$E
9	$(\exists x) \sim Ax$	2 R
10	$\sim(\exists x) \sim Ax$	2-9 $\sim$I
11	$\sim(\exists x) \sim Ax$	Assumption
12	$\sim Ac$	Assumption
13	$(\exists x) \sim Ax$	12 $\exists$I
14	$\sim(\exists x) \sim Ax$	11 R
15	Ac	12-14 $\sim$E
16	$(\forall x)Ax$	15 $\forall$I
17	$(\forall x)Ax \equiv \sim(\exists x) \sim Ax$	1-10, 11-16 $\equiv$ I

e. Derive: (∃x)(B ⊃ Ax) ≡ (B ⊃ (∃x)Ax)

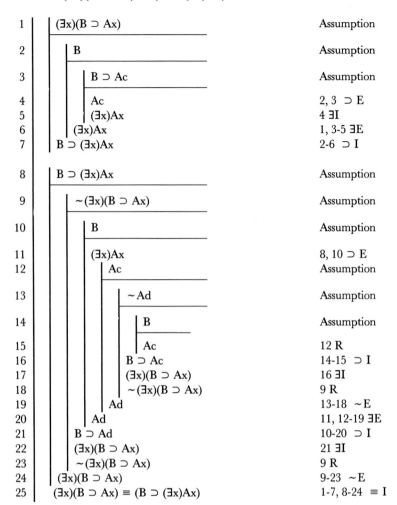

1	(∃x)(B ⊃ Ax)	Assumption
2	B	Assumption
3	B ⊃ Ac	Assumption
4	Ac	2, 3 ⊃ E
5	(∃x)Ax	4 ∃I
6	(∃x)Ax	1, 3-5 ∃E
7	B ⊃ (∃x)Ax	2-6 ⊃ I
8	B ⊃ (∃x)Ax	Assumption
9	~(∃x)(B ⊃ Ax)	Assumption
10	B	Assumption
11	(∃x)Ax	8, 10 ⊃ E
12	Ac	Assumption
13	~Ad	Assumption
14	B	Assumption
15	Ac	12 R
16	B ⊃ Ac	14-15 ⊃ I
17	(∃x)(B ⊃ Ax)	16 ∃I
18	~(∃x)(B ⊃ Ax)	9 R
19	Ad	13-18 ~E
20	Ad	11, 12-19 ∃E
21	B ⊃ Ad	10-20 ⊃ I
22	(∃x)(B ⊃ Ax)	21 ∃I
23	~(∃x)(B ⊃ Ax)	9 R
24	(∃x)(B ⊃ Ax)	9-23 ~E
25	(∃x)(B ⊃ Ax) ≡ (B ⊃ (∃x)Ax)	1-7, 8-24 ≡ I

9. Equivalence

a. Derive: (∀x)(Bx ⊃ Bx)

1	(∀x)(Ax ⊃ Ax)	Assumption
2	Ba	Assumption
3	Ba	2 R
4	Ba ⊃ Ba	2-3 ⊃ I
5	(∀x)(Bx ⊃ Bx)	4 ∀I

Derive: (∀x)(Ax ⊃ Ax)

1	(∀x)(Bx ⊃ Bx)	Assumption
2	Aa	Assumption
3	Aa	2 R
4	Aa ⊃ Aa	2-3 ⊃ I
5	(∀x)(Ax ⊃ Ax)	4 ∀I

c. Derive: (∃y) ~ By ⊃ (∀x) ~ Ax

1	(∀x)(∀y)(Ax ⊃ By)	Assumption
2	(∃y) ~ By	Assumption
3	~ Ba	Assumption
4	(∀y)(Ab ⊃ By)	1 ∀E
5	Ab ⊃ Ba	4 ∀E
6	Ab	Assumption
7	Ba	5, 6 ⊃ E
8	~ Ba	3 R
9	~ Ab	6-8 ~ I
10	(∀x) ~ Ax	9 ∀I
11	(∀x) ~ Ax	2, 3-10 ∃E
12	(∃y) ~ By ⊃ (∀x) ~ Ax	2-11 ⊃ I

Derive: (∀x)(∀y)(Ax ⊃ By)

1	(∃y) ~ By ⊃ (∀x) ~ Ax	Assumption
2	Aa	Assumption
3	~ Bb	Assumption
4	(∃y) ~ By	3 ∃I
5	(∀x) ~ Ax	1, 4 ⊃ E
6	~ Aa	5 ∀E
7	Aa	2 R
8	Bb	3-7 ~ E
9	Aa ⊃ Bb	2-8 ⊃ I
10	(∀y)(Aa ⊃ By)	9 ∀I
11	(∀x)(∀y)(Ax ⊃ By)	10 ∀I

e. Derive: $\sim(\forall x)Ax \lor (\forall y)By$

1	$(\exists x)(\forall y)(Ax \supset By)$	Assumption
2	$(\forall y)(Aa \supset By)$	Assumption
3	$Aa \supset Bb$	2 $\forall$E
4	$\sim(\sim(\forall x)Ax \lor (\forall y)By)$	Assumption
5	$(\forall x)Ax$	Assumption
6	Aa	5 $\forall$E
7	Bb	3, 6 $\supset$ E
8	$(\forall y)By$	7 $\forall$I
9	$\sim(\forall x)Ax \lor (\forall y)By$	8 $\lor$I
10	$\sim(\sim(\forall x)Ax \lor (\forall y)By)$	4 R
11	$\sim(\forall x)Ax$	5-10 $\sim$I
12	$\sim(\forall x)Ax \lor (\forall y)By$	11 $\lor$I
13	$\sim(\sim(\forall x)Ax \lor (\forall y)By)$	4 R
14	$\sim(\forall x)Ax \lor (\forall y)By$	4-13 $\sim$E
15	$\sim(\forall x)Ax \lor (\forall y)By$	1, 2-14 $\exists$E

Derive: (∃x)(∀y)(Ax ⊃ By)

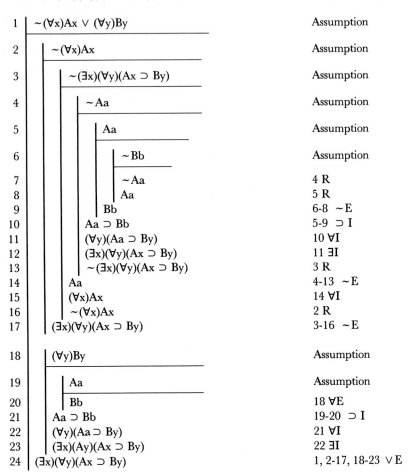

1	~(∀x)Ax ∨ (∀y)By	Assumption
2	~(∀x)Ax	Assumption
3	~(∃x)(∀y)(Ax ⊃ By)	Assumption
4	~Aa	Assumption
5	Aa	Assumption
6	~Bb	Assumption
7	~Aa	4 R
8	Aa	5 R
9	Bb	6-8 ~E
10	Aa ⊃ Bb	5-9 ⊃I
11	(∀y)(Aa ⊃ By)	10 ∀I
12	(∃x)(∀y)(Ax ⊃ By)	11 ∃I
13	~(∃x)(∀y)(Ax ⊃ By)	3 R
14	Aa	4-13 ~E
15	(∀x)Ax	14 ∀I
16	~(∀x)Ax	2 R
17	(∃x)(∀y)(Ax ⊃ By)	3-16 ~E
18	(∀y)By	Assumption
19	Aa	Assumption
20	Bb	18 ∀E
21	Aa ⊃ Bb	19-20 ⊃I
22	(∀y)(Aa ⊃ By)	21 ∀I
23	(∃x)(Ay)(Ax ⊃ By)	22 ∃I
24	(∃x)(∀y)(Ax ⊃ By)	1, 2-17, 18-23 ∨E

10. Inconsistency

a. 1	(∀y)(∃z)Byz	Assumption
2	(∀w) ~Baw	Assumption
3	(∃z)Baz	1 ∀E
4	Bab	Assumption
5	(∀w) ~Baw	Assumption
6	~Bab	5 ∀E
7	Bab	4 R
8	~(∀w) ~Baw	5-7 ~I
9	~(∀w) ~Baw	3, 4-8 ∃E
10	(∀w) ~Baw	2 R

c. 1 | $(\exists x)(\sim Bx \And Lxx)$ | Assumption
2 | $(\forall z)(Cz \And Bz)$ | Assumption
3 | $(\forall y)[(By \And \sim Cy) \equiv Lyy]$ | Assumption

4 | $\sim Bi \And Lii$ | Assumption

5 | $(Bi \And \sim Ci) \equiv Lii$ | $3 \forall E$
6 | Lii | $4 \And E$
7 | $Bi \And \sim Ci$ | $5, 6 \equiv E$
8 | $\sim(M \And \sim M)$ | Assumption

9 | Bi | $7 \And E$
10 | $\sim Bi$ | $4 \And E$
11 | $M \And \sim M$ | $8\text{-}10 \sim E$
12 | $M \And \sim M$ | $1, 4\text{-}11 \exists E$
13 | M | $12 \And E$
14 | $\sim M$ | $12 \And E$

e. 1 | $(\exists x)(\exists y)Fxy \lor (\forall x)(\forall y)(\forall z)Hxxyz$ | Assumption
2 | $(\exists x)(\exists y)Fxy \supset \sim Haaab$ | Assumption
3 | $(Hbbba \lor \sim Haaab) \equiv (\forall x) \sim (Ax \lor \sim Ax)$ | Assumption

4 | $(\exists x)(\exists y)Fxy$ | Assumption

5 | $\sim Haaab$ | $2, 4 \supset E$
6 | $Hbbba \lor \sim Haaab$ | $5 \lor I$

7 | $(\forall x)(\forall y)(\forall z)Hxxyz$ | Assumption

8 | $(\forall y)(\forall z)Hbbyz$ | $7 \forall E$
9 | $(\forall z)Hbbbz$ | $8 \forall E$
10 | $Hbbba$ | $9 \forall E$
11 | $Hbbba \lor \sim Haaab$ | $10 \lor I$
12 | $Hbbba \lor \sim Haaab$ | $1, 4\text{-}6, 7\text{-}11 \lor E$
13 | $(\forall x) \sim (Ax \lor \sim Ax)$ | $3, 12 \equiv E$
14 | Ac | Assumption

15 | $Ac \lor \sim Ac$ | $14 \lor T$
16 | $\sim(Ac \lor \sim Ac)$ | $13 \forall E$
17 | $\sim Ac$ | $14\text{-}16 \sim I$
18 | $Ac \lor \sim Ac$ | $17 \lor I$
19 | $\sim(Ac \lor \sim Ac)$ | $13 \forall E$

11. Validity

a. Derive: (∃x)(Fxg & Cx)

```
1  │ (∀x)[Sx ⊃ (Cx ∨ Bx)]                      Assumption
2  │ (∃x)[Fxg & (Sx & ~Bx)]                    Assumption

3  │  ┌ Fkg & (Sk & ~Bk)                        Assumption

4  │  │ Sk ⊃ (Ck ∨ Bk)                          1 ∀E
5  │  │ Sk & ~Bk                                3 & E
6  │  │ Sk                                      5 & E
7  │  │ Ck ∨ Bk                                 4, 6 ⊃ E
8  │  │  ┌ Ck                                   Assumption

9  │  │  │ Ck                                   8 R

10 │  │  ┌ Bk                                   Assumption

11 │  │  │  ┌ ~Ck                               Assumption
12 │  │  │  │ Bk                                10 R
13 │  │  │  │ ~Bk                               5 & E
14 │  │  │ Ck                                   11-13 ~E
15 │  │ Ck                                      7, 8-9, 10-14 ∨ E
16 │  │ Fkg                                     3 & E
17 │  │ Fkg & Ck                                16, 15 & I
18 │  │ (∃x)(Fxg & Cx)                          17 ∃I
19 │ (∃x)(Fxg & Cx)                             2, 3-18 ∃E
```

c. Derive: Fnm

```
1  │ (∀x)[(∃y)(∃z)[ ~Iyz & (Lyx & Lzx)] ⊃
   │    (∀z)((∃y)[Lyz & (∀w)(Lwz ⊃ Iwy)] ⊃ Fxz)]    Assumption
2  │ ~Ihg & (Lhn & Lgn)                              Assumption
3  │ Ldm & (∀w)(Lwm ⊃ Iwd)                           Assumption

4  │ (∃y)(∃z)[ ~Iyz & (Lyn & Lzn)] ⊃
   │    (∀z)((∃y)[Lyz & (∀w)(Lwz ⊃ Iwy)] ⊃ Fnz)      1 ∀E
5  │ (∃z)[ ~Ihz & (Lhn & Lzn)]                       2 ∃I
6  │ (∃y)(∃z)[ ~Iyz & (Lyn & Lzn)]                   5 ∃I
7  │ (∀z)((∃y)[Lyz & (∀w)(Lwz ⊃ Iwy)] ⊃ Fnz)         4, 6 ⊃ E
8  │ (∃y)[Lym & (∀w)(Lwm ⊃ Iwy)] ⊃ Fnm               7 ∀E
9  │ (∃y)[Lym & (∀w)(Lwm ⊃ Iwy)]                     3 ∃I
10 │ Fnm                                             8, 9 ⊃ E
```

e. Derive: $(\forall x)[Hx \supset \sim(\exists y)(Hy \ \& \ Sxy)] \supset (\exists z)(Lz \ \& \ Szz)$

1	$(\exists x)[Hx \ \& \ (\exists y)(Dy \ \& \ Sxy)]$		Assumption
2	$(\exists x)[Hx \ \& \ (\forall y)(Dy \supset \sim Sxy)]$		Assumption
3	$(\forall x)(\forall y)([(Px \ \& \ Sxy) \ \& \ (Dy \lor Hy)] \supset Lx)$		Assumption
4	$(\forall x)[Hx \supset (Px \ \& \ (\forall y)[Sxy \supset (Dy \lor Hy)])]$		Assumption
5	$(\forall x)(Hx \supset (\exists y)Sxy)$		Assumption
6	$\qquad (\forall x)[Hx \supset \sim(\exists y)(Hy \ \& \ Sxy)]$		Assumption
7	$\qquad\quad Ha \ \& \ (\forall y)(Dy \supset \sim Say)$		Assumption
8	$\qquad\quad Ha \supset (Pa \ \& \ (\forall y)[Say \supset (Dy \lor Hy)])$		4 $\forall$E
9	$\qquad\quad Ha$		7 & E
10	$\qquad\quad Pa \ \& \ (\forall y)[Say \supset (Dy \lor Hy)]$		8, 9 $\supset$ E
11	$\qquad\quad (\forall y)[Say \supset (Dy \lor Hy)]$		10 & E
12	$\qquad\quad Ha \supset (\exists y)Say$		5 $\forall$E
13	$\qquad\quad (\exists y)Say$		9, 12 $\supset$ E
14	$\qquad\qquad Sab$		Assumption
15	$\qquad\qquad Sab \supset (Db \lor Hb)$		11 $\forall$E
16	$\qquad\qquad Db \lor Hb$		14, 15 $\supset$ E
17	$\qquad\qquad\quad Db$		Assumption
18	$\qquad\qquad\quad (\forall y)(Dy \supset \sim Say)$		7 & E
19	$\qquad\qquad\quad Db \supset \sim Sab$		18 $\forall$E
20	$\qquad\qquad\qquad \sim Hb$		Assumption
21	$\qquad\qquad\qquad \sim Sab$		17, 19 $\supset$ E
22	$\qquad\qquad\qquad Sab$		14 R
23	$\qquad\qquad\quad Hb$		20-22 $\sim$ E
24	$\qquad\qquad\quad Hb$		Assumption
25	$\qquad\qquad\quad Hb$		24 R
26	$\qquad\qquad Hb$		16, 17-23, 24-25 $\lor$ E
27	$\qquad\qquad Hb \ \& \ Sab$		26, 14 & I
28	$\qquad\qquad (\exists y)(Hy \ \& \ Say)$		27 $\exists$I
29	$\qquad\quad (\exists y)(Hy \ \& \ Say)$		13, 14-28 $\exists$E
30	$\qquad\qquad \sim(\exists z)(Lz \ \& \ Szz)$		Assumption
31	$\qquad\qquad (\exists y)(Hy \ \& \ Say)$		29 R
32	$\qquad\qquad Ha \supset \sim(\exists y)(Hy \ \& \ Say)$		6 $\forall$E
33	$\qquad\qquad \sim(\exists y)(Hy \ \& \ Say)$		9, 32 $\supset$ E
34	$\qquad\quad (\exists z)(Lz \ \& \ Szz)$		30-33 $\sim$ E
35	$\qquad (\exists z)(Lz \ \& \ Szz)$		2, 7-34 $\exists$E
36	$(\forall x)[Hx \supset \sim(\exists y)(Hy \ \& \ Sxy)] \supset (\exists z)(Lz \ \& \ Szz)$		6-35 $\supset$ I

12. Inconsistency

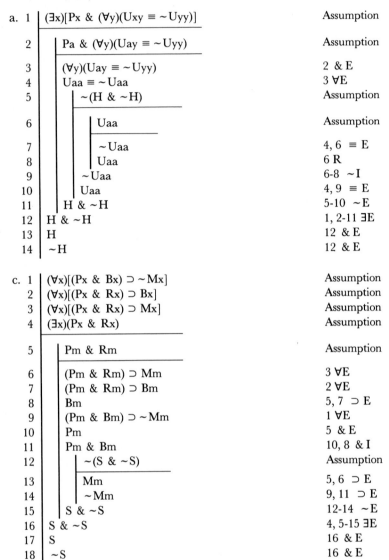

a.

1	(∃x)[Px & (∀y)(Uxy ≡ ~Uyy)]	Assumption
2	Pa & (∀y)(Uay ≡ ~Uyy)	Assumption
3	(∀y)(Uay ≡ ~Uyy)	2 & E
4	Uaa ≡ ~Uaa	3 ∀E
5	~(H & ~H)	Assumption
6	Uaa	Assumption
7	~Uaa	4, 6 ≡ E
8	Uaa	6 R
9	~Uaa	6-8 ~I
10	Uaa	4, 9 ≡ E
11	H & ~H	5-10 ~E
12	H & ~H	1, 2-11 ∃E
13	H	12 & E
14	~H	12 & E

c.

1	(∀x)[(Px & Bx) ⊃ ~Mx]	Assumption
2	(∀x)[(Px & Rx) ⊃ Bx]	Assumption
3	(∀x)[(Px & Rx) ⊃ Mx]	Assumption
4	(∃x)(Px & Rx)	Assumption
5	Pm & Rm	Assumption
6	(Pm & Rm) ⊃ Mm	3 ∀E
7	(Pm & Rm) ⊃ Bm	2 ∀E
8	Bm	5, 7 ⊃ E
9	(Pm & Bm) ⊃ ~Mm	1 ∀E
10	Pm	5 & E
11	Pm & Bm	10, 8 & I
12	~(S & ~S)	Assumption
13	Mm	5, 6 ⊃ E
14	~Mm	9, 11 ⊃ E
15	S & ~S	12-14 ~E
16	S & ~S	4, 5-15 ∃E
17	S	16 & E
18	~S	16 & E

10.5E

1. Derivability

a. Derive: $(\exists y)(\sim Fy \lor \sim Gy)$

1	$\sim(\forall y)(Fy \ \& \ Gy)$	Assumption
2	$(\exists y) \sim (Fy \ \& \ Gy)$	1 QN
3	$(\exists y)(\sim Fy \lor \sim Gy)$	2 DeM

c. Derive: $(\exists z)(Az \ \& \ \sim Cz)$

1	$(\exists z)(Gz \ \& \ Az)$	Assumption
2	$(\forall y)(Cy \supset \sim Gy)$	Assumption
3	Gh & Ah	Assumption
4	Ch $\supset \sim$ Gh	2 $\forall$E
5	Gh	3 & E
6	$\sim\sim$ Gh	5 DN
7	$\sim$ Ch	4, 6 MT
8	Ah	3 & E
9	Ah & $\sim$ Ch	8, 7 & I
10	$(\exists z)(Az \ \& \ \sim Cz)$	9 $\exists$I
11	$(\exists z)(Az \ \& \ \sim Cz)$	1, 3-10 $\exists$E

e. Derive: $(\exists x)Cxb$

1	$(\forall x)[(\sim Cxb \lor Hx) \supset Lxx]$	Assumption
2	$(\exists y) \sim Lyy$	Assumption
3	$\sim$ Lmm	Assumption
4	$(\sim Cmb \lor Hm) \supset Lmm$	1 $\forall$E
5	$\sim(\sim Cmb \lor Hm)$	3, 4 MT
6	$\sim\sim$ Cmb & $\sim$ Hm	5 DeM
7	$\sim\sim$ Cmb	6 & E
8	Cmb	7 DN
9	$(\exists x)Cxb$	8 $\exists$I
10	$(\exists x)Cxb$	2, 3-9 $\exists$E

2. Validity

a. Derive: $(\forall y) \sim (Hby \lor Ryy)$

1	$(\forall y) \sim Jx$	Assumption
2	$(\exists y)(Hby \lor Ryy) \supset (\exists x)Jx$	Assumption
3	$\sim(\exists x)Jx$	1 QN
4	$\sim(\exists y)(Hby \lor Ryy)$	2, 3 MT
5	$(\forall y) \sim (Hby \lor Ryy)$	4 QN

c. Derive: $(\forall x)(\forall y)Hxy \ \& \ (\forall x) \sim Tx$

1	$(\forall x) \sim ((\forall y)Hyx \lor Tx)$	Assumption
2	$\sim (\exists y)(Ty \lor (\exists x) \sim Hxy)$	Assumption
3	$(\forall y) \sim (Ty \lor (\exists x) \sim Hxy)$	2 QN
4	$\sim (Ta \lor (\exists x) \sim Hxa)$	3 $\forall$E
5	$\sim Ta \ \& \sim (\exists x) \sim Hxa$	4 DeM
6	$\sim (\exists x) \sim Hxa$	5 & E
7	$(\forall x) \sim\sim Hxa$	6 QN
8	$\sim\sim Hba$	7 $\forall$E
9	Hba	8 DN
10	$(\forall y)Hby$	9 $\forall$I
11	$(\forall x)(\forall y)Hxy$	10 $\forall$I
12	$\sim Ta$	5 & E
13	$(\forall x) \sim Tx$	12 $\forall$I
14	$(\forall x)(\forall y)Hxy \ \& \ (\forall x) \sim Tx$	11, 13 & I

e. Derive: $(\exists x) \sim Kxx$

1	$(\forall z)[Kzz \supset (Mz \ \& \ Nz)]$	Assumption
2	$(\exists z) \sim Nz$	Assumption
3	$\quad \sim Ng$	Assumption
4	$\quad Kgg \supset (Mg \ \& \ Ng)$	1 $\forall$E
5	$\quad \sim Mg \lor \sim Ng$	3 $\lor$I
6	$\quad \sim (Mg \ \& \ Ng)$	5 DeM
7	$\quad \sim Kgg$	4, 6 MT
8	$\quad (\exists x) \sim Kxx$	7 $\exists$I
9	$(\exists x) \sim Kxx$	2, 3-8 $\exists$E

g. Derive: $(\exists w)(Qw \And Bw) \supset (\forall y)(Lyy \supset \sim Ay)$

1	$(\exists z)Qz \supset (\forall w)(Lww \supset \sim Hw)$	Assumption
2	$(\exists x)Bx \supset (\forall y)(Ay \supset Hy)$	Assumption
3	$(\exists w)(Qw \And Bw)$	Assumption
4	$Qm \And Bm$	Assumption
5	Qm	4 & E
6	$(\exists z)Qz$	5 ∃I
7	$(\forall w)(Lww \supset \sim Hw)$	1, 6 ⊃ E
8	$Lcc \supset \sim Hc$	7 ∀E
9	Bm	4 & E
10	$(\exists x)Bx$	9 ∃I
11	$(\forall y)(Ay \supset Hy)$	2, 10 ⊃ E
12	$Ac \supset Hc$	11 ∀E
13	$\sim Hc \supset \sim Ac$	12 Trans
14	$Lcc \supset \sim Ac$	8, 13 HS
15	$(\forall y)(Lyy \supset \sim Ay)$	14 ∀I
16	$(\forall y)(Lyy \supset \sim Ay)$	3, 4-15 ∃E
17	$(\exists w)(Qw \And Bw) \supset (\forall y)(Lyy \supset \sim Ay)$	3-16 ⊃ I

i. Derive: $\sim(\forall x)(\forall y)Bxy \supset (\forall x)(\sim Px \lor \sim Hx)$

1	$\sim(\forall x)(\sim Px \lor \sim Hx) \supset (\forall x)[Cx \And (\forall y)(Ly \supset Axy)]$	Assumption
2	$(\exists x)[Hx \And (\forall y)(Ly \supset Axy)] \supset (\forall x)(Rx \And (\forall y)Bxy)$	Assumption
3	$\sim(\forall x)(\sim Px \lor \sim Hx)$	Assumption
4	$(\exists x) \sim (\sim Px \lor \sim Hx)$	3 QN
5	$\sim(\sim Pi \lor \sim Hi)$	Assumption
6	$\sim\sim Pi \And \sim\sim Hi$	5 DeM
7	$\sim\sim Hi$	6 & E
8	Hi	7 DN
9	$(\forall x)[Cx \And (\forall y)(Ly \supset Axy)]$	1, 3 ⊃ E
10	$Ci \And (\forall y)(Ly \supset Aiy)$	9 ∀E
11	$(\forall y)(Ly \supset Aiy)$	10 & E
12	$Hi \And (\forall y)(Ly \supset Aiy)$	8, 11 & I
13	$(\exists x)[Hx \And (\forall y)(Ly \supset Axy)]$	12 ∃I
14	$(\forall x)(Rx \And (\forall y)Bxy)$	2, 13 ⊃ E
15	$Rj \And (\forall y)Bjy$	14 ∀E
16	$(\forall y)Bjy$	15 & E
17	$(\forall x)(\forall y)Bxy$	16 ∀I
18	$(\forall x)(\forall y)Bxy$	4, 5-17 ∃E
19	$\sim(\forall x)(\sim Px \lor \sim Hx) \supset (\forall x)(\forall y)Bxy$	3-18 ⊃ I
20	$\sim(\forall x)(\forall y)Bxy \supset \sim\sim(\forall x)(\sim Px \lor \sim Hx)$	19 Trans
21	$\sim(\forall x)(\forall y)Bxy \supset (\forall x)(\sim Px \lor \sim Hx)$	20 DN

3. Theorems

a. Derive: $(\forall x)(Ax \supset Bx) \supset (\forall x)(Bx \lor \sim Ax)$

1	$(\forall x)(Ax \supset Bx)$	Assumption
2	$(\forall x)(\sim Ax \lor Bx)$	1 Impl
3	$(\forall x)(Bx \lor \sim Ax)$	2 Com
4	$(\forall x)(Ax \supset Bx) \supset (\forall x)(Bx \lor \sim Ax)$	1-3 $\supset$ I

c. Derive: $\sim(\exists x)(Ax \lor Bx) \supset (\forall x) \sim Ax$

1	$\sim(\exists x)(Ax \lor Bx)$	Assumption
2	$(\forall x) \sim(Ax \lor Bx)$	1 QN
3	$\sim(Ac \lor Bc)$	2 $\forall$E
4	$\sim Ac \;\&\; \sim Bc$	3 DeM
5	$\sim Ac$	4 & E
6	$(\forall x) \sim Ax$	5 $\forall$I
7	$\sim(\exists x)(Ax \lor Bx) \supset (\forall x) \sim Ax$	1-6 $\supset$ I

e. Derive: $((\exists x)Ax \supset (\exists x)Bx) \supset (\exists x)(Ax \supset Bx)$

1	$\sim(\exists x)(Ax \supset Bx)$	Assumption
2	$(\forall x) \sim(Ax \supset Bx)$	1 QN
3	$\sim(Ac \supset Bc)$	2 $\forall$E
4	$\sim(\sim Ac \lor Bc)$	3 Impl
5	$\sim\sim Ac \;\&\; \sim Bc$	4 DeM
6	$\sim\sim Ac$	5 & E
7	$(\exists x) \sim\sim Ax$	6 $\exists$I
8	$\sim(\forall x) \sim Ax$	7 QN
9	$\sim\sim(\exists x)Ax$	8 QN
10	$\sim Bc$	5 & E
11	$(\forall x) \sim Bx$	10 $\forall$I
12	$\sim(\exists x)Bx$	11 QN
13	$\sim\sim(\exists x)Ax \;\&\; \sim(\exists x)Bx$	9, 12 & I
14	$\sim(\sim(\exists x)Ax \lor (\exists x)Bx)$	13 DeM
15	$\sim((\exists x)Ax \supset (\exists x)Bx)$	14 Impl
16	$\sim(\exists x)(Ax \supset Bx) \supset \sim((\exists x)Ax \supset (\exists x)Bx)$	1-15 $\supset$ I
17	$((\exists x)Ax \supset (\exists x)Bx) \supset (\exists x)(Ax \supset Bx)$	16 Trans

4. Equivalence

a. Derive: $(\exists x)(Ax \;\&\; \sim Bx)$

1	$\sim(\forall x)(Ax \supset Bx)$	Assumption
2	$(\exists x) \sim(Ax \supset Bx)$	1 QN
3	$(\exists x) \sim(\sim Ax \lor Bx)$	2 Impl
4	$(\exists x)(\sim\sim Ax \;\&\; \sim Bx)$	3 DeM
5	$(\exists x)(Ax \;\&\; \sim Bx)$	4 DN

Derive: $\sim(\forall x)(Ax \supset Bx)$

1	$(\exists x)(Ax \;\&\; \sim Bx)$	Assumption
2	$(\exists x)(\sim\sim Ax \;\&\; \sim Bx)$	1 DN
3	$(\exists x) \sim(\sim Ax \lor Bx)$	2 DeM
4	$(\exists x) \sim(Ax \supset Bx)$	3 Impl
5	$\sim(\forall x)(Ax \supset Bx)$	4 QN

c. Derive: $(\exists x)[\sim Ax \lor (\sim Cx \supset \sim Bx)]$

1	$\sim(\forall x) \sim[(Ax \;\&\; Bx) \supset Cx]$	Assumption
2	$(\exists x) \sim\sim[(Ax \;\&\; Bx) \supset Cx]$	1 QN
3	$(\exists x)[(Ax \;\&\; Bx) \supset Cx]$	2 DN
4	$(\exists x)[Ax \supset (Bx \supset Cx)]$	3 Exp
5	$(\exists x)[\sim Ax \lor (Bx \supset Cx)]$	4 Impl
6	$(\exists x)[\sim Ax \lor (\sim Cx \supset \sim Bx)]$	5 Trans

Derive: $\sim(\forall x) \sim[(Ax \;\&\; Bx) \supset Cx]$

1	$(\exists x)[\sim Ax \lor (\sim Cx \supset \sim Bx)]$	Assumption
2	$(\exists x)[\sim Ax \lor (Bx \supset Cx)]$	1 Trans
3	$(\exists x)[Ax \supset (Bx \supset Cx)]$	2 Impl
4	$(\exists x)[(Ax \;\&\; Bx) \supset Cx]$	3 Exp
5	$\sim\sim(\exists x)[(Ax \;\&\; Bx) \supset Cx]$	4 DN
6	$\sim(\forall x) \sim[(Ax \;\&\; Bx) \supset Cx]$	5 QN

e. Derive: $\sim(\exists x)[(\sim Ax \lor \sim Bx) \;\&\; (Ax \lor Bx)]$

1	$(\forall x)(Ax \equiv Bx)$	Assumption
2	$\sim\sim(\forall x)(Ax \equiv Bx)$	1 DN
3	$\sim(\exists x) \sim(Ax \equiv Bx)$	2 QN
4	$\sim(\exists x) \sim[(Ax \;\&\; Bx) \lor (\sim Ax \;\&\; \sim Bx)]$	3 Equiv
5	$\sim(\exists x)[\sim(Ax \;\&\; Bx) \;\&\; \sim(\sim Ax \;\&\; \sim Bx)]$	4 DeM
6	$\sim(\exists x)[(\sim Ax \lor \sim Bx) \;\&\; \sim(\sim Ax \;\&\; \sim Bx)]$	5 DeM
7	$\sim(\exists x)[(\sim Ax \lor \sim Bx) \;\&\; (\sim\sim Ax \lor \sim\sim Bx)]$	6 DeM
8	$\sim(\exists x)[(\sim Ax \lor \sim Bx) \;\&\; (Ax \lor \sim\sim Bx)]$	7 DN
9	$\sim(\exists x)[(\sim Ax \lor \sim Bx) \;\&\; (Ax \lor Bx)]$	8 DN

Derive: $(\forall x)(Ax \equiv Bx)$

1	$\sim(\exists x)[(\sim Ax \lor \sim Bx) \& (Ax \lor Bx)]$	Assumption
2	$\sim(\exists x)[(\sim Ax \lor \sim Bx) \& (Ax \lor \sim\sim Bx)]$	1 DN
3	$\sim(\exists x)[(\sim Ax \lor \sim Bx) \& (\sim\sim Ax \lor \sim\sim Bx)]$	2 DN
4	$\sim(\exists x)[(\sim Ax \lor \sim Bx) \& \sim(\sim Ax \& \sim Bx)]$	3 DeM
5	$\sim(\exists x)[\sim(Ax \& Bx) \& \sim(\sim Ax \& \sim Bx)]$	4 DeM
6	$\sim(\exists x) \sim[(Ax \& Bx) \lor (\sim Ax \& \sim Bx)]$	5 DeM
7	$\sim(\exists x) \sim(Ax \equiv Bx)$	6 Equiv
8	$\sim\sim(\forall x)(Ax \equiv Bx)$	7 QN
9	$(\forall x)(Ax \equiv Bx)$	8 DN

5. Inconsistency

a.

1	$[(\forall x)(Mx \equiv Jx) \& \sim Mc] \& (\forall x)Jx$	Assumption
2	$(\forall x)(Mx \equiv Jx) \& \sim Mc$	1 & E
3	$(\forall x)(Mx \equiv Jx)$	2 & E
4	$Mc \equiv Jc$	3 $\forall$E
5	$(Mc \supset Jc) \& (Jc \supset Mc)$	4 Equiv
6	$Jc \supset Mc$	5 & E
7	$\sim Mc$	2 & E
8	$\sim Jc$	6, 7 MT
9	$(\forall x)Jx$	1 & E
10	Jc	9 $\forall$E

c.

1	$(\forall x)(\forall y)Lxy \supset \sim(\exists z)Tz$	Assumption
2	$(\forall x)(\forall y)Lxy \supset ((\exists w)Cww \lor (\exists z)Tz)$	Assumption
3	$(\sim(\forall x)(\forall y)Lxy \lor (\forall z)Bzzk)$	
	$\& (\sim(\forall z)Bzzk \lor \sim(\exists w)Cww)$	Assumption
4	$(\forall x)(\forall y)Lxy$	Assumption
5	$\sim(\exists z)Tz$	1, 4 $\supset$ E
6	$(\exists w)Cww \lor (\exists z)Tz$	2, 4 $\supset$ E
7	$(\exists w)Cww$	5, 6 DS
8	$\sim(\forall x)(\forall y)Lxy \lor (\forall z)Bzzk$	3 & E
9	$(\forall x)(\forall y)Lxy \supset (\forall z)Bzzk$	8 Impl
10	$(\forall z)Bzzk$	4, 9 $\supset$ E
11	$\sim(\forall z)Bzzk \lor \sim(\exists w)Cww$	3 & E
12	$(\forall z)Bzzk \supset \sim(\exists w)Cww$	11 Impl
13	$\sim(\exists w)Cww$	10, 12 $\supset$ E

e.	1	$(\forall x)(\forall y)(Gxy \supset Hc)$	Assumption
	2	$(\exists x)Gix \ \& \ (\forall x)(\forall y)(\forall z)Lxyz$	Assumption
	3	$Lcib \supset \sim Hc$	Assumption
	4	$(\exists x)Gix$	2 & E
	5	Gik	Assumption
	6	$(\forall y)(Giy \supset Hc)$	1 $\forall$E
	7	$Gik \supset Hc$	6 $\forall$E
	8	Hc	5, 7 MP
	9	$\sim\sim Hc$	8 DN
	10	$\sim Lcib$	3, 9 MT
	11	$(\forall x)(\forall y)(\forall z)Lxyz$	2 & E
	12	$(\forall y)(\forall z)Lcyz$	11 $\forall$E
	13	$(\forall z)Lciz$	12 $\forall$E
	14	$Lcib$	13 $\forall$E
	15	$Lcib \lor (Am \ \& \ \sim Am)$	14 $\lor$I
	16	$Am \ \& \ \sim Am$	10, 15 DS
	17	$Am \ \& \ \sim Am$	4, 5-16 $\exists$E
	18	Am	17 & E
	19	$\sim Am$	17 & E

6.a. Suppose there is a sentence on an accessible line i of a derivation to which Universal Elimination can be properly applied at line n. The sentence that would be derived by Universal Elimination can also be derived by using the routine beginning at line n:

i	$(\forall x)\mathscr{P}$	
n	$\sim \mathscr{P}(a/x)$	Assumption
$n + 1$	$(\exists x)\sim \mathscr{P}$	$n \ \exists$I
$n + 2$	$\sim (\forall x)\mathscr{P}$	$n + 1$ QN
$n + 3$	$(\forall x)\mathscr{P}$	i R
$n + 4$	$\mathscr{P}(a/x)$	n-$n + 3 \ \sim$ E

Suppose there is a sentence on an accessible line i of a derivation to which Universal Introduction can be properly applied at line n. The sentence that would be derived by Universal Introduction can also be derived by using the routine beginning at line n:

$$
\begin{array}{lll}
i & \mathcal{P}(a/x) & \\
\\
n & \quad \sim (\forall x)\mathcal{P} & \text{Assumption} \\
n+1 & \quad (\exists x) \sim \mathcal{P} & n \text{ QN} \\
n+2 & \quad\quad \sim \mathcal{P}(a/x) & \text{Assumption} \\
\\
n+3 & \quad\quad\quad \sim (\forall x)\mathcal{P} & \text{Assumption} \\
n+4 & \quad\quad\quad\quad \mathcal{P}(a/x) & i \text{ R} \\
n+5 & \quad\quad\quad\quad \sim \mathcal{P}(a/x) & n+2 \text{ R} \\
n+6 & \quad\quad\quad (\forall x)\mathcal{P} & n+3\text{-}n+5 \ \sim \text{E} \\
n+7 & \quad\quad (\forall x)\mathcal{P} & n+1, \\
& & \quad n+2\text{-}n+6 \ \exists\text{E} \\
n+8 & \quad \sim (\forall x)\mathcal{P} & n \text{ R} \\
n+9 & (\forall x)\mathcal{P} & n\text{-}n+8 \ \sim \text{E}
\end{array}
$$

No restriction on the use of Existential Elimination was violated at line $n + 7$. We assumed that we could have applied Universal Introduction at line n to $\mathcal{P}(a/x)$ on line i. So a does not occur in any undischarged assumption prior to line n, and a does not occur in $(\forall x)\mathcal{P}$. So a does not occur in $\mathcal{P}$. Hence

(i) a does not occur in any undischarged assumption prior to $n + 7$. Note that the assumptions on lines $n + 2$ and $n + 3$ have been discharged and that a cannot occur in the assumption on line n, for a does not occur in $\mathcal{P}$.

(ii) a does not occur in $(\exists x) \sim \mathcal{P}$, for a does not occur in $\mathcal{P}$.

(iii) a does not occur in $(\forall x)\mathcal{P}$, for a does not occur in $\mathcal{P}$.

10.6E

1.a. Derive: $a = b \supset b = a$

$$
\begin{array}{lll}
1 & \quad a = b & \text{Assumption} \\
2 & \quad a = a & 1, 1 \ = \text{E} \\
3 & \quad b = a & 1, 2 \ = \text{E} \\
4 & a = b \supset b = a & 1\text{-}3 \ \supset \text{I}
\end{array}
$$

c. Derive: (~ a = b & b = c) ⊃ ~ a = c

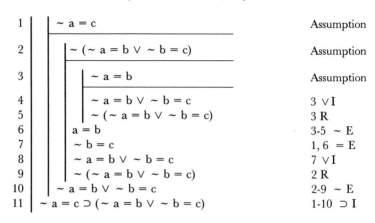

1	~ a = b & b = c	Assumption
2	~ a = b	1 & E
3	b = c	1 & E
4	~ a = c	2, 3 = E
5	(~ a = b & b = c) ⊃ ~ a = c	1-4 ⊃ I

e. Derive: ~ a = c ⊃ (~ a = b ∨ ~ b = c)

1	~ a = c	Assumption
2	~ (~ a = b ∨ ~ b = c)	Assumption
3	~ a = b	Assumption
4	~ a = b ∨ ~ b = c	3 ∨ I
5	~ (~ a = b ∨ ~ b = c)	3 R
6	a = b	3-5 ~ E
7	~ b = c	1, 6 = E
8	~ a = b ∨ ~ b = c	7 ∨ I
9	~ (~ a = b ∨ ~ b = c)	2 R
10	~ a = b ∨ ~ b = c	2-9 ~ E
11	~ a = c ⊃ (~ a = b ∨ ~ b = c)	1-10 ⊃ I

2.a. Derive: ~ (∀x)Bxx

1	a = b & ~ Bab	Assumption
2	~ Bab	1 & E
3	a = b	1 & E
4	(∀x)Bxx	Assumption
5	Baa	4 ∀E
6	~ Baa	2, 3 = E
7	~ (∀x)Bxx	4-6 ~ I

c. Derive: Hii

1	(∀z)[Gz ⊃ (∀y)(Ky ⊃ Hzy)]	Assumption
2	(Ki & Gj) & i = j	Assumption
3	Gj ⊃ (∀y)(Ky ⊃ Hjy)	1 ∀E
4	Ki & Gj	2 & E
5	Gj	4 & E
6	(∀y)(Ky ⊃ Hjy)	3, 5 ⊃ E
7	Ki ⊃ Hji	6 ∀E
8	Ki	4 & E
9	Hji	7, 8 ⊃ E
10	i = j	2 & E
11	Hii	9, 10 = E

e. Derive: Ka ∨ ~ Kb

1	a = b		Assumption
2		~ (Ka ∨ ~ Ka)	Assumption
3			Ka	Assumption
4			Ka ∨ ~ Ka	3 ∨I
5			~ (Ka ∨ ~ Ka)	2 R
6		~ Ka	3-5 ~ I
7		Ka ∨ ~ Ka	6 ∨I
8		~ (Ka ∨ ~ Ka)	2 R
9	Ka ∨ ~ Ka		2-8 ~ E
10	Ka ∨ ~ Kb		1, 9 = E

3.a. Derive: (∀x)(x = x ∨ ~ x = x)

1	(∀x)x = x	= I
2	a = a	1 ∀E
3	a = a ∨ ~ a = a	2 ∨I
4	(∀x)(x = x ∨ ~ x = x)	3 ∀I

c. Derive: (∀x)(∀y)(x = y ≡ y = x)

1		a = b	Assumption
2		a = a	1, 1 = E
3		b = a	1, 2 = E
4		b = a	Assumption
5		b = b	4, 4 = E
6		a = b	4, 5 = E
7	a = b ≡ b = a		1-3, 4-6 ≡ I
8	(∀y)(a = y ≡ y = a)		7 ∀I
9	(∀x)(∀y)(x = y ≡ y = x)		8 ∀I

e. Derive: ~ (∃x) ~ x = x

1		(∃x) ~ x = x	Assumption
2			~ a = a	Assumption
3				(∃x) ~ x = x	Assumption
4				(∀x)x = x	= I
5				a = a	4 ∀E
6				~ a = a	2 R
7			~ (∃x) ~ x = x	3-6 ~ I
8		~ (∃x) ~ x = x	1, 2-7 ∃E
9		(∃x) ~ x = x	1 R
10	~ (∃x) ~ x = x		1-9 ~ I

4.a. Derive: $(\exists x)(\exists y)[(Ex \mathbin{\&} Ey) \mathbin{\&} \sim x = y]$

1	$\sim t = f$	Assumption
2	$Et \mathbin{\&} Ef$	Assumption
3	$(Et \mathbin{\&} Ef) \mathbin{\&} \sim t = f$	1, 2 & I
4	$(\exists y)[(Et \mathbin{\&} Ey) \mathbin{\&} \sim t = y]$	3 ∃I
5	$(\exists x)(\exists y)[(Ex \mathbin{\&} Ey) \mathbin{\&} \sim x = y]$	4 ∃I

c. Derive: $\sim s = b$

1	$\sim Ass \mathbin{\&} Aqb$	Assumption
2	$(\forall x)[(\exists y)Ayx \supset Abx]$	Assumption
3	$\quad s = b$	Assumption
4	$\quad (\exists y)Ayb \supset Abb$	2 ∀E
5	$\quad Aqb$	1 & E
6	$\quad (\exists y)Ayb$	5 ∃I
7	$\quad Abb$	4, 6 ⊃ E
8	$\quad \sim Ass$	1 & E
9	$\quad \sim Abb$	3, 8 = E
10	$\sim s = b$	3-9 ~ I

e. Derive: $(\exists x)[(Rxe \mathbin{\&} Pxa) \mathbin{\&} (\sim x = e \mathbin{\&} \sim x = a)]$

1	$(\exists x)(Rxe \mathbin{\&} Pxa)$	Assumption
2	$\sim Ree$	Assumption
3	$\sim Paa$	Assumption
4	$\quad Rie \mathbin{\&} Pia$	Assumption
5	$\quad\quad i = e$	Assumption
6	$\quad\quad Rie$	4 & E
7	$\quad\quad Ree$	5, 6 = E
8	$\quad\quad \sim Ree$	2 R
9	$\quad \sim i = e$	5-8 ~ I
10	$\quad\quad i = a$	Assumption
11	$\quad\quad Pia$	4 & E
12	$\quad\quad Paa$	10, 11 = E
13	$\quad\quad \sim Paa$	3 R
14	$\quad \sim i = a$	10-13 ~ I
15	$\quad \sim i = e \mathbin{\&} \sim i = a$	9, 14 & I
16	$\quad (Rie \mathbin{\&} Pia) \mathbin{\&} (\sim i = e \mathbin{\&} \sim i = a)$	4, 15 & I
17	$\quad (\exists x)[(Rxe \mathbin{\&} Pxa) \mathbin{\&} (\sim x = e \mathbin{\&} \sim x = a)]$	16 ∃I
18	$(\exists x)[(Rxe \mathbin{\&} Pxa) \mathbin{\&} (\sim x = e \mathbin{\&} \sim x = a)]$	1, 4-17 ∃E

11.1E

5. Let $\Gamma \cup \{(\exists x)\mathscr{P}\}$ be a quantificationally consistent set of sentences, none of which contains the constant a. Then there is some interpretation **I** on which every member of $\Gamma \cup \{(\exists x)\mathscr{P}\}$ is true. Because $(\exists x)\mathscr{P}$ is true on **I**, we know that for any variable assignment **d**, there is a member **u** of the U.D. such that $\mathbf{d}[\mathbf{u}/x]$ satisfies $\mathscr{P}$ on **I**. Let **I′** be the interpretation that is just like **I** except that $\mathbf{I}'(a) = \mathbf{u}$. Because a does not occur in $\Gamma \cup \{(\exists x)\mathscr{P}\}$, it follows from 11.1.7 that every member of $\Gamma \cup \{(\exists x)\mathscr{P}\}$ is true on **I′**.

On our assumption that $\mathbf{d}[\mathbf{u}/x]$ satisfies $\mathscr{P}$ on **I**, it follows from 11.1.6 that $\mathbf{d}[\mathbf{u}/x]$ satisfies $\mathscr{P}$ on **I′**. By the way that we have constructed **I′**, **u** is $\mathbf{I}'(a)$ and so $\mathbf{d}[\mathbf{u}/x]$ is $\mathbf{d}[\mathbf{I}'(a)/x]$. From result 11.1.1, we therefore know that **d** satisfies $\mathscr{P}(a/x)$ on **I′**. By 11.1.3, then, every variable assignment on **I** satisfies $\mathscr{P}(a/x)$, so it is true on **I**.

Every member of $\Gamma \cup \{(\exists x)\mathscr{P}, \mathscr{P}(a/x)\}$ being true on **I′**, we conclude that the extended set is quantificationally consistent.

6. Assume that **I** is an interpretation on which each member of the U.D. is assigned to at least one individual constant and that every substitution instance of $(\forall x)\mathscr{P}$ is true on **I**. Now $(\forall x)\mathscr{P}$ is true on **I** if every variable assignment satisfies $(\forall x)\mathscr{P}$ and, by 11.1.3, if some variable assignment **d** satisfies $(\forall x)\mathscr{P}$. The latter is the case if for every member **u** of the U.D., $\mathbf{d}[\mathbf{u}/x]$ satisfies $\mathscr{P}$. Consider an arbitrary member **u** of the U.D. By our assumption, $\mathbf{u} = \mathbf{I}(a)$ for some individual constant a. Also by assumption, $\mathscr{P}(a/x)$ is true on **I**—so **d** satisfies $\mathscr{P}(a/x)$. By 11.1.1, then, $\mathbf{d}[\mathbf{I}(a)/x]$, which is $\mathbf{d}[\mathbf{u}/x]$, satisfies $\mathscr{P}$. We conclude that for every member **u** of the U.D., $\mathbf{d}[\mathbf{u}/x]$ satisfies $\mathscr{P}$, that **d** therefore satisfies $(\forall x)\mathscr{P}$, and that $(\forall x)\mathscr{P}$ is true on **I**.

11.2E

1.a. Assume that an argument of *PL* is valid in *PD*. Then the conclusion is derivable in *PD* from the set consisting of the premises. By Metatheorem 11.1, it follows that the conclusion is quantificationally entailed by the set consisting of the premises. Therefore the argument is quantificationally valid.

 b. Assume that a sentence $\mathscr{P}$ is a theorem in *PD*. Then $\varnothing \vdash \mathscr{P}$. So $\varnothing \vDash \mathscr{P}$, by Metatheorem 11.1, and $\mathscr{P}$ is quantificationally true.

2. Our induction will be on the number of occurrences of *logical operators* in $\mathscr{P}$, for we must now take into account the quantifiers as well as the truth-functional connectives.

Basis clause: Thesis 11.2.3 holds for every atomic formula of *PL*.

> Proof: Assume that $\mathcal{P}$ is an atomic formula and that $\mathcal{Q}$ is a subformula of $\mathcal{P}$. Then $\mathcal{P}$ and $\mathcal{Q}$ are identical. For any formula $\mathcal{Q}_1$, then, $[\mathcal{P}](\mathcal{Q}_1//\mathcal{Q})$ is simply $\mathcal{Q}_1$. It is trivial that the thesis holds in this case.

Inductive step: Let $\mathcal{P}$ be a formula with $k+1$ occurrences of logical operators, let $\mathcal{Q}$ be a subformula of $\mathcal{P}$, and let $\mathcal{Q}_1$ be a formula related to $\mathcal{Q}$ as stipulated. Assume (the inductive hypothesis) that 11.2.3 holds for every formula with k or fewer occurrences of logical operators. We now establish that 11.2.3 holds for $\mathcal{P}$ as well. Suppose first that $\mathcal{Q}$ and $\mathcal{P}$ are identical. In this case, that 11.2.3 holds for $\mathcal{P}$ and $[\mathcal{P}](\mathcal{Q}_1//\mathcal{Q})$ is established as in the proof of the basis clause. So assume that $\mathcal{Q}$ is a subformula of $\mathcal{P}$ that is not identical with $\mathcal{P}$ (in which case we say that $\mathcal{Q}$ is a *proper subformula* of $\mathcal{P}$). We consider each form that $\mathcal{P}$ may have.

(i) $\mathcal{P}$ is of the form $\sim\mathcal{R}$. Since $\mathcal{Q}$ is a proper subformula of $\mathcal{P}$, $\mathcal{Q}$ is a subformula of $\mathcal{R}$. Therefore $[\mathcal{P}](\mathcal{Q}_1//\mathcal{Q})$ is $\sim[\mathcal{R}](\mathcal{Q}_1//\mathcal{Q})$. Since $\mathcal{R}$ has fewer than $k+1$ occurrences of logical operators, it follows from the inductive hypothesis that, on any interpretation, a variable assignment satisfies $\mathcal{R}$ if and only if it satisfies $[\mathcal{R}](\mathcal{Q}_1//\mathcal{Q})$. Since an assignment satisfies a formula if and only if it fails to satisfy the negation of the formula, it follows that on any interpretation a variable assignment satisfies $\sim\mathcal{R}$ if and only if it satisfies $\sim[\mathcal{R}](\mathcal{Q}_1//\mathcal{Q})$.

(ii)–(v) $\mathcal{P}$ is of the form $\mathcal{R}\,\&\,\mathcal{S}$, $\mathcal{R}\lor\mathcal{S}$, $\mathcal{R}\supset\mathcal{S}$, or $\mathcal{R}\equiv\mathcal{S}$. These cases are handled similarly to case (ii) in the inductive proof of Lemma 6.1 (in Chapter Six), with obvious adjustments as in case (i).

(vi) $\mathcal{P}$ is of the form $(\forall x)\mathcal{R}$. Since $\mathcal{Q}$ is a proper subformula of $\mathcal{P}$, $\mathcal{Q}$ is a subformula of $\mathcal{R}$. Therefore $[\mathcal{P}](\mathcal{Q}_1//\mathcal{Q})$ is $(\forall x)[\mathcal{R}](\mathcal{Q}_1//\mathcal{Q})$. Since $\mathcal{R}$ has fewer than $k+1$ occurrences of logical operators, it follows, by the inductive hypothesis, that on any interpretation a variable assignment satisfies $\mathcal{R}$ if and only if that assignment satisfies $[\mathcal{R}](\mathcal{Q}_1//\mathcal{Q})$. Now $(\forall x)\mathcal{R}$ is satisfied by a variable assignment $\mathbf{d}$ if and only if for each member $\mathbf{u}$ of the U.D., $\mathbf{d}[\mathbf{u}/x]$ satisfies $\mathcal{R}$. The latter is the case just in case $[\mathcal{R}](\mathcal{Q}_1//\mathcal{Q})$ is satisfied by every variant $\mathbf{d}[\mathbf{u}/x]$. And this is the case if and only if $(\forall x)[\mathcal{R}](\mathcal{Q}_1//\mathcal{Q})$ is satisfied by $\mathbf{d}$. Therefore on any interpretation $(\forall x)\mathcal{R}$ is satisfied by a variable assignment if and only if $(\forall x)[\mathcal{R}](\mathcal{Q}_1//\mathcal{Q})$ is satisfied by that assignment.

(vii) $\mathcal{P}$ is of the form $(\exists x)\mathcal{R}$. This case is similar to case (vi).

3. $\mathcal{Q}_{k+1}$ is justified at position $k+1$ by Quantifier Negation. Then $\mathcal{Q}_{k+1}$ is derived as follows:

h	$\mathcal{S}$	
$k+1$	$\mathcal{Q}_{k+1}$	h QN

where some component $\mathcal{R}$ of $\mathcal{S}$ has been replaced by a component $\mathcal{R}_1$ to obtain $\mathcal{Q}_{k+1}$ and the four forms that $\mathcal{R}$ and $\mathcal{R}_1$ may have are

$\mathcal{R}$ is	$\mathcal{R}_1$ is
$\sim(\forall x)\mathcal{P}$	$(\exists x)\sim\mathcal{P}$
$(\exists x)\sim\mathcal{P}$	$\sim(\forall x)\mathcal{P}$
$\sim(\exists x)\mathcal{P}$	$(\forall x)\sim\mathcal{P}$
$(\forall x)\sim\mathcal{P}$	$\sim(\exists x)\mathcal{P}$

Whichever pair $\mathcal{R}$ and $\mathcal{R}_1$ constitute, the two sentences contain exactly the same nonlogical constants. We first establish that on any interpretation variable assignment $\mathbf{d}$ satisfies $\mathcal{R}$ if and only if $\mathbf{d}$ satisfies $\mathcal{R}_1$.

(i) Either $\mathcal{R}$ is $\sim(\forall x)\mathcal{P}$ and $\mathcal{R}_1$ is $(\exists x)\sim\mathcal{P}$, or $\mathcal{R}$ is $(\exists x)\sim\mathcal{P}$ and $\mathcal{R}_1$ is $\sim(\forall x)\mathcal{P}$. Assume that a variable assignment $\mathbf{d}$ satisfies $\sim(\forall x)\mathcal{P}$. Then $\mathbf{d}$ does not satisfy $(\forall x)\mathcal{P}$. There is then at least one variant $\mathbf{d}[u/x]$ that does not satisfy $\mathcal{P}$. Hence $\mathbf{d}[u/x]$ satisfies $\sim\mathcal{P}$. It follows that $\mathbf{d}[u/x]$ satisfies $(\exists x)\sim\mathcal{P}$. Now assume that a variable assignment $\mathbf{d}$ satisfies $(\exists x)\sim\mathcal{P}$. Then some variant $\mathbf{d}[u/x]$ satisfies $\sim\mathcal{P}$. This variant does not satisfy $\mathcal{P}$. Therefore $\mathbf{d}$ does not satisfy $(\forall x)\mathcal{P}$ and does satisfy $\sim(\forall x)\mathcal{P}$.

(ii) Either $\mathcal{R}$ is $\sim(\exists x)\mathcal{P}$ and $\mathcal{R}_1$ is $(\forall x)\sim\mathcal{P}$, or $\mathcal{R}$ is $(\forall x)\sim\mathcal{P}$ and $\mathcal{R}_1$ is $\sim(\exists x)\mathcal{P}$. This case is similar to case (i).
$\mathcal{R}$ and $\mathcal{R}_1$ contain the same nonlogical symbols and variables, so it follows, by 11.2.3 (Exercise 2), that $\mathcal{S}$ is satisfied by a variable assignment if and only if $\mathcal{Q}_{k+1}$ is satisfied by that assignment. So on any interpretation $\mathcal{S}$ and $\mathcal{Q}_{k+1}$ have the same truth-value.

By the inductive hypothesis, $\Gamma_k \vDash \mathcal{S}$. But Γ_k is a subset of Γ_{k+1}, so $\Gamma_{k+1} \vDash \mathcal{S}$, by 11.2.1. Since $\mathcal{S}$ and $\mathcal{Q}_{k+1}$ have the same truth-value on any interpretation, it follows that $\Gamma_{k+1} \vDash \mathcal{Q}_{k+1}$.

11.3E

2. Assume that $\Gamma \cup \{\sim\mathcal{P}\}$ is inconsistent in *PD*. Then there is a derivation of the following sort, where $\mathcal{Q}_1, \ldots, \mathcal{Q}_n$ are members of Γ:

1	$\mathcal{Q}_1$	Assumption
.	.	
n	$\mathcal{Q}_n$	Assumption
$n+1$	$\sim\mathcal{P}$	Assumption
.	.	
m	$\mathcal{S}$	
.	.	
p	$\sim\mathcal{S}$	

We construct a new derivation as follows:

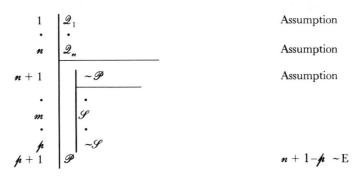

1	$\mathcal{Q}_1$	Assumption
$\cdot$	$\cdot$	
n	$\mathcal{Q}_n$	Assumption
$n+1$	$\sim\mathcal{P}$	Assumption
$\cdot$	$\cdot$	
m	$\mathcal{S}$	
$\cdot$	$\cdot$	
p	$\sim\mathcal{S}$	
$p+1$	$\mathcal{P}$	$n+1$–p $\sim$E

where lines 1–p are as in the original derivation, except that $\sim\mathcal{P}$ is now an auxiliary assumption. This shows that $\Gamma \vdash \mathcal{P}$.

    3.a. Assume that an argument of *PL* is quantificationally valid. Then the set consisting of the premises quantificationally entails the conclusion. By Metatheorem 11.2, the conclusion is derivable from that set in *PD*. Therefore the argument is valid in *PD*.

    b. Assume that a sentence $\mathcal{P}$ is quantificationally true. Then $\varnothing \vDash \mathcal{P}$. By Metatheorem 11.2, $\varnothing \vdash \mathcal{P}$. So $\mathcal{P}$ is a theorem in *PD*.

    4. We shall associate with each symbol of *PL* a numeral as follows. With each symbol of *PL* that is a symbol of *SL*, associate the two-digit numeral that is associated with that symbol in the enumeration of Section 6.4. With the symbol ' (the prime) associate the numeral '66'. With the nonsubscripted lower-case letters 'a', 'b', ..., 'z', associate the numerals '67', '68', ..., '92', respectively. With the symbols '∀' and '∃' associate the numerals '93' and '94', respectively. (Note that the numerals '66'–'94' are not associated with any symbol of *SL*.) We then associate with each sentence of *PL* the numeral that consists of the associated numerals of each of the symbols that occur in the sentence, in the order in which the symbols occur. We now enumerate the sentences of *PL* by letting the first sentence be the sentence whose numeral designates a number that is smaller than the number designated by any other sentence's associated numeral; the second sentence is the sentence whose numeral designates the next largest number designated by the associated numeral of any sentence; and so on.

    5. Assume that $\Gamma \vdash \mathcal{P}$. Then there is a derivation

1	$\mathcal{Q}_1$
$\cdot$	$\cdot$
n	$\mathcal{Q}_n$
$\cdot$	$\cdot$
m	$\mathcal{P}$

where $\mathcal{Q}_1, \ldots, \mathcal{Q}_m$ are all members of Γ. The primary assumptions are all members of any superset Γ' of Γ, so $\Gamma' \vdash \mathcal{P}$ as well.

6.a. Assume that a does not occur in any member of the set $\Gamma \cup \{(\exists x)\mathcal{P}\}$, and that the set is consistent in PD. Assume, contrary to what we want to prove, that $\Gamma \cup \{(\exists x)\mathcal{P}, \mathcal{P}(a/x)\}$ is *in*consistent in PD. Then there is a derivation of the sort

$$
\begin{array}{r|l}
1 & \mathcal{Q}_1 \\
\cdot & \cdot \\
n & \mathcal{Q}_n \\
n+1 & (\exists x)\mathcal{P} \\
n+2 & \mathcal{P}(a/x) \\
m & \mathcal{R} \\
\cdot & \cdot \\
p & \sim\!\mathcal{R}
\end{array}
$$

where $\mathcal{Q}_1, \ldots, \mathcal{Q}_n$ are all members of Γ. We may convert this into a derivation that shows that $\Gamma \cup \{(\exists x)\mathcal{P}\}$ is inconsistent in PD, contradicting our initial assumption:

$$
\begin{array}{r|l}
1 & \mathcal{Q}_1 \\
\cdot & \cdot \\
n & \mathcal{Q}_n \\
n+1 & (\exists x)\mathcal{P} \\
\\
n+2 & \quad \mathcal{P}(a/x) \\
\\
n+3 & \quad\quad (\exists x)\mathcal{P} \\
\cdot & \quad\quad \cdot \\
m+1 & \quad\quad \mathcal{R} \\
\cdot & \quad\quad \cdot \\
p+1 & \quad\quad \sim\!\mathcal{R} \\
p+2 & \quad \sim\!(\exists x)\mathcal{P} \\
p+3 & \sim\!(\exists x)\mathcal{P} \\
p+4 & (\exists x)\mathcal{P}
\end{array}
$$

$$
\begin{array}{ll}
n+3 & p+1 \sim\!\mathrm{I} \\
n+2 & p+2 \; \exists\mathrm{E} \\
n+1 & \mathrm{R}
\end{array}
$$

(Note that use of $\exists$E is legitimate at line $p+3$ because a, by our initial hypothesis, does not occur in $(\exists x)\mathcal{P}$ or in any member of Γ.)

We conclude that if the set $\Gamma \cup \{(\exists x)\mathcal{P}\}$ is consistent in PD and a does not occur in any member of that set, then $\Gamma \cup \{(\exists x)\mathcal{P}(a/x)\}$ is also consistent in PD.

b. Let Γ^* be constructed as in our proof of Lemma 11.2. Assume that $(\exists x)\mathcal{P}$ is a member of Γ^* and that $(\exists x)\mathcal{P}$ is the ith sentence in our enumeration of the sentences of PL. Then, by the way each member of the infinite sequence

$\Gamma_1, \Gamma_2, \Gamma_3, \ldots$ is constructed, Γ_{i+1} contains $(\exists x)\mathscr{P}$ and a substitution instance of $(\exists x)\mathscr{P}$ if $\Gamma_i \cup \{(\exists x)\mathscr{P}\}$ is consistent in PD. Since each member of the infinite sequence is consistent in PD, Γ_i is consistent in PD. So assume that $\Gamma_i \cup \{(\exists x)\mathscr{P}\}$ is inconsistent in PD. Then, since we assumed that $\mathscr{P}_i$, that is, $(\exists x)\mathscr{P}$, is a member of Γ^* and since every member of Γ_i is a member of Γ^*, it follows that Γ^* is inconsistent in PD. But this contradicts our original assumption, so $\Gamma_i \cup \{(\exists x)\mathscr{P}\}$ is consistent in PD. Hence Γ_{i+1} is $\Gamma_i \cup \{(\exists x)\mathscr{P}, \mathscr{P}(a/x)\}$ for some constant a, so some substitution instance of $(\exists x)\mathscr{P}$ is a member of Γ_{i+1} and thus of Γ^*.

7. We shall prove that the sentence at each position i in the new derivation can be justified by the same rule that was used at position i in the original derivation.

Basis clause: Let $i = 1$. The sentence at position 1 of the original derivation is an assumption, and so the sentence at position 1 of the new sequence can be justified similarly.

Inductive step: Assume (the inductive hypothesis) that at every position i prior to position $k + 1$, the new sequence contains a sentence that may be justified by the rule justifying the sentence at position i of the original derivation. We now prove that the sentence at position $k + 1$ of the new sequence can be justified by the rule justifying the sentence at position $k + 1$ of the original derivation. We shall consider the rules by which the sentence at position $k + 1$ of the original derivation could have been justified:

1. $\mathscr{P}$ is justified at position $k + 1$ by Assumption. Obviously, $\mathscr{P}^*$ can be justified by Assumption at position $k + 1$ of the new sequence.

2. $\mathscr{P}$ is justified at position $k + 1$ by Reiteration. Then $\mathscr{P}$ occurs at an accessible earlier position in the original derivation. Therefore $\mathscr{P}^*$ occurs at an accessible earlier position in the new sequence, so $\mathscr{P}^*$ can be justified at position $k + 1$ by Reiteration.

3. $\mathscr{P}$ is a conjunction $\mathscr{Q} \& \mathscr{R}$ justified at position $k + 1$ by Conjunction Introduction. Then the conjuncts $\mathscr{Q}$ and $\mathscr{R}$ of $\mathscr{P}$ occur at accessible earlier positions in the original derivation. Therefore $\mathscr{Q}^*$ and $\mathscr{R}^*$ occur at accessible earlier positions in the new sequence. So $\mathscr{P}^*$, which is just $\mathscr{Q}^* \& \mathscr{R}^*$, can be justified at position $k + 1$ by Conjunction Introduction.

4–12. $\mathscr{P}$ is justified by one of the other truth-functional connective introduction or elimination rules. These cases are as straightforward as case 3, so we move on to the quantifier rules.

13. $\mathscr{P}$ is a sentence $\mathscr{Q}(a/x)$ justified at position $k + 1$ by $\forall$E, appealing to an accessible earlier position with $(\forall x)\mathscr{Q}$. Then $(\forall x)\mathscr{Q}^*$ occurs at the accessible earlier position of the new sequence, and $\mathscr{Q}(a/x)^*$ occurs at position $k + 1$. But $\mathscr{Q}(a/x)^*$ is just a substitution instance of $(\forall x)\mathscr{Q}^*$. So $\mathscr{Q}(a/x)^*$ can be justified at position $k + 1$ by $\forall$E.

14. $\mathscr{P}$ is a sentence $(\exists x)\mathscr{Q}$ and is justified at position $k + 1$ by $\exists$I. This case is similar to case 13.

15. $\mathscr{P}$ is a sentence $(\forall x)\mathscr{Q}$ and is justified at position $k + 1$ by $\forall$I. Then some substitution instance occurs at an accessible earlier position j, where a is a constant that does not occur in any undischarged assumption prior to position $k + 1$ or in $(\forall x)\mathscr{Q}$. $\mathscr{Q}(a/x)^*$ and $(\forall x)\mathscr{Q}^*$ occur at positions j and $k + 1$ of the new sequence. $\mathscr{Q}(a/x)^*$ is a substitution instance of $(\forall x)\mathscr{Q}^*$. The instantiating constant a in $\mathscr{Q}(a/x)$ is some a_i, and so the instantiating constant in $\mathscr{Q}(a/x)^*$ is a_{m+i}. Since a_i did not occur in any undischarged assumption before position $k + 1$ or in $(\forall x)\mathscr{Q}$ in the original derivation and a_{m+i} does not occur in the original derivation, a_{m+i} does not occur in any undischarged assumption prior to position $k + 1$ of the new sequence or in $(\forall x)\mathscr{Q}^*$. So $(\forall x)\mathscr{Q}^*$ can be justified by $\forall$I at position $k + 1$ in the new sequence.

16. $\mathscr{P}$ is justified at position $k + 1$ by $\exists$E. This case is similar to case 15.

Since every sentence in the new sequence can be justified by a rule of PD, it follows that the new sequence is indeed a derivation of PD.

10. We require that Γ^* be $\exists$-complete so that we could construct an interpretation $\mathbf{I}^*$ for which we could *prove* that every member of Γ^* is true on $\mathbf{I}^*$. In requiring that Γ^* be $\exists$-complete in addition to being maximally consistent in PD, we were guaranteed that Γ^* had property g of sets that are both maximally consistent in PD and $\exists$-complete; and we used this fact in case 4 of the proof that every member of Γ^* is true on $\mathbf{I}^*$.

11. To prove that PD^* is complete for predicate logic, it will suffice to show that with $\forall$E* instead of $\forall$E, every set Γ^* of PD^* that is both maximally consistent in PD^* and $\exists$-complete has property f (i.e., $(\forall x)\mathscr{P} \in \Gamma^*$ if and only if for every constant a, $\mathscr{P}(a/x) \in \Gamma^*$). For the properties a–e and g can be shown to characterize such sets by appealing to the rules of PD^* that are rules of PD. Here is our proof:

Assume that $(\forall x)\mathscr{P} \in \Gamma^*$. Then, since $\{(\forall x)\mathscr{P}\} \vdash \sim(\exists x) \sim \mathscr{P}$ by $\forall$E*, it follows from 11.3.1 that $\sim(\exists x) \sim \mathscr{P} \in \Gamma^*$. Then $(\exists x) \sim \mathscr{P} \notin \Gamma^*$, by a. Assume that for some substitution instance $\mathscr{P}(a/x)$ of $(\forall x)\mathscr{P}$, $\mathscr{P}(a/x) \notin \Gamma^*$. Then, by a, $\sim \mathscr{P}(a/x) \in \Gamma^*$. Since $\{\sim\mathscr{P}(a/x)\} \vdash (\exists x) \sim \mathscr{P}$ (without use of $\forall$E), it follows that $(\exists x) \sim \mathscr{P} \in \Gamma^*$. But we have just shown that $(\exists x) \sim \mathscr{P} \notin \Gamma^*$. Hence, if $(\forall x)\mathscr{P} \in \Gamma^*$, then every substitution instance $\mathscr{P}(a/x)$ of $(\forall x)\mathscr{P}$ is a member of Γ^*.

Now assume that $(\forall x)\mathscr{P} \notin \Gamma^*$. Then, by a, $\sim(\forall x)\mathscr{P} \in \Gamma^*$. But then, since $\{\sim(\forall x)\mathscr{P}\} \vdash (\exists x) \sim \mathscr{P}$ (without use of $\forall$E), it follows that $(\exists x) \sim \mathscr{P} \in \Gamma^*$. Since Γ^* is $\exists$-complete, some substitution instance $\sim\mathscr{P}(a/x)$ of $(\exists x) \sim \mathscr{P}$ is a member of Γ^*. By a, $\mathscr{P}(a/x) \notin \Gamma^*$.

13. Assume that some sentence $\mathscr{P}$ is not quantificationally false. Then $\mathscr{P}$ is true on at least one interpretation, so $\{\mathscr{P}\}$ is quantificationally consistent. Now suppose that $\{\mathscr{P}\}$ is inconsistent in PD. Then some sentences $\mathscr{Q}$ and $\sim\mathscr{Q}$ are

derivable from $\{\mathscr{P}\}$ in *PD*. By Metatheorem 11.1, it follows that $\{\mathscr{P}\} \vDash \mathscr{Q}$ and $\mathscr{P} \vDash \sim\mathscr{Q}$. But then $\mathscr{P}$ cannot be true on any interpretation, contrary to our assumption. So $\{\mathscr{P}\}$ is consistent in *PD*. By Lemma 11.2, $\{\mathscr{P}_e\}$—the set resulting from doubling the subscript of every individual constant in $\mathscr{P}$—is a subset of a set Γ^* that is both maximally consistent in *PD* and ∃-complete. It follows from Lemma 11.3 that Γ^* is quantificationally consistent. But, in proving 11.3, we actually showed more—for the characteristic interpretation $\mathbf{I}^*$ that we constructed for Γ^* has the set of positive integers as U.D. Hence every member of Γ^* is true on some interpretation with the set of positive integers as U.D., and thus $\mathscr{P}_e$ is true on some interpretation with the set of positive integers as U.D. $\mathscr{P}$ can also be shown true on some interpretation with that U.D., using 11.1.13.

16. Consider the sentence '$(\forall x)(\forall y)x = y$'. This sentence is not quantificationally false; it is true on every interpretation with a one-member U.D. In addition, however, it is true on *only* those interpretations that have one-member U.D.s. (This is because for any variable assignment and any members $\mathbf{u}_1$ and $\mathbf{u}_2$ of a U.D., $\mathbf{d}[\mathbf{u}_1/x, \mathbf{u}_2/y]$ satisfies '$x = y$' as required for the truth of '$(\forall x)(\forall y)x = y$' if and only if $\mathbf{u}_1$ and $\mathbf{u}_2$ are the same object.) So there can be no interpretation with the set of positive integers as U.D. on which the sentence is true.

11.4E

2.a. Assume that for some sentence $\mathscr{P}$, $\{\mathscr{P}\}$ has a closed systematic truth-tree. Then, by Metatheorem 11.3, $\{\mathscr{P}\}$ is quantificationally inconsistent. Hence there is no interpretation on which $\mathscr{P}$, the sole member of $\{\mathscr{P}\}$, is true. Therefore $\mathscr{P}$ is quantificationally false.

b. Assume that for some sentence $\mathscr{P}$, $\{\sim\mathscr{P}\}$ has a closed systematic truth-tree. Then, by Metatheorem 11.3, $\{\sim\mathscr{P}\}$ is quantificationally inconsistent. Hence there is no interpretation on which $\sim\mathscr{P}$ is true. So $\mathscr{P}$ is true on every interpretation; that is, $\mathscr{P}$ is quantificationally true.

d. Assume that $\Gamma \cup \{\sim\mathscr{P}\}$ has a closed systematic truth-tree. Then, by Metatheorem 11.3, $\Gamma \cup \{\sim\mathscr{P}\}$ is quantificationally inconsistent. Hence there is no interpretation on which every member of Γ is true and $\sim\mathscr{P}$ is also true. That is, there is no interpretation on which every member of Γ is true and $\mathscr{P}$ is false. But then $\Gamma \vDash \mathscr{P}$.

3.a. $\mathscr{P}$ is obtained from $\sim\sim\mathscr{P}$ by $\sim\sim$D. It is straightforward that $\{\sim\sim\mathscr{P}\} \vDash \mathscr{P}$.

d. $\mathscr{P}$ or $\sim\mathscr{Q}$ is obtained from $\sim(\mathscr{P} \supset \mathscr{Q})$ by $\sim\supset$ D. On any interpretation on which $\sim(\mathscr{P} \supset \mathscr{Q})$ is true, $\mathscr{P} \supset \mathscr{Q}$ is false—hence $\mathscr{P}$ is true and $\mathscr{Q}$ is false. But, if $\mathscr{Q}$ is false, then $\sim\mathscr{Q}$ is true. Thus $\{\sim(\mathscr{P} \supset \mathscr{Q})\} \vDash \mathscr{P}$, and $\{\sim(\mathscr{P} \supset \mathscr{Q})\} \vDash \sim\mathscr{Q}$.

e. $\mathscr{P}(a/x)$ is obtained from $(\forall x)\mathscr{P}$ by $\forall$D. It follows, from 11.1.4, that $\{(\forall x)\mathscr{P}\} \vDash \mathscr{P}(a/x)$.

4.a. $\sim\mathscr{P}$ and $\sim\mathscr{Q}$ are obtained from $\sim(\mathscr{P}\mathbin{\&}\mathscr{Q})$ by $\sim\mathbin{\&}$ D. On any interpretation on which $\sim(\mathscr{P}\mathbin{\&}\mathscr{Q})$ is true, $\mathscr{P}\mathbin{\&}\mathscr{Q}$ is false. But then either $\mathscr{P}$ is false, or $\mathscr{Q}$ is false. Hence on such an interpretation either $\sim\mathscr{P}$ is true, or $\sim\mathscr{Q}$ is true.

5. The path is extended to form two paths to level $\mathscr{k}+1$ as a result of applying one of the branching rules $\equiv$ D or $\sim\equiv$ D to a sentence $\mathscr{P}$ on $\Gamma_\mathscr{k}$. We consider four cases.

a. Sentences $\mathscr{P}$ and $\sim\mathscr{P}$ are entered at level $\mathscr{k}+1$ as the result of applying $\equiv$ D to a sentence $\mathscr{P}\equiv\mathscr{Q}$ on $\Gamma_\mathscr{k}$. On any interpretation on which $\mathscr{P}\equiv\mathscr{Q}$ is true, so is either $\mathscr{P}$ or $\sim\mathscr{P}$. Therefore either $\mathscr{P}$ and all the sentences on $\Gamma_\mathscr{k}$ are true on $I_{\Gamma_\mathscr{k}}$, which is a path-variant of I for the new path containing $\mathscr{P}$, or $\sim\mathscr{P}$ and all the sentences on $\Gamma_\mathscr{k}$ are true on $I_{\Gamma_\mathscr{k}}$, which is a path-variant of I for the new path containing $\sim\mathscr{P}$.

b. Sentence $\mathscr{Q}$ (or $\sim\mathscr{Q}$) is entered at level $\mathscr{k}+1$ as the result of applying $\equiv$ D to a sentence $\mathscr{P}\equiv\mathscr{Q}$ on $\Gamma_\mathscr{k}$. Then $\mathscr{P}$ (or $\sim\mathscr{P}$) occurs on $\Gamma_\mathscr{k}$ at level $\mathscr{k}$ (application of $\equiv$ D involves making entries at two levels, and $\mathscr{Q}$ and $\sim\mathscr{Q}$ will be entries made on the second of these levels). Since $\{\mathscr{P}\equiv\mathscr{Q}, \mathscr{P}\}$ quantificationally entails $\mathscr{Q}$ (and $\{\mathscr{P}\equiv\mathscr{Q}, \sim\mathscr{P}\}$ quantificationally entails $\sim\mathscr{Q}$), it follows that $\mathscr{Q}$ and all the sentences on $\Gamma_\mathscr{k}$ ($\sim\mathscr{Q}$ and all the sentences on $\Gamma_\mathscr{k}$) are all true on $I_{\Gamma_\mathscr{k}}$, which is a path-variant of I for the new path containing $\mathscr{Q}$ ($\sim\mathscr{Q}$).

c. Sentences $\mathscr{P}$ and $\sim\mathscr{P}$ are entered at level $\mathscr{k}+1$ as the result of applying $\sim\equiv$ D to a sentence $\sim(\mathscr{P}\equiv\mathscr{Q})$ on $\Gamma_\mathscr{k}$. This case is similar to case a.

d. Sentence $\mathscr{Q}$ (or $\sim\mathscr{Q}$) is entered at level $\mathscr{k}+1$ as the result of applying $\sim\equiv$ D to a sentence $\sim(\mathscr{P}\equiv\mathscr{Q})$ on $\Gamma_\mathscr{k}$. This case is similar to case b.

6. Yes. Dropping a rule would not make the method unsound, for, with the remaining rules, it would still follow that if a branch on a tree for a set Γ closes, then Γ is quantificationally inconsistent. That is, the remaining rules would still be consistency-preserving.

7. In proving that the tree method for SL is sound, there are obvious adjustments that must be made in the proof of Metatheorem 11.3. First, of course, not all the tree rules for PL are tree rules for SL. In proving Lemma 11.4, then, we take only the tree rules for SL into consideration. And in the case of SL we would be proving that certain sets are truth-functionally consistent or inconsistent, rather than quantificationally consistent or inconsistent. The basic semantic concept for SL is that of a truth-value assignment, rather than an interpretation. With these stipulations, the proof of Metatheorem 11.3 can be converted straightforwardly into a proof of the parallel metatheorem for SL.

11.5E

1.a. Assume that a sentence $\mathscr{P}$ is quantificationally false. Then $\{\mathscr{P}\}$ is quantificationally inconsistent. It follows from Metatheorem 11.5 that every systematic tree for $\{\mathscr{P}\}$ closes.

b. Assume that a sentence $\mathcal{P}$ is quantificationally true. Then $\sim\mathcal{P}$ is quantificationally false, and $\{\sim\mathcal{P}\}$ is quantificationally inconsistent. It follows from Metatheorem 11.5 that every systematic tree for $\{\sim\mathcal{P}\}$ closes.

d. Assume that $\Gamma \vDash \mathcal{P}$. Then on every interpretation on which every member of Γ is true, $\mathcal{P}$ is true, and $\sim\mathcal{P}$ is therefore false. So $\Gamma \cup \{\sim\mathcal{P}\}$ is quantificationally inconsistent. It follows from Metatheorem 11.5 that every systematic tree for $\Gamma \cup \{\sim\mathcal{P}\}$ closes.

2.a. The lengths are 6, 2, and 6, respectively.

b. Assume that the length of a sentence $\sim(\mathcal{Q}\ \&\ \mathcal{R})$ is k. Then, since $\sim(\mathcal{Q}\ \&\ \mathcal{R})$ contains an occurrence of the tilde and an occurrence of the ampersand that neither $\mathcal{Q}$ nor $\mathcal{R}$ contains, the length of $\mathcal{Q}$ is $k-2$ or less and the length of $\mathcal{R}$ is $k-2$ or less. Hence the length of $\sim\mathcal{Q}$ is $k-1$ or less, and the length of $\sim\mathcal{R}$ is $k-1$ or less.

d. Assume that the length of a sentence $\sim(\forall x)\mathcal{Q}$ is k. Then the length of the formula $\mathcal{Q}$ is $k-2$. Hence the length of $\mathcal{Q}(a/x)$ is $k-2$—since $\mathcal{Q}(a/x)$ differs from $\mathcal{Q}$ only in containing a wherever $\mathcal{Q}$ contains x and neither constants nor variables are counted in computing the length of a formula. Hence the length of $\sim\mathcal{Q}(a/x)$ is $k-1$.

3.a. $\mathcal{P}$ is of the form $\mathcal{Q} \vee \mathcal{R}$. Assume that $\mathcal{P} \in \Gamma$. Then, by e, either $\mathcal{Q} \in \Gamma$, or $\mathcal{R} \in \Gamma$. If $\mathcal{Q} \in \Gamma$, then $\mathbf{I}(\mathcal{Q}) = \mathbf{T}$, by the inductive hypothesis. If $\mathcal{R} \in \Gamma$, then $\mathbf{I}(\mathcal{R}) = \mathbf{T}$, by the inductive hypothesis. Either way, it follows that $\mathbf{I}(\mathcal{Q} \vee \mathcal{R}) = \mathbf{T}$.

c. $\mathcal{P}$ is of the form $\mathcal{Q} \supset \mathcal{R}$. Assume that $\mathcal{P} \in \Gamma$. Then, by g, either $\sim\mathcal{Q} \in \Gamma$ or $\mathcal{R} \in \Gamma$. By the inductive hypothesis, then, either $\mathbf{I}(\sim\mathcal{Q}) = \mathbf{T}$ or $\mathbf{I}(\mathcal{R}) = \mathbf{T}$. So either $\mathbf{I}(\mathcal{Q}) = \mathbf{F}$ or $\mathbf{I}(\mathcal{R}) = \mathbf{T}$. Consequently, $\mathbf{I}(\mathcal{Q} \supset \mathcal{R}) = \mathbf{T}$.

f. $\mathcal{P}$ is of the form $\sim(\mathcal{Q} \equiv \mathcal{R})$. Assume that $\mathcal{P} \in \Gamma$. Then, by j, either both $\mathcal{Q} \in \Gamma$ and $\sim\mathcal{R} \in \Gamma$, or both $\sim\mathcal{Q} \in \Gamma$ and $\mathcal{R} \in \Gamma$. In the former case, $\mathbf{I}(\mathcal{Q}) = \mathbf{T}$ and $\mathbf{I}(\sim\mathcal{R}) = \mathbf{T}$, by the inductive hypothesis; so $\mathbf{I}(\mathcal{Q}) = \mathbf{T}$ and $\mathbf{I}(\mathcal{R}) = \mathbf{F}$. In the latter case, $\mathbf{I}(\sim\mathcal{Q}) = \mathbf{T}$ and $\mathbf{I}(\mathcal{R}) = \mathbf{T}$, by the inductive hypothesis; hence $\mathbf{I}(\mathcal{Q}) = \mathbf{F}$ and $\mathbf{I}(\mathcal{R}) = \mathbf{T}$. Either way, it follows that $\mathbf{I}(\mathcal{Q} \equiv \mathcal{R}) = \mathbf{F}$, and so $\mathbf{I}(\sim(\mathcal{Q} \equiv \mathcal{R})) = \mathbf{T}$.

g. $\mathcal{P}$ is of the form $(\exists x)\mathcal{Q}$. Assume that $\mathcal{P} \in \Gamma$. Then, by m, there is some constant a such that $\mathcal{Q}(a/x) \in \Gamma$. By the inductive hypothesis, $\mathbf{I}(\mathcal{Q}(a/x) = \mathbf{T}$. By 11.1.5, $\{\mathcal{Q}(a/x)\} \vDash (\exists x)\mathcal{Q}$. So $\mathbf{I}((\exists x)\mathcal{Q}) = \mathbf{T}$ as well.

5. Clauses 7 and 9. First consider clause 7. Suppose that $\mathcal{Q} \supset \mathcal{R}$ has k occurrences of logical operators. Then $\mathcal{Q}$ certainly has fewer than k occurrences of logical operators, and so does $\mathcal{R}$. But, in the proof for case 7, once we assume that $\mathcal{Q} \supset \mathcal{R} \in \Gamma$, we know that $\sim\mathcal{Q}$ or $\mathcal{R}$ is a member of Γ by property g of Hintikka sets. The problem is that we cannot apply the inductive hypothesis to $\sim\mathcal{Q}$, since $\sim\mathcal{Q}$ might contain k occurrences of logical operators. In the sentence '(Am & Bm) $\supset$ Bm', for instance, this happens. The entire sentence has two occurrences of logical operators, but so does the negation of the antecedent '$\sim$(Am & Bm)'. However, it can easily be shown that the *length* of $\sim\mathcal{Q}$ is less than the *length* of $\mathcal{Q} \supset \mathcal{R}$.

Similarly, in the case of clause 9 we know that if $\mathscr{Q} \equiv \mathscr{R} \in \Gamma$, then either both $\mathscr{Q} \in \Gamma$ and $\mathscr{R} \in \Gamma$ or both $\sim\mathscr{Q} \in \Gamma$ and $\sim\mathscr{R} \in \Gamma$. But then we are not guaranteed that either $\sim\mathscr{Q}$ or $\sim\mathscr{R}$ has fewer occurrences of logical operators than does $\mathscr{Q} \equiv \mathscr{R}$. For instance, ' $\sim$ Am' and ' $\sim$ Bm' each contain one occurrence of a logical operator, and so does 'Am $\equiv$ Bm'.

6. If $\exists$D were not included, then we could not be assured that the set of sentences on each nonclosed branch of a systematic tree has property m of Hintikka sets. And in the inductive proof that every Hintikka set is quantificationally consistent we made use of this property in steps (12) and (13).

7. Yes, it would. For let us trace those places in our proof of Metatheorem 11.4 where we appealed to the rule $\sim\forall$D. We used it to establish that the set of sentences on a nonclosed branch of a systematic tree has property l of Hintikka sets, and we appealed to property l in step 12 of our inductive proof of Lemma 11.7. So let us first replace property l by the following:

> l*. If $\sim(\forall x)\mathscr{P} \in \Gamma$, then, for some constant $\boldsymbol{a}$ that occurs in some sentence in Γ, $\sim\mathscr{P}(\boldsymbol{a}/x) \in \Gamma$.

It is then easily established that every nonclosed branch of a systematic tree has properties a–k, l*, and m–n. In our inductive proof of Lemma 11.7, change step 12 to the following:

> 12*. $\mathscr{P}$ is of the form $\sim(\forall x)\mathscr{Q}$. Assume that $\mathscr{P} \in \Gamma$. Then, by l*, there is some constant $\boldsymbol{a}$ such that $\sim\mathscr{Q}(\boldsymbol{a}/x) \in \Gamma$. By the inductive hypothesis, $I(\sim\mathscr{Q}(\boldsymbol{a}/x)) = T$, and so $I(\mathscr{Q}(\boldsymbol{a}/x)) = F$. Since $\{(\forall x)\mathscr{Q}\} \vDash \mathscr{Q}(\boldsymbol{a}/x)$, by 11.1.4, it follows that $I((\forall x)\mathscr{Q}) = F$ and $I(\sim(\forall x)\mathscr{Q}) = T$.

8. Certain adjustments are obvious if we are to convert the proof of Metatheorem 11.4 into a proof that the tree method for *SL* is complete for sentential logic. The tree method for *SL* contains only some of the rules of the tree method for *PL*; hence we have fewer rules to work with. We replace talk of quantificational concepts (consistency and the like) with talk of truth-functional concepts, hence talk of interpretations with talk of truth-value assignments.

A Hintikka set of *SL* will have only properties a–j of Hintikka sets for *PL*. And trees for *SL* are *all* finite, so we have only finite open branches to consider in this case. (Thus Lemma 11.6 would not be used in the proof for *SL*.) Finally, the construction of the characteristic truth-value assignment for a Hintikka set of *SL* requires only clause 2 of the construction of the characteristic interpretation for a Hintikka set of *PL*.

9. We must first show that a set Γ^* that is both maximally consistent in *PD* and $\exists$-complete has the fourteen properties of Hintikka sets. We list those properties here. (And we refer to the seven properties a–g of sets that are both maximally consistent in *PD* and $\exists$-complete as 'M(a)', 'M(b)', ..., 'M(g)'.)

a. For any atomic sentence $\mathcal{P}$, not both $\mathcal{P}$ and $\sim\mathcal{P}$ are members of Γ^*.

Proof: This follows immediately from property M(a) of Γ^*.

b. If $\sim\sim\mathcal{P}$ is a member of Γ^*, then $\mathcal{P}$ is a member of Γ^*.

Proof: If $\sim\sim\mathcal{P} \in \Gamma^*$, then $\sim\mathcal{P} \notin \Gamma^*$, by M(a), and $\mathcal{P} \in \Gamma^*$, by M(a).

c. If $\mathcal{P} \,\&\, \mathcal{Q} \in \Gamma^*$, then $\mathcal{P} \in \Gamma^*$ and $\mathcal{Q} \in \Gamma^*$.

Proof: This follows from property M(b) of Γ^*.

d. If $\sim(\mathcal{P} \,\&\, \mathcal{Q}) \in \Gamma^*$, then either $\sim\mathcal{P} \in \Gamma^*$ or $\sim\mathcal{Q} \in \Gamma^*$.

Proof: If $\sim(\mathcal{P} \,\&\, \mathcal{Q}) \in \Gamma^*$, then $\mathcal{P} \,\&\, \mathcal{Q} \notin \Gamma^*$, by M(a). By M(b), either $\mathcal{P} \notin \Gamma^*$ or $\mathcal{Q} \notin \Gamma^*$. By M(a), either $\sim\mathcal{P} \in \Gamma^*$ or $\sim\mathcal{Q} \in \Gamma^*$.

e–j are established similarly.

k. If $(\forall x)\mathcal{P} \in \Gamma^*$, then, for every constant a that occurs in some sentence in Γ^*, $\mathcal{P}(a/x) \in \Gamma^*$.

Proof: This follows from property M(f) of Γ^*.

l. If $\sim(\forall x)\mathcal{P} \in \Gamma^*$, then $(\exists x) \sim\mathcal{P} \in \Gamma^*$.

Proof: If $\sim(\forall x)\mathcal{P} \in \Gamma^*$, then $(\forall x)\mathcal{P} \notin \Gamma^*$, by M(a). Then, for some constant a, $\mathcal{P}(a/x) \notin \Gamma^*$, by M(f). Then $\sim\mathcal{P}(a/x) \in \Gamma^*$, by M(a). So $(\exists x) \sim\mathcal{P} \in \Gamma^*$, by M(g).

m. If $(\exists x)\mathcal{P} \in \Gamma^*$, then, for at least one constant a, $\mathcal{P}(a/x) \in \Gamma^*$.

Proof: This follows from property M(g) of Γ^*.

n. If $\sim(\exists x)\mathcal{P} \in \Gamma^*$, then $(\forall x) \sim\mathcal{P} \in \Gamma^*$.

Proof: If $\sim(\exists x)\mathcal{P} \in \Gamma^*$, then $(\exists x)\mathcal{P} \notin \Gamma^*$, by M(a). Then, for every constant a, $\mathcal{P}(a/x) \notin \Gamma^*$, by M(g). So, for every constant a, $\sim\mathcal{P}(a/x) \in \Gamma^*$, by M(a). And $(\forall x) \sim\mathcal{P} \in \Gamma^*$, by M(f).

Second, that every Hintikka set is ∃-complete follows from property m of Hintikka sets.

Third, we show that some Hintikka sets are *not* maximally consistent in *PD*. Here is an example of such a set:

$$\{(\forall x)Fx, (\exists y)Fy, Fa\}$$

It is easily verified that this set is a Hintikka set. And the set is of course consistent in *PD*. But this set is *not* such that the addition to the set of any sentence that is not already a member will create an inconsistent set. For instance, the sentence 'Fb' may be added, and the resulting set also consistent in *PD*:

$$\{(\forall x)Fx, (\exists y)Fy, Fa, Fb\}$$

Hence the set is not maximally consistent in *PD*.